D1187755

# Honourable
# Warriors

Dedication

*To Emily and Henry*


A tale of two mottoes:

*Data Fata Secuutus*
*Celer et Audax*

# Honourable Warriors

*Fighting the Taliban in Afghanistan*

A Front-line Account of the British Army's
Battle for Helmand

Richard Streatfeild

Pen & Sword
**MILITARY**

First published in Great Britain by
**PEN AND SWORD MILITARY**
*an imprint of*
Pen and Sword Books Ltd
47 Church Street
Barnsley
South Yorkshire S70 2AS

Copyright © Richard Streatfeild 2014

ISBN 978 1 78346 227 8

Printed and bound by Guntenberg Press


Typeset in Times by CHIC GRAPHICS

*Pen & Sword Books Ltd incorporates the imprints of*
Pen & Sword Books Ltd incorporates the imprints of Pen & Sword
Archaeology, Atlas, Aviation, Battleground, Discovery,
Family History, History, Maritime, Military, Naval, Politics,
Railways, Select, Social History, Transport, True Crime, and
Claymore Press, Frontline Books, Leo Cooper, Praetorian Press,
Remember When, Seaforth Publishing and Wharncliffe.

*For a complete list of Pen and Sword titles please contact*
Pen and Sword Books Limited
47 Church Street, Barnsley, South Yorkshire, S70 2AS, England
E-mail: enquiries@pen-and-sword.co.uk
Website: www.pen-and-sword.co.uk

# Contents

Acknowledgements ............................................................vii

Glossary...........................................................................viii

Maps ..................................................................................ix

Chapter 1      Salaam Alaikum ................................................1

Chapter 2      Training: Darwin's Theory will apply ..............13

Chapter 3      Training Part 2 ...............................................25

Chapter 4      Leave, Leaving, Left........................................36

Chapter 5      Heeellloooo Hellllmand...................................48

Chapter 6      How on earth did I end up here, and what the hell
               am I going to do about it? ..............................58

Chapter 7      Buckle Up.......................................................69

Chapter 8      Reality Bites ..................................................80

Chapter 9      Afghans ..........................................................95

Chapter 10     The Road into Hel(mand)..............................115

Chapter 11     Hellfire and Resurrection .............................132

Chapter 12     Afghans on the March...................................146

Chapter 13     Return to Hell ..............................................165

Chapter 14     Honourable Warriors....................................178

Chapter 15     Coming Home ..............................................189

Appendix 1.................................................................................204

Appendix 2.................................................................................208

Appendix 3.................................................................................210

Appendix 4.................................................................................213

# Acknowledgements

The greatest debt I have is to the men and women under my command who put themselves into harm's way during the winter of 2009–10 in Afghanistan. Ten made the ultimate sacrifice; forty more came home bearing the physical wounds of battle and many more had traumatic memories to reconcile. This book is my acknowledgement of that effort; I hope I have done you justice. And where I have failed to recall or recount some vital element that is now lost, I am sorry. I know that everyone had a 'moment'. There are, for some, painful memories that will be brought to mind by this account, for which I acknowledge another debt.

In the writing, production and publication of this book there are those who I would like to thank publicly: Andrew Gordon at David Higham Associates, Rupert Harding and Susan Last at Pen and Sword, John Shields at Radio 4 and James Shelley and Crispin Lockhart in the MoD, all of whom have been key at various stages. My thanks to family and friends who have worried, listened and encouraged, too numerous to mention by name; I am extremely grateful for your time and patience. Finally to Rachel, irresistible as ever, and much more besides, my eternal gratitude, love and thanks.

# Glossary

| | |
|---|---|
| ANA | Afghan National Army |
| ANSF | Afghan National Security Forces (Police and Army). There are four or five different types of police. |
| AO | Area of Operations |
| ATO | Ammunition Technical Officer or bomb-disposal officer. |
| BG | Battle Group |
| BGHQ | Battle Group Head Quarters |
| Herc | C130 aircraft |
| CH-47 | Chinook helicopter |
| CMT | Combat Medic Technician |
| CO | Commanding Officer |
| CP | Checkpoint |
| COIN | Counter Insurgency |
| CQMS | Company Quarter Master Sergeant |
| CSM | Company Sergeant Major |
| Dishdash | generic term for clothing worn by Afghans |
| EHT | Environmental Health Team |
| FAC | Forward Air Controller |
| FOB | Forward Operating Base |
| FOO | Forward Observation Officer |
| FMHT | Field Mental Health Team |
| FSG | Fire Support Group |
| GMG | Grenade Machine-Gun, 40mm grenade launcher |
| GPMG | General Purpose Machine-Gun 7.62 mm (diameter bullet) belt fed |
| H-Hour | Start time for an operation |
| HLS | Helicopter Landing Site, also an EHLS Emergency Helicopter Landing Site |
| HMG | Heavy Machine-Gun 12.7mm (diameter bullet) belt fed |
| IDF | Indirect Fire. Generic term for enemy artillery or mortar fire |
| IED | Improvised Explosive Device. Of which a number of types |

| | |
|---|---|
| CWIED | Command Wire Improvised Explosive Device |
| PPIED | Pressure Pad Improvised Explosive Device |
| RCIED | Radio-Controlled Improvised Explosive Device |
| VBIED | Vehicle-Borne Improvised Explosive Device |
| DBIED | Donkey-Borne Improvised Explosive Device |
| MFC | Mortar Fire Controller |
| NCO | Non-Commissioned Officer |
| NVG | Night Vision Goggles |
| OC | Officer Commanding |
| OMLT | Operational mentoring and liaison team |
| Op | Operation |
| OP | Observation Post |
| OPTAG | Operational Training Advisory Group |
| PB | Patrol Base |
| QM | Quarter Master |
| QRF | Quick Reaction Force |
| RiP | Relief in Place |
| RMP | Royal Military Police |
| RPG | Rocket-Propelled Grenade |
| R and R | Rest and Recuperation |
| SA80 | Assault Rifle |
| SIB | Special Investigations Branch |
| Sitrep | Situation Report |
| SPG-9 | Russian recoilless anti-tank gun |
| TAC | Company Commander's Tactical Headquarters |
| UAV | Unmanned Aerial Vehicle or Drone |
| 107mm | Chinese Rocket |
| 611 | Road running down the Helmand Valley from Kajaki via Sangin to Geresk |

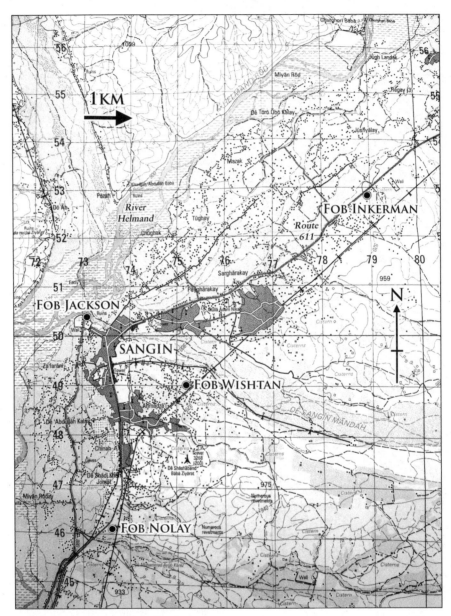

*3 Rifles area of operations (Sangin)*

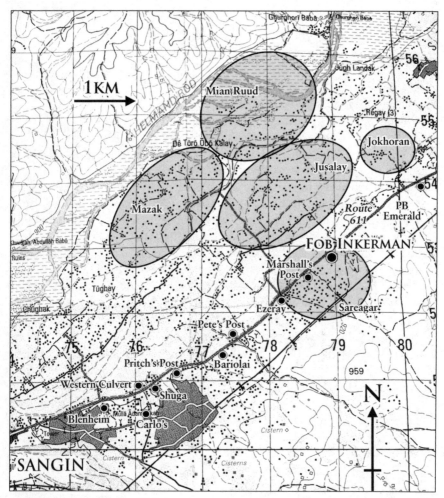

*A Company area of operations.*

## Chapter 1

# Salaam Alaikum

'Begin at the beginning and go on until you reach the end.' Through ditches, over mountains, down dusty tracks in the dark of an Afghan night, while preparing kit for inspections at the Royal Military Academy Sandhurst, and on operational tours I have said this to myself a thousand times. And now again. This book, a narrative of a year of my life punctuated by reminiscent conversation, recollection and analysis, begins in March 2009 and ends in May 2010. During that time, of the 364 nights that I could have been sleeping soundly in my bed I was, instead, at least for 264 of them, 'away': away training, away conducting reconnaissance, and for seven months based just north of Sangin, Northern Helmand, Afghanistan. This is not just my story. It is, in most part, the tale of A Company 4 Rifles and those who served with us on Operation Herrick.

I have had the opportunity to examine these events with the benefit of hindsight. I will try to keep that hindsight in perspective because the story is, though I say it myself, extraordinary. Many Afghans, soldiers, civilians and Taliban were killed or wounded. Ten British soldiers died and over fifty were wounded. The 200 improvised devices should provide enough explosive content and over 800 fire-fights should inject enough adrenaline for even the most hardened junkie. The snares of grief, anger, euphoria, revenge and addiction lace the account. It is fraught with danger. Most of all it is about triumph and disaster and our success and failure to meet those two imposters just the same.

## Introductions

There are some people I need to introduce, albeit briefly, before I go on.

Pat Hyde, my company sergeant major, 5ft 9in, thick set, a Gloucestershire man, small nose. Durch. (Royal Green Jacket idiom for 'not', i.e. to render the meaning opposite of what had just been stated. Commonly used when something was truly excellent, 'Wank-durch'.) Has been in the army since he was a boy, guarded a safe haven in Bosnia aged seventeen and is now in his mid-thirties. My right-hand man.

Ben Shuttleworth my second in command. Educated at Winchester, New College and the Royal Military Academy, commissioned into the Royal Green Jackets – a Wykehamist's Wykehamist. A description that sounds too traditional, too archetypal. A candidate for entitled arrogance were it not for his modesty.

Manners hath indeed maketh that man. Five foot seven, sandy hair, intelligent, enthusiastic and tenacious, in a manner befitting a Springer Spaniel–Jack Russell cross.

Tim Lush, my company quarter master sergeant (CQMS). Calm. Quiet. Diligent and stoic. A Dorsetshire motorbike enthusiast. Responsible for making sure the right kit was in the right place at the right time. A slightly careworn look under a thinning, greying pate.

Then there are the platoon commanders. Five in all: Mike, 1 Platoon; Charlie, 2 Platoon; Tom, 3 Platoon; Rob, 7 Platoon (attached from C Company 3 Rifles in December 2009), and Fred, Fire Support Group. Four young bucks relatively fresh from training at Sandhurst and Fred who had been there, done it, drunk the beer and got the T-shirt and the medals to prove it. And their respective platoon sergeants: 'Jona' Jones, 'H' Henry, 'Jimmy' Houston, 'Billy' Baines and 'Bog-eyed Will' Williams. I'll leave the detailed description of these guys but we will catch up with them all on the way.

Then there are the men and women of A Company, 4 Rifles. Recruited from all over the UK and all over the globe. The Rifles sign up an eclectic mix. 4 Rifles, based as it was on 2nd Battalion the Royal Green Jackets (2RGJ), included the scallies, yam-yams and sparrows of inner-city Liverpool, Birmingham and London – 'norf' and 'saarf', as well as, in the modern era, newer recruits from the north-east and south-west of the UK. And, due to extensive recruiting of commonwealth soldiers, the ranks included Australians, South Africans, Sierra Leoneans, Gambians, Fijians, Jamaicans and Kenyans. All based in Bulford and setting out to train for what we knew would be the ultimate test of soldiering for our generation.

Others from 3 Rifles battlegroup who were attached to us for various operations should be mentioned: the Recce Platoon and various platoons from A and B Company 3 Rifles; Pilots – Army, RAF and NATO alliance – who guarded us from the air and came to fetch our casualties out of some very sticky situations; the men and women of the Chestnut Troop 1st Regiment Royal Horse Artillery; the Bengal Rocket Troop of the Royal Artillery, the Troop of Engineers from 42 Field Squadron Royal Engineers, the combat logistic patrols that supplied us; the signallers, chefs, the Afghan National Army, the interpreters... all of whom deserve far more than a passing mention and who will all feature.

Then there is me. I hope I will not let either modesty or vanity cloud this autobiographical introduction. At the start of this story I was a thirty-six-year-old father of two (Emily, four and Henry, two). A husband to Rachel, a teacher, who had been forced into full-time motherhood by the gypsy existence of army life. Or, as the sticker on our fridge said, 'Hardest job in the army? Army Wife.'

We were living in a major's quarter, a four-bed box, on the edge of the meteorologically-challenged Salisbury plain. All army training areas are meteorologically challenged. Apparently it's character-building to be soaked, baked, boiled and frozen and in common with all Army officers I'd had my fair share of personality construction by this method. I had commanded A Company, 4 Rifles for eight months. I had been lucky enough to have commanded another company before I went on the intermediate staff and command course: eighteen months in Northern Ireland commanding R Company 2RGJ had given me a taste both of and for life in command. It had included preparation for operations in Northern Ireland and the planning and the execution of those operations. We conducted a number of operations in support of the police service of Northern Ireland, dealing with terrorist activities and public order situations.

In my schooling and academic record there is nothing particularly remarkable. I went to a boys' Grammar School in Tonbridge called the Judd School, where I got good enough A-levels to go to the University of Warwick to read Politics with French. From commissioning in 1998 until 2003 I was a junior officer in 2RGJ. As a platoon commander I did a six-month tour of Bosnia, as a company second in command I did a tour of Kosovo and as the battalion operations officer I did another tour of Bosnia. I only offer this by way of context to the narrative that follows. There are obvious gaps. I had the good fortune never to serve in Iraq.

I was the Officer Commanding, C Company, Army Foundation College, Harrogate from October 2002 until December 2003. The Army Foundation College is a college of further education teaching English, Maths and IT to junior soldiers aged sixteen. Those who one day will become the brightest and the best. The job included responsibility for the welfare, training and development of 350 junior soldiers and fifty staff; I was a glorified military house master or head of year.

During the academic year 2005/6 I attended the intermediate staff and command course. This course is the training given to each generation of army officers when they are promoted to major, designed to equip them with the skills and knowledge to fulfil jobs in headquarters and advising the civil service. On leaving the course I became a desk officer in the public relations department of the MoD, attempting to get the 'best reputation for defence consistent with the facts' or, as my brother put it, 'lying for my country'. I reported to the director of defence public relations, helping him manage media organisations to go to the operational theatres, and handling media project management including TV documentaries, media coverage of events and newspaper articles. I was lucky enough to be the uniformed ministry representative on the first Help for Heroes Bike Ride and 'City Salutes' events.

But my real luck was that half of my last ten years in the Army had been served as a company commander.

\*  \*  \*  \*  \*

On 30 March 2009, at seventeen minutes past eleven, or 23:17 to be military about it, I finished preparing a talk to A Company. It set out what I knew of Afghanistan and proposed a narrative for the company to follow. What follows is based on that talk: forgive me for reminding you that this was a talk, not prose for publication, and that the audience were all that we could muster of the 141 who would be posted to Afghanistan seven months later. The average Rifleman does not have a GCSE to his name, but by and large they are canny, if undereducated. At this point we did not know where we were going in Helmand; I only knew it would be with 3 Rifles. I have tried to explain the three-letter abbreviations and the army patois in this version. Otherwise, it is as I delivered it then:

Why are we in Afghanistan? According to the president of the United States it is because the Pashtun areas of Southern Afghanistan and Northern Pakistan are the most dangerous places in the world. They have protected terrorist cells that plan to attack the UK and other countries in the West. Both countries have weak governments, but they are democratically elected. They have asked for our help. We are helping them extend the rule of law. We do this in three ways: we secure the local population; we neutralise the insurgent; and we help build up the local forces of law and order – the army and the police force.

I am going to give you the way I see it. For hundreds of years the people in that part of the world have found themselves squeezed on one side by the ambition and fear of the Russian empires and on the other by Britain through India and Pakistan. So the average Pashtu tribesman has developed a historic aversion to this constant encroachment. He is loyal to his family, his tribe, and his religion. He does not like outsiders. We are outsiders… but so are the Taliban. He likes a fight; he will change sides to side with whoever he thinks is winning. He will talk to anyone. But basically he, like everyone else, does not want to be pushed around and wants to earn a living for himself and his family. Rule one for A Company – do not give him any more reasons to fight us than is absolutely necessary to achieve our mission.

And to achieve that we have rules of engagement. Why do we have rules of engagement? Because we adhere to the law. We are there to enforce the law, therefore we must not act outside the law. Murder is murder. It is the difference between right and wrong. It is the difference between being able to look at yourself in the mirror and a lifetime of regret and conflicting emotions. You will be able to plead honest belief, i.e. if you honestly believe that you acted in self-defence or to save a life then you acted within the rules of engagement. But be under no illusion – I am not going to give a nod and a wink that you did honestly believe. You have to act within your honest belief but it is not good enough for you to say it, you must believe it.

During training you need to soak up is what is going on out there. I am not going to pretend that it is anything other than complicated. But you need to understand what is going on. Just like you do when you walk into your road back at home. The commanders amongst you will recognise this as the first question in the seven questions of the combat estimate. The rest of you will recognise it as the best question a Rifleman can ask…why?

Who are the Taliban? Their HQ is in Northern Pakistan. They ruled Afghanistan from 1996 to 2001. They are religious zealots. They believe in an extreme form of Muslim law. They recruit foreign fighters. They enforce their will on the local population by terror.

Who are the drug lords? This is where it gets complicated. The Afghan economy relies on opium growth. The farmers are paid to grow poppy. It is their best form of livelihood… the Foreign Office are working to try and provide them with alternative crops. Those who sell the drugs pay off the government officials and the police to turn a blind eye. This means that the police turn a blind eye to most things, which allows the Taliban to move in.*

So how will we out manoeuvre the enemy? Patrolling. The other day the intelligence officer gave you a patrol scenario. He based it on threat. What is the point of patrolling? Have an effect. What are the effects we want to achieve? We want to secure the local population; we want to neutralise the insurgent; and we want to help build up the local forces of law and order.

The first two require information. We need to know what is going on. We can do this in a number of ways. The HQ has an Int[elligence] cell. It will be working incredibly hard in the first few weeks to give us a history of incidents in the local area. What is the method of operation of the local Taliban groups? Where are the local minefields? What does the local pattern of life look like? Who are the key leaders? We then need to speak to people.

How do we win? We might not. The final reason why the peace bids will probably fail is that the Taliban, whatever their internal problems, give little sign of believing they need to negotiate. 'If they win, it is victory; if they are killed, it is victory,' said Zaeef (a quote from article in the *Observer* in March 2009). From total defeat in 2001 through the grand offensive of 2006 to today's bloody stalemate, the insurgents have suffered tactical defeats and heavy casualties, but have made significant strategic progress.

We have to find a way of winning.

---

*In six months of training I never heard anyone give a convincing explanation of how the narcotics industry was related to the insurgency, but it was widely accepted that it was. When in Afghanistan it always seemed that the narcotics industry had much closer links to the government than the insurgency.

[I started with a quote from CO 4 Rifles training direction on the application of violence.]

'From the outset you must focus on the effect of our operations on the population. Commanders will have at their disposal a vast array of weapons and, when required, we must be confident in their employment. However we must use them responsibly. Commanders will need to decide whether it is appropriate to employ Offensive Support assets (artillery, mortars and bombs) and what the consequences of doing so are: by dropping ordnance on the enemy have you destroyed the home of a local farmer and taken away his livelihood? …. He then has a reason to fight us.

We must not always default to using a mallet to crack a nut. Be confident that you are better warriors than the enemy and, if you choose to, you can outmanoeuvre and destroy him by employing old-fashioned infantry skills. When violence is required you must be ready to apply it in a clinical and decisive manner, using whatever assets are appropriate, but always ask whether there is another way and what the consequences of your actions are. In sum, while we can be confident of winning our tactical engagements, campaign success will not follow if we lose the population.'

[I wanted to apply violence but I wanted to do it at a time and place of my own choosing on the precise people that we wanted to kill. Those who terrorised and those who did not want to submit of the rule of law. In order to do this I impressed on the company that they, and I, would need information. We needed to know who they were, when they moved, where they came from, and we would prefer to turn members of the local population so that they felt that they could tell us. If we were attacked in villages it was the enemy that would get the blame. The enemy were also trying to secure and hold.]

The lessons from other counter insurgencies are clear. You have to work very hard to get these opportunities. It is easy to go out there tooled up and exchange bullets. But death is victory for them. We need to work hard to try to capture the enemy. There is no greater humiliation.

[I talked about force protection, or those measures that give us the best chance of survival in a very hostile environment:]

There are a multitude of things to be done. There is a certain amount of knowledge that we must all have. It is contained in the Tactical Aide Memoire. You must know this stuff, the reports and the drills. It is all there and you must know it. It will save your life and save the lives of your mates.

A Company will be a fit company. As the brigade commander has said, you will be fitter than you have ever been before. Fitness is a personal responsibility. If you are not fit enough you will not come to Afghanistan. We are going to do the Advanced Combat Fitness Test on 29/30 June. This is about carrying heavy weight over long distance. It is about strength and endurance, it is not about speed. Fitness will also save your life if you get injured. Be under no illusion, being fit is a life insurance policy and your part of the team effort.

Many of the things we are going to learn are about keeping ourselves safe. Barma drills, contact drills, IED threat, mines awareness, helicopter drills, electronic counter-measures training. We need to do these until they are second nature. So you know them so well you do them automatically. There can be no room for complacency. They must be carried out completely every time you have to do them.

But doing the drill for the sake of the drill is not the point. We do the drill to get to the population, to be able to give them a sense of security. Of not being threatened. We need to be able to select the appropriate drill for the job in hand. It is about a balance of risk.

[I had a bit to say about administration, or combat service support, as it known in the army. Some think this is the task of the quarter master and the platoon sergeants. They execute much of the plan, but it is still the commander's plan.]

Admin: this is the bedrock of success on operations. Even if the plan is a good one, if the kit does not work or there is not the right kit it will fail. You must have serviceable kit. What does this mean? A rifle that works – that you have confidence in because you have trained with it. Know how to fault-find with the electronic counter-measures equipment. The right amount of ammo, food, water, suncream, in the middle of winter being able to keep yourself warm. All these things are admin. This is not just a platoon sergeant responsibility. This is your responsibility. You must administrate yourselves and take responsibility as an individual and for each other.

Success. So what is success going to look like? It is going to be avoiding contact unless it is at a time and place of our choosing. It is a find of an IED or a weapons cache. It is a development project. Maslow had a theory that everybody needs security, shelter, food, water; they also need to be part of society, they both need and want to be valued. We are going to give them those things. It is changing people's perception. Give them knowledge, make it possible for them to understand, trust and support. It is going to be that piece of info. It will be individuals feeling that they can stand up for themselves. It is the ANA leading operations. It is the civil police making an arrest. Those are the things that represent success.

This is the future story of A Company from April 2009 to April 2010. It is going to give you an idea of the path we are going to travel. It represents a mix of what I want to happen and the most likely scenario.

We are a company group of 141 individuals, a command structure, and a good deal of experience. We represent a breadth and a depth of the British Army. This is because I want you to understand where we come from. We will let others judge us by the standards they set; we will judge ourselves by the standards we set. This is important for what we must do but also the way we do it.

So this is a story about a group of blokes who are going on operations in Northern Helmand. We are from all over the UK and abroad. We all have different opinions, attitudes, strengths and weaknesses. Some of you will be nervous about going, some even a bit fearful. In the next twelve months we are all likely to find out a lot about ourselves that we do not know now. We are going to train, live and fight together in order to secure the local population; neutralise the insurgent; and build up the local forces of law and order – the Afghan army and the police force.

In the training we are constantly going to go over and over the basics. Our heads are going to get crammed with knowledge so that when we are on patrol we know what to do automatically. We are going to get the knowledge then we are going to practice it time and again in different scenarios. We are going to talk about Afghanistan constantly to try and understand as much as possible before setting a foot in that country. PPPPPPP. Or Prior Preparation and Planning Prevents Piss Poor Performance.

We are going to be marksmen of the highest order. So that when we do get the opportunity to neutralise the insurgent we can take it with a single shot, not a javelin missile, or a 500lb bomb. We will have the highest standards of fieldcraft. Being able to frustrate and deny the enemy opportunities to attack us on patrol, but at the same time being able to manoeuvre against them to attack the enemy at a time and place of our choosing.

We are going to get fit, very fit; fit enough to be able to carry seventy pounds for three hours or more. By being this fit we are going to be able to compete physically with the enemy and the elements. Because where we are going to is at altitude. The air is thinner and the sun is hotter. We need to be fit to survive, because a fit body helps to keep a fit mind. The threat is such that at the end of the patrol we need to be alert enough to get the information down so we can use it to inform the next operation. And it helps to keep us alive if we get blown up or shot.

We need to have knowledge of the enemy and the locals. We need to understand and respect the local culture. We respect it in the sense that it is the local culture and part of the country that we're in. If we have opinions about the locals we know better than to voice them in public because we know that securing the population requires them to be on our side.

We know that image is important and that perception is everything. We need to convince the enemy and the local population that we are a bunch of serious individuals not a bunch of cowboys. Self-disciplined in the way we go about our business. We will show restraint in our dealings with the locals but we are prepared to unleash hell on the enemy and them alone.

Having prepared we will then execute. We know that excellence in training is good but the true measure of being good is to put it into practice in the theatre of operations. In theatre we get a whole load of new kit that we must adjust to quickly. But by this stage we know the basics so well that we can get the maximum operational effect out of the new kit.

We will do the relief in place. There is not a whisper of shit handovers or slagging the outgoing unit. They will have been at it for six months and will be very tired. No, our job is to get every piece of information from the outgoing unit about the enemy and the ground. I don't care about people's opinion; I need you to get the facts.

Then we are going to go patrolling. This will start off with familiarisation. The enemy will know we have changed over. After all, we do flag changes at Bastion just to let them know. They will be looking for weakness and early success. We will deny it to them. We will gather new information and confirm what we have been told in the handover and we will seek to make friends in the local population. The important people have to trust us, but it is those who observe us and support the Taliban through fear that we must concentrate on. They need to be able to talk to us. After all, they know who they are giving information to. Where does it go? Follow the trail.

We know that this will be a long and painstaking business. The first two months are critical. It is the understanding gained at this time that will allow us to have success later in the tour. It is when we are best manned before R&R [The two-week break from the front line that all soldiers on tour get, taken from month two to month five]. It is when we will have most freedom of manoeuvre before the weather hampers us.

As the R&R plot kicks in, those who go back normally get two weeks off; occasionally this comes down to eleven days because of flights. But it is well-deserved time off. Plan your rest and recuperation. Make the most of it, but you are still on ops on return. The company must remain focussed.

Month four is always the longest month. We will keep fresh by mixing it up a bit in the middle of the tour. Setting patterns is a killer. Sloppy drills are a killer. The way we are going to try and go about this means that we will need to remain on top of our game as the enemy makes more extravagant attempts to try and take us on.

Then, with the R&R window closed, we will be back to full strength and by making use of all our experience we will try to generate a very high tempo to allow the break clean. We need the enemy off-balance before we start handing over. In this way it will give us the best opportunity for handing over as we can. There will be projects that we are working on that will not be finished off. Informants who we know and use, leaders who we engage and people that we recognise as sympathisers, either with us or the Taliban.

We will keep the home fires burning. You all have families who are concerned for your welfare. We need to use the communications systems available to us. Your families can use Army net. We will write a regular blog. You will all fill out a factsheet about yourself and your army career. This will be used to supply 'local boy' stories to your local newspapers so that people continue to support the army and know what we are doing in Afghanistan on their behalf. And, in what is a sensitive subject, this information is also critical if you get badly injured or killed.

On that subject, which is a difficult one for all of us, a few words. If I am in a vehicle that gets blown up on patrol and I am breathing my last, I want to know that I have done everything to reduce that possibility, but also that in death I have had some hand in how I am remembered and might even serve as an inspiration to others.

It would be irresponsible for all of us not to make a will. This is part of that process. It is how I want to be remembered if it comes to it, but let me tell you now that it is my responsibility to design the training and make the plans that reduce this possibility to a minimum. If we make a plan for the worst-case scenario we can face up to it and ease what is a legitimate fear. Enough said.

Then there is coming home. This can be as difficult as going. It depends on how the tour goes. Suffice to say that we will take a well-earned break and the company will change very quickly as people go off to courses and other postings. But it is important that we spend some time together back here. That we all get a chance to talk about the tour, get drunk and remember the good, the bad and the ugly. The trick with homecoming is to keep talking to each other. Friends and family cannot possibly understand completely what it is like to be in Afghanistan. We will try and tell them, and they will try and understand. But we must look after each other in this regard. You won't like me for saying it, but getting back to work is the best way of dealing with it.

And that is the story of the A Company tour as I see it now. In twelve months' time, when I stand here and look at your faces I want to be filled with pride. Pride that there is a small patch in Afghanistan where the people live better lives than they do now, that the rule of law is extended just a little bit further and the streets of the UK are that much more secure as a result of our efforts. Pride that we trained hard and fought easy. Pride that we have done the right thing in the right way.

\*  \*  \*  \*  \*

Much has been written about the training for operations. I remember thinking in September 2009, and indeed saying as much, that I thought it had been an incredibly long period of training for an operation. Looking back there are some things I might have done rather differently.

It began with the brigade study week. The army had created a new brigade to command Operation Herrick 11, the winter tour of 2009–10 to Afghanistan. Commanded by Brigadier James Cowan, its units had been poached from all over the army. In a well tried and tested method of getting everyone thinking along the same lines, the first thing I did in May 2009 was attend the brigade study week. The 11 Brigade HQ had assembled a group of notables to speak to us, including Michael Semple, an Irishman who had worked for the UN but had recently been thrown out of Afghanistan by the Afghan government for 'spying'. It was rumoured that he had been trying to broker a deal with the Taliban, and it has subsequently emerged that he was, but with what he thought was the agreement of the Karzai government.

There were two striking elements to this week that I remember, other than Michael Semple's insights. The first was the lecture from a sociologist. Over the course of an hour he constructed an argument in which he suggested that our continued presence in Afghanistan after the fall of the Taliban, and certainly since the move south in 2006, was a source of inspiration to disaffected youth in our indigenous radical Muslim populations. Far from making our streets safer, it was probably doing more to promote disaffection than to solve it. I précis his argument and do not do it justice, because it is a complicated subject. What I do not need to précis is the audience reaction. You could have heard a pin drop. The silence was like grey granite: hard and abrasive.

Someone asked a question in such a tone as to be utterly dismissive and from then on it was never mentioned again. Even James Cowan could not bring himself to touch on the argument in his summary speech two days later. It was my last exposure to the idea that 'Whatever the rights and wrongs of this, I am going'. The alternative was, 'If I accept this argument I should resign'. But my hand was far too far into the mangle of company command. This is what I was training for, what my whole professional existence had worked towards. I remembered the words I once uttered to the captain in the Royal Green Jackets in 1996, to whom I had been sent for a 'chat' to see if I was the right 'type' for the regiment. 'I want to join the infantry because if there are tough decisions to be made I want to see if I am up to them'. This was it. We closed our minds to the possibility that the ostensible reason we were being sent to Afghanistan, Achilles-like in our armour, had a heel in Bradford West, Birmingham or London.

The brigade commander gave the last talk of the week. Sixty-four slides in just under two hours. The first twelve were a brisk walk through his distinguished family and regimental history – hoo-rah. Then he went through the more difficult aspects of fighting a counter-insurgency.

> Counter-insurgency is a battle of wills. It is not simply a matter of contesting will but finding where you can bring those contesting wills closer together, through diplomacy, dialogue, negotiation and discussion. In war, you do not have to kill a man, merely his courage. But in Counter Insurgency (COIN) you must kill his resentment. The most courageous act an insurgent can make is to change sides.
>
> You can't commute to this fight. Position Forward Operating Bases and Patrol Bases in the neighbourhoods we intend to secure. Living among the people is essential to securing them and defeating the insurgents. Dilemma: the more you live among the people, the more Forward Operating Bases you build. The more Forward Operating Bases you build, the more you protect. And the more you protect, the less you live among the people.

I was a little relieved that what I had told the company a couple of weeks before was not a million miles away from what the boss wanted, even if the overall effect was not what any of us wanted to hear.

Next stop for A Company was six weeks of training, culminating in a 'Confirmatory Exercise' in Norfolk. The Army gets to train in all the most picturesque places in the UK. A wide landscape is a prerequisite for the training cognoscenti; landscape and weather. The microclimates of Sennybridge, Stanford in Norfolk, Otterburn and Lydd are well known to all ranks of the army. We have all shivered and baked around the country, combat uniform moistened from outside and in, by day and by night on very little sleep – still, one would expect nothing less.

# Chapter 2

# Training: Darwin's Theory will apply

Lydd was the first stop. Flat, windswept, with a magnificent view over the nuclear power station. The early summer of 2009 was hot, damn hot, at least by British standards. This I thought to be a good thing, because on arrival in Afghanistan the temperature would still be over 35°C. Unlike our counterparts on the summer tour, who trained for that temperature in the freezing cold of English winter, at least we were training in roughly the same temperatures as we would fight in. The shooting camp at Lydd was first time that we had a chance to interact with our new parent unit, 3 Rifles.

It is worth explaining that due to the vagaries of the way that the army prepares for operations, A Company had been selected to be an 'independent' rifle company, meaning that we were with a new 'battlegroup' and not entirely responsible to the headquarters we normally reported to. This was made more complicated by our new Battlegroup HQ being based in Edinburgh and we in Bulford. Just to make things harder still, our normal unit was 4 Rifles and our new battlegroup was under the command of 3 Rifles. The Rifles had formed into a new regiment in 2007 and achieved almost instantaneous public recognition and sympathy, if only for the seemingly endless casualties we had suffered in Iraq and Afghanistan. So recently amalgamated were the former regiments of the Rifles that the memories of old allegiances were still fresh in some minds; there were those who still saw this as a Green Jacket company going to a Light Infantry battalion.

Lydd would be the first chance to see how we all shaped up. Lydd is a live-firing camp – rifle shooting on a plethora of different ranges and scenarios. I was really unreasonably keen that we gave a good account of ourselves. Both in how 'wilco' or cooperative we could be and that we should also set down a marker to the rest by a demonstration of our shooting prowess, like an over-keen father at the first school match of the term. The camp is set up to conduct a mandatory set of shooting ranges as individuals and then up to platoon level. The highlight for many, although not all, is the Forward Operating Base defence shoot, where over the course of forty minutes a thousand targets come up at ranges up to 800m. It requires command and control, preservation of the ammunition by disciplined fire, and of course accurate shooting at the limit of the ranges of the various weapon systems. A Company from 3 Rifles set the early pace and posted a benchmark score in the 500s. One of the platoons from B Company 3 Rifles then went into the 600s. The company commander of B Company was a good friend. We had served together in 2RGJ as junior officers and James was as keen as I was to lay down the early marker. The platoons were all on different timetables and I cannot remember which of my platoons posted the first score over 700, but it was game on.

The following day I got a text from James saying that one of his platoons had just scored 805. My return text was as magnanimous as I could muster, but inside I sincerely hoped that 1 Platoon under Mike would be able to top it. Unfortunately 1 Platoon were having a shocker. On one of the previous ranges one of the Riflemen had negligently fired his rifle, meaning he had fired it when he didn't intend to. Luckily he had followed the drills well enough to fire it in a safe direction and no one had been injured. In the army we all take that kind of lapse very seriously – it can and has cost lives. The commanding officer, with the power of a JP, will more often than not fine the individual concerned a month's wages. When you are in the public glare of independent range staff and a new battlegroup, the whole company pays the price in shame. I spoke to Michael on the back of the range.

> You can't do anything about it now. If he's re-passed his weapon handling test and re-zeroed a spare weapon he can go back on. You'll need every man you've got and you're going to have to shoot bloody well to beat B Company. It would go some way to making amends.

Michael grunted his acknowledgement: 823 downed targets later he was nothing other than a broad smile. I just texted the number to James.

For my money the reason we did as well as that was because we had yet to receive our allocation of light machine guns. I hear you take a short breath. 'You mean you were going through the ranges that were supposed to prepare you for operations without the equipment you were going to use on the operation?' Yes. That is absolutely true and it wasn't the only time. On this occasion it had a rather better outcome than it did for the other items we were missing in our preparation.

The light machine gun is only accurate for the first round or two out of the barrel. After that it leaps around so much that relatively inexperienced firers can't hit a barn door beyond 200m. So with all our firers using their normal rifle, the SA80 A2, which is extremely accurate even when firing automatic, we were able to score well. It was also the first time I was able to demonstrate categorically to the company the trap that the army had fallen into of wanting something that looked and sounded good, but did not deliver the required effect.

This is very much a live debate in the army. I am continually dismayed by the weight given to the psychological benefit of having an automatic weapon firing next to you. My intuition then and my experience now would suggest that the maxim 'ineffective suppression is absolutely ineffective' is absolutely true. And the psychological effect of actually being able to hit the enemy outweighs the narcissistic benefit of having your military wet dream played out against the prophylactic soundtrack of automatic fire.

One member of the permanent range team down at Lydd was Sergeant Dave Rider. I had served with Dave in Kosovo in 1999. His older brother, Lee, had been my second platoon sergeant in Bosnia in 1998 and just for good measure Lee's son Danny was now in 3 Platoon. Dave had been on the ranges for six weeks solid. He had seen all the units go through and was not a man to mince his words. The kind of man it takes a little time to get to know, but once mutual trust has been established, a diamond. In any case he was complimentary enough about our performance. At least by comparison to 'those other red coat muppets', which is a Green Jacket term of affection for the rest of the line infantry regiments in the army. It was a typical backhanded compliment delivered in a 'Well, you don't have to be that good to beat this lot, so don't get too big for your boots' kind of way. Six weeks later Dave Rider was posted to A Company for the tour and became the operations room sergeant, assistant CQMS, and any other job we could dream up for him.

So we escaped from Lydd to Bulford with pride intact – just – and with one of our number a little lighter in his wallet.

A few weeks later we were in Norfolk. In the intervening time the commanding officer had been on a recce to Sangin. We now knew we would be part of Battlegroup North based in the Sangin district of northern Helmand. He was close to deciding which company would get which task in Sangin. If we had put down a marker in Lydd it was now time to pull out all the stops, or we might get six months of dam guarding in Kajaki. Not, of course, that the Kajaki dam wasn't strategically important to the economic future of Afghanistan, but it hardly represented what the company wanted. I had seen other commanders at other times lobbying hard for a particular role and I had decided not to. I had not asked for the company to be the independent rifle company, nor was I going to lobby one way or another for a particular task. When going to Afghanistan you have to be very careful what you wish for. We would just do our best and let the commanding officer (CO) decide. That's not to say there weren't some strong opinions within the company. Being based with the Battlegroup HQ in the middle of Sangin would bring daily contact with the CO, and for the Riflemen the prospect of sharing a camp with a regimental sergeant major (RSM). This was not all that enticing for anyone. The other three choices were Forward Operating Bases Wishtan, Nolay and Inkerman; all were independent company bases and at that stage level-pegging in the Riflemen's estimation, although Inkerman had slightly more status due to the *Ross Kemp in Afghanistan* series, some of which had been filmed in the green zone near the base.

We arrived in Norfolk for the confirmatory exercise after five hours on a coach negotiating vile traffic on the M25. We were late. Not that late, but late enough that our arrival in Rollestone Camp on the edge of Stanford training area was greeted with much shouting, designed to indicate just how urgently we should get off one mode of transport and on to the next, to get on with the first part of the exercise.

Each element of the exercise would test a different aspect of operations that we might conduct in Helmand. The first was a clearance of a village where the insurgents had removed the inhabitants and set up a base. Our task was to recapture the village. We moved into a Forward Operating Base where for two hours there was the form of ordered chaos that the army does so well. We had to maximise concurrent activity. While I digested the task at hand the CSM issued the ammunition. The CQMS issued the food and other stores and equipment that we would need for the operation. The Riflemen fed, watered and repacked their kit. Ben set up a briefing area and an operations room. It was just a little unfortunate that the first base we moved into was only two rooms big, so everything happened concurrently and in the same space.

I gave a short set of orders. Not enough detail, not enough contingent plans, but enough to get us out of the gate. The platoons managed a short patrol brief. As we set off into the night I vowed that if I ever did this for real then more time in preparation was going to be vital. My particular bugbear was platoons not giving formal orders. For the chain of command to work, for mission command to work, subordinates need to know what to obey by way of orders. There is, of course, a balance to be struck. The danger of the 100 per cent plan delivered too late is as great as the danger of people going into battle not knowing what to do.

Once the time estimate was done the 'one-third, two-thirds' rule had to be applied. This rule of thumb for the army states that the commander should only use one third of the time available for his planning and briefing of subordinates if there is a deadline to meet. So on that first evening of the exercise I had precisely forty minutes to come up with a plan and brief it to the team. They would then have thirty minutes to do likewise. And the corporals would have twenty minutes, at best, to sort out their sections.

This sounds bad. The only mitigating factor is that we were briefing trained soldiers, thinking Riflemen, and many of the things we were going to do would have to rely on the standard operating procedures that we had practised up to this point. Even so, as we left camp to clear the village I had little confidence that everyone had a firm grip on what was supposed to be happening. It was even more disconcerting when the first two platoons walked off in what can only be described as the wrong direction. We were on an 'all-informed' company network of radios, which meant that the corporals could hear what I was telling the platoon commanders. In a large company this promotes rapid dissemination of information, but requires rigorous 'net discipline'; you have to keep the transmission to the point. Those with a garrulous tongue can inadvertently prevent important information getting round. One also becomes attuned to the tone and timbre of people's voices. It is easy to sound stressed, cross, unsure or timid, but conversely a good radio manner promotes confidence and efficiency. By the time we had done three months in Helmand we were pretty good at getting the balance right, but right now, under a little pressure, it was taking some self-control not to explode down the net.

We were half an hour late on to the line of departure. The attack started, and after a bit of a stutter gathered enough momentum to be completed in the early hours. Momentum is critical in attack. It is infinitely easier to delay or defend. The ratio of attacker to defender has to be as high as possible and ideally at least seven to one. The idea is to concentrate force at the enemy's weak point and then keep him moving backwards. He'll nearly always have a well-defended strong point, so once identified, maximum resources are required to neutralise or defeat it. But should the enemy inflict casualties or you use up too much ammo in the initial stages, then having the right amount of men and materiel for the defeat of this strong point is difficult. There were a number of lessons given to us by the staff to work on after the exercise, but all in all 'a fair crack' was the final verdict.

Next up the Afghan village. We did two operations in Stanford's new Afghan village. We were only the second battlegroup to use it. It was an excellent insight into the difficulty of coping with eighteen-foot walls, narrow alleyways and limited access. But time, on this occasion, was on our side. I managed to give a full set of orders and the platoons had time for theirs as well. For the first time in a long time it all went like clockwork. I had taken over A Company ten months earlier, been on exercise on four separate occasions, and initially had some decidedly mixed results. Some very good things seemed always to be undermined by a moment of individual or collective failure. The company had been through a long period of transition where all the key members of the team had changed over. Finally it felt like it was coming together, and not before time. We had only settled the personnel issues at the beginning of May and now in the third week of June we began to hit our stride. As we went into the next phase of the exercise confidence began to course through the platoons. Napoleon said 'that the moral is to the physical as three is to one', a quote I have often used because I have found it to be as true today as 200 years ago. I might even put the ratio up to four or five to one.

There were still many individual lessons to be learned at every level. I started an operation going into the 'Green Zone' with the company in single file. It confused the 'enemy' temporarily, but soon meant we were being outflanked. The platoons had to work incredibly hard to regain the initiative. But they did and they won praise for doing so and I learned my lesson. The great thing about the rest of that week is that all those lessons were being learned in the context of successful missions. No one minds owning up to a mistake if it has not fatally undermined the company effort, and most importantly if it is an isolated error. A former CO of 2 RGJ used to say 'You must underwrite the honest mistakes of your subordinates'. Often easier said than done, and a whole lot easier if the mistake is made in training rather than on operations.

A commander must always prove himself tactically if those he is commanded by and those he commands are to really trust him. Whilst collectively the machine was functioning well and disaster had been averted in the green zone, I still felt I personally had something to prove. My next chance was the urban arrest operation. Back in the new village again we had to cordon and search a compound in a known insurgent area. There was a strong likelihood of having to effect an opposed detention. I had done plenty of these types of operations in preparation for operations in Northern Ireland. The tactics of putting in a cordon to protect a crime scene or conduct a search was something I had done for real in Northern Ireland in 2004. The trick is to invest covertly and then get in quickly, search thoroughly and get out as fast and efficiently as possible before anyone has time to react. If you have to stay to guard the place then better to be well set before the enemy shows up. The company moved in without being seen. A car blocked the route as the vehicles moved in, but the inimitable Freddie Fryer moved it out of the way with a quick drag and we were on our way. The search complete, weapons found and arrest made, we were getting the hell out of Dodge in under forty-five minutes.

What happened after that was classic training politics. The training colour sergeant monitoring us summed up as we came back to camp with somewhat breathless excitement. 'Wow, that was fantastic.... Been here two years, best I've seen. You went so fast that we never had time to give you half the problems we meant to. The last lot were in there for five hours.'

As you might imagine, the company was abuzz and I was little short of elated. They had heard the debrief and they knew they had done outstandingly well. We were told to rest easy while the colour sergeant went back to see what we should do next. He came back an hour later with four other monitors.

'Right. You were obviously far too aggressive with the arrest. You have upset the locals and you need to set up a Shura with the elders to sort it out.'

I knew what that meant. We were going to walk into everything that the training team could throw at us to try and take us down a peg or two. I was dismayed. I did not want to end the phase on a low. I gathered the team, made a plan and briefed in short order. There was no option but to play this straight. Cordon in different locations – don't set patterns. Quick reaction force in place.

And a close protection force for me in the Shura. The cordon was attacked, there was a suicide bomber in the village, etc, etc, etc. The section commanders were inundated with points about their application of the rules of engagement, route selection, command and control, tactics. It was an orgy of debriefing. In hindsight I can see why overconfidence is as dangerous as no confidence. At the time I was spitting feathers and so were most of the team. There were two more serials to go and time still to make or break a fledgling reputation.

The next phase involved the defence of a Forward Operating Base or 'Fob' as they are universally known in the Army. It practised the procedures we would have in place for protection of the base, dealing with casualties and our ability to do all this while keeping our higher headquarters fully informed. As we changed over I ran into James who told me that he had let his second in command take charge for this one. He reasoned that we were all going to be away on R&R at some point, so it was a chance to give them a run out on a demanding, but not impossible, phase. It had given him a chance to observe, which he had found very useful. It seemed like sound argument all round. So up stepped Ben to be the commander. Needless to say he carried the whole thing off with his usual efficiency. There were plenty of observers in to watch. One particular moment stands out in my memory. The base suddenly came under mortar fire. 4 Rifles had been deployed to Iraq on Op Telic in 2007. They were the last unit in Basra Palace. They had endured endless days of enemy mortar fire. Whilst many of the Riflemen had never been under this type of attack, the platoon sergeants and corporals all knew exactly what to do. Lie down, fast, head down, count the rounds as they get fired and make sure you hear all the explosions when they drop. Wait at least a minute from the end of the last firing and then get back up as quickly as possible to carry on the defence. It was all done immaculately well and the CO, who also happened to be observing, disappeared giving nothing away. I didn't see how he could fail to be impressed. I was, but then I was biased.

The last twenty-four hours of the exercise were at the CO's discretion and had in the past been given over to a battlegroup attack. But on this occasion the CO indicated he wanted to go in the opposite direction. The companies had been put through their paces. It was time to give the platoons some more independence. For A Company this meant setting up a rural ambush to capture an insurgent leader in transit; setting up a platoon-size Patrol Base and conducting platoon-level framework patrols to secure the area round the base to gain local intelligence. There were some who were sceptical of this approach, but for A Company it proved remarkably prescient. Those twenty-four hours in Norfolk gave us the starting point for understanding what some of the potential difficulties might be.

At the end of the exercise the CO got all the company commanders into a meeting. Decision time. He explained that he was not going to say in any detail why different companies were going to different locations, but that he had his reasons, some of which he would be prepared to share with us individually.

| Tim | A Company 3 Rifles, Nolay, South of Sangin. |
| James | B Company, 3 Rifles Sangin District Centre, based with the Battalion HQ |
| Mike | C Company, 3 Rifles, Kajaki on the dam |
| Richard | A Company, 4 Rifles, to Inkerman |
| Graeme | B Company, 1 Scots to Wishtan |

Inkerman. 'Bloody Hell', was my first reaction. 'CSM'll be happy. It'll make it a busy tour.'

As we stepped outside of the meeting I asked 'So why Inkerman then, Colonel?' 'Fighting spirit, Dickie,' he replied. 'Your company showed fighting spirit. Perhaps occasionally too much, but you'll need that in Inkerman'. And as if to prove a point, as I strode back to where the rest of the battlegroup were sitting neatly laid out in squares cleaning their weapons, two of my platoons were engaged in a mass brawl that was friendly enough not to cause any casualties. They were on a high. They knew they had done well and the CO's decision had proved it. For my part pride was mixed with uncertainty about what we had got ourselves into. The following week I was going on the recce to Afghanistan, so I was about to find out.

* * * * *

The day before we left for the recce there was some startling news. Lieutenant Colonel Rupert Thorneloe, the commanding officer of the Welsh Guards Battlegroup, had been killed in Afghanistan. This came as something of a shock. The other two rifle companies of 4 Rifles were under his command; it was a big blow. Major Sean Birchall, also of the Welsh Guards, had been killed a few weeks previously, something I had tried to write off, at least to Rachel, as an unhappy accident. I was constantly trying to give some perspective to the risks that I might face. My favourite line was that it was statistically more dangerous to cross the road than go on ops. This was just about true up to that point in Afghanistan. But the week of the recce was to be the bloodiest week in the campaign thus far. Operation Panther's Claw had just started and now a CO had been killed. There was just no hiding from this one.

If there are seven degrees of separation between everyone in the world, in the British Army you get one degree. Everyone will have been on a course or on ops with someone that you know. This is particularly true of officers. I had met Rupert Thorneloe when he was adjutant of the Welsh Guards and then again while I was working in the MoD. But far more significantly, we lived about fifty metres from the Thorneloes on the 'patch' in Wandsworth and our daughters were exactly the same age. This meant that despite the disparity in rank and position in the MoD – he the military adviser to the Secretary of State, me a desk officer in the communications department – our lives brushed through our wives and children. I only ever had one thing to do with him at work and I have rarely met such gentle candour in someone so capable. But now he was dead and I was off to Afghanistan.

I knew Sally Thorneloe had been informed, but we were still in the twenty-four-hour 'grace' period before the media would publish his name. (Nothing could be less gracious.) Should I tell Rachel before I left? I felt I had to. She could not hear it first from a TV news presenter. The military get very touchy about how this news gets out. Husbands in privileged positions know, then wives, then Facebook, and before you know it, if the next of kin has not been informed because he or she is by some misfortune uncontactable, the worst-case scenario, which happened with early deaths in Iraq, is that next of kin are told their loved one has died by friends rather than by the army chain of command. The system now is a good one, if it is strictly adhered to, but it still needs discretion. Rupert's death dispelled any notion of how safe it might or might not be for me to go to Afghanistan. It cast a shadow longer than even Rachel or I could imagine over Emily. Emily was four years and seven months old when Rupert was killed. Two and a half years later, and never having seen Rupert's eldest daughter again, when asked to say something to her new school on Remembrance Day about what it was like to have a daddy in Afghanistan she uttered the unforgettable; 'I don't want to say anything about daddy in Afghanistan, I just want to say a prayer for Hannah whose daddy did not come back'.

The next day I got up at very early o'clock to wait in time-honoured tradition at RAF Brize Norton for a flight to Camp Bastion as the television screens filled with images of Lieutenant Colonel Rupert Thorneloe and Trooper Hammond. I was thinking about what it was really going to be like. Hot, damn hot. Afghanistan is a land of extremes. It is physically a brutal environment in which to exist. As you step off the plane in July you get smacked across the eyeballs by fifty degrees of heat. It blinds you, wrings the water out of you at the rate of six litres a day and generally makes life pretty unpleasant. And that's before you strap fifty-five kilograms to your back and try to fight a man who is wearing a dishdash (Arab tunic) and trainers.

We were booked in by the quarter master's staff, billeted in the 2 Rifles 'Officers' mess'. Same tents as everyone else, same air conditioning blowing all night, same camp cots only slightly less crowded, same dust. Gone are the days when officers might dine with the mess silver every night at home and abroad. As far as accommodation and rations went Camp Bastion was equal opportunities; less for the base rats in their portacabins. Later we had a brief on when we were due to travel to our various Forward Operating Bases. The rest were going the following morning and I would have to wait until the afternoon when the first flight to Inkerman was scheduled. As we finished the brief the lance corporal from 2 Rifles said, 'But don't hold your breath. The CO was kept waiting here for a week early on in the tour.' I'm glad I didn't – hold my breath that is – four days later I was on a flight to Inkerman, which meant I would have precisely thirty-six hours to glean what I could from Iain, company commander of B Company 2 Rifles.

Those four days in Bastion did not pass by in a flash. They amounted to a surreal set of fleeting meetings coupled with long hours, in searing heat, sitting under a high-roofed bus shelter that counted for the airport lounge at Camp Bastion Heliport. The Helicopter Landing Site, or HLS as it is more properly called in military parlance, is at one end of the camp. There was only one HLS actually inside the camp, where casualties were brought, close to the hospital. The inside HLS was busier than the outside one. Panther's Claw was beginning to take its toll. It seemed to me at the time that the hospital HLS was in perpetual use. A chance encounter with the regimental sergeant major of the Light Dragoons confirmed that this was not business as usual.

'We've had forty-five through that facility already. Mainly heat injury but a few nasty ones as well.' I bumped into Charlie, a squadron commander from the Royal Tank Regiment who drove the Viking vehicles. 'They're calling us the 20 minuters', he said in reference to Blackadder and the Army Flying Corps, 'But its proper soldiering.' Adding a dash of cavalry swagger to the black-humoured reality.

The conversation did not make me feel any better. I went off to find the 4 Rifles administrative headquarters, which housed a frustrated CO and RSM who were in Afghanistan to provide personnel and logistic support to the two companies of 4 Rifles who had been mobilised at fairly short notice as the Election Support Force. In reality the two companies held some of the ground, while the Welsh Guards manoeuvred to clear the ground to be taken in Panther's Claw. The RSM of 4 Rifles was an old friend. He had been my CQMS in Northern Ireland. He told me something of the camp rumours and how the other companies were getting on.

'It's fucking mad, sir' was his considered opinion.

The CO was like a bear with a sore head, frustrated as hell by the deployment of all of his fighting companies and he not in command of any of it. Despite being on hand he was not picked to take over from Rupert Thorneloe. I stayed long enough to be briefed but no longer. He was right though. It is curious that we form battalions to promote professional efficiency and morale and then break them up at very short notice, thereby undoing all that good. The quicker the British Army finds a way to preserve but get over its 'regimental traditions' and starts building structures that can live and fight together, the better. Yet I suspected a confluence of what was good for the Army might also be good for him and vice versa, a reasonably common disease in ambitious officers from major up.

Also on our flight was the commander of another of the 2 Rifles companies. His son had been seriously ill so he had been flown home, arriving in a British hospital intensive care unit in desert combats in eighteen hours. Luckily the boy made a speedy recovery and with the alarm over his father was back in Afghanistan four days later. He had lost two men to IEDs and he was about to go to enlarge the base in Sangin called Wishtan. He talked about the highs and lows of command, full of insight and honesty. He gave me a copy of the set of orders he had written for the company on arrival. Within ten days of that conversation he was back in the UK, having been seriously injured in a patrol that saw five men killed.

Finally, after four excruciating days, I got on a helicopter to Inkerman. I arrived just minutes after B Company had got in from patrol. They had been attacked and the medic had been wounded. Iain was just about to start his after-action review when I arrived, hot and pale. It was even hotter here than Bastion, like being roasted alive. For the next thirty-six hours, less about six hours of sweaty sleep, Iain talked through everything from the management of locally employed civilians to tactics in the green zone (although by the time we arrived in October the green zone would be turning brown). The maze that grew above head height would come down and the jungle tactics of the summer fight would turn into something more conventional.

The large Afghan compound named Forward Operating Base Inkerman had been occupied to act as some kind of a buffer and to take the fighting out of the centre of Sangin in 2007. This in turn would allow the economic regeneration of Sangin. Inkerman was designed to keep the hornets out of Sangin. To its north, east and south lay ground where the Taliban had complete freedom of movement; an entirely safe area from which to launch attacks. Iain had two platoons, a section of mortars and a troop of light guns from the Royal Artillery. They had arrived in the middle of the poppy harvest in late spring and been left unmolested for six weeks. They conducted long patrols into the green zone and met many of the local population. To the south and east of Inkerman is desert. Scattered compounds with deep wells but sparsely inhabited. Large hills rise up out of the desert like dogs' teeth to provide a jagged edge above the shimmer. To the west of Inkerman is the small village of Sareagar. As the fighting intensified from 2006 to 2008 many people moved from the green zone into Sareagar to escape the violence. As a result there were none of the traditional tribal or village relationships. It was essentially a new town.

Then, two weeks before I got there for the recce, Iain's world had suddenly become very small. They could hardly step out of the gate without being attacked. In 2008 this had happened to 2 Para on 13 June. Iain had been given until 16 June. They could not get near the farmers as they fled on sight. We talked on, agreeing on most things, but I came away with three abiding impressions, borne out by the video of the camp that I took back to show the company and families. I was glad that there were far fewer IED incidents in the Inkerman area than in other areas. It was, as my notebook says, a 'clean fight'. Secondly, whilst Iain had two platoons I would bring four, and that would give me the freedom to do a good deal more, so there was plenty of opportunity. And finally, what was not apparent to me as I took my video shots but was very important a week later when I showed it to the families, was that the enemy mortar threat, or Indirect Fire (IDF), as it is colloquially known in the military, was greatly reduced compared to Iraq in 2007. The random nature of most artillery-type bombardment erodes morale. From the Western Front to Basra Palace soldiers who have been exposed to this threat do not forget it. They were all glad it was not going to be this way again. So, despite the cruel context of much of this recce I came away emboldened. It seemed very much as though I could dictate the pace of operations and that we would be saved from the worst excesses of the insurgency.

# Chapter 3

# Training Part 2

The next instalment in the training regime was the Final Test Exercise, or FTX in the Army lexicon of three-letter abbreviations. This took place on, over and around Salisbury Plain and we were based in Imber village in the very centre of Salisbury Plain West. Imber was taken over by the army after the Second World War. It remains much like any other Wiltshire village; a pub, a church, a manor house. And a small, tight-knit population that still comes back to celebrate the Christian festivals in Imber Church, which has remained consecrated. Except for the occasional church service it is now dilapidated and devoid of human social life; its purpose now to provide the architecture for trial by arms.

I was distinctly dubious about the merits of being stuck in Imber for two weeks trying to train. For a start we had people all over the rest of the country on courses and this exercise was designed largely to give the Brigade Headquarters practice at their planning cycle. A brigade plan takes at least thirty-six hours to work up and a battlegroup one can take twelve hours, with a company usually able to plan in less than four hours. Put that little lot together and Rifleman Smith spends two days doing not very much before he is asked to get out of his scratcher and do something useful. Of course there is the necessary discipline of camp routine to nail down. Feeding, sleeping and washing arrangements are a vital part of force protection on a tour and I was anxious to get it right. One of the messages from the recce was that the long-drop latrines needed constant attention and were a source of the worst kind of ailment. D and V, once it takes hold, can be difficult to stop. B Company 2 Rifles had sixteen men with the 'squits' at one stage, which had forced the delay of a planned operation. Both Y Company 45 Commando and B Company 2 Para had suffered similarly before them. The likelihood of other injuries is significantly enhanced after illness. Dehydration causing heat injury is the most common, as soldiers head out on patrol thinking they are better, but are not yet fully recovered.

Prevention is far better than cure. Therefore rigorous hand-washing before meals is a must. Provision of sufficient water for washing and shaving, as well as drinking, is fairly high on the list. To achieve this, a Rifle company has an administrative chain. The CSM enforces discipline and is in charge of ammunition, rations, casualty evacuation and force protection. The CQMS deals with everything else. Any bit of equipment that you get comes through the quarter master's chain via the CQMS. At platoon level all of this work is undertaken by the platoon serjeant and his team of section second in commands who hold the rank of lance corporal. Hiving off this aspect of our preparations to this group allows concurrent activity to take place. As the OC (me), the platoon commanders and the section commanders are formulating their plans, the CSM, CQMS, platoon serjeants and section seconds in command are conducting the necessary administration. Getting this work started requires a Warning Order. True to form, the army has drills and procedures to ensure this happens as efficiently as possible. Like most military activity, learning it in theory is very simple, while doing it wet, cold, tired, hungry or afraid turns even the simplest of activities into a herculean task. So if the Final Test Exercise was going to be at all useful, it was as an opportunity to really test those procedures.

Much has been written and said about the inadequate state of equipment procurement in the military. I am ashamed to say, having been a sponsoring officer for soldier equipment in the MoD for the last two years of my military career, it is absolutely true and if anything underestimates the scale of the problem. The equipment provided to soldiers in Afghanistan is just about adequate. Unfortunately, getting it once you are in Afghanistan or even just before you go means that you do not really know how to use it. The final exercise was a prime example of this. In 2008 and early 2009 most of the improvised explosive devices had some metal content. The equipment we used to help find the bombs at that time was called a Vallon, and this was supported by a list of tactics, techniques and procedures to counter the threat of IEDs, known as Barma drills. But key to it all in 2009 was the Vallon. In Helmand we had thirty-five for the company; on the Final Test Exercise we had three. I had just come back from a recce where no one went out of the gate without the ground in front of them being swept by a Vallon. So for the first operation I was given a Hobson's choice of setting platoons in lines of thirty behind a Vallon or breaking them down into their more normal tactical formations. We considered broomsticks; but the image of a soldier practicing for combat in Afghanistan with a broomstick might severely undermine the confidence of young Riflemen and the public alike. The Barma drills have a severe impact on patrolling speed so it is important to get used to going slower than one might do normally.

We set off on day three in three long lines behind a Vallon. Our task was to meet up with the recce platoon and investigate a reported IED factory. The recce platoon was being commanded by Captain Ben Coward – a great name for an officer! Ben had commanded 2 Platoon in A Company in Iraq, but moved to 3 Rifles via a training job in Catterick. He still knew a few of those who were left of the old hands. He was shocked at the number of new faces. He briefed me on what they had seen overnight. Then I noticed none of them were carrying a Vallon. He told me that they had not had any issued and were in the traditional recce role for this operation. The recce platoon was to be hard hit by IEDs in Afghanistan, as were we. Whilst one cannot say that not having the Vallons in training caused those deaths, one can say for absolute certain that if you are going to send an army to war, it is not just about the equipment that is in the theatre, it needs to be there in training. The army, the MoD and most importantly Her Majesty's Treasury continue to fail to make this happen despite ten years to get it right.

On the way in to the suspected IED factory the company was attacked. The cry came up the line, 'Man down!' Treating the casualty promptly and getting him away to hospital inside the golden hour is very difficult when you are under fire. Maintaining the momentum of a patrol in that context is even harder, especially if the drill includes the use of a Vallon from the point of wounding to the HLS. It requires relentless practice, and is a key part of training. The report that gets the medical assets on their way is a '9 liner' and we practised long and hard getting the information required quickly to be able to send these as soon as possible. Marking and preparing a Helicopter Landing Site must also be completed quickly and safely, and skills are required to marshal the aircraft. We had sent a number of people away on courses so that each platoon could do this task. Now was a chance to confirm that training. Except, of course, that we never saw a helicopter. Well, we did see some flying about, but not once in two weeks, despite repeated requests, did a helicopter come and pick up a casualty. This had also been true on the exercise in Norfolk, where the excellent blokes from Amputees in Action, who give a phenomenally realistic edge to the training, had to be left in the middle of a field. In Afghanistan we evacuated over fifty casualties, often under fire. We became all too familiar with the process, and for the most part were extremely proficient, but we learned that skill on the job, not in training.

This exercise was also an opportunity to meet some of the people we might work with, the attachments or 'atts' for short. A peace-time infantry company consists of 110 men at full strength, but a company group on operations can be up to three times that number. The extras come from elsewhere in the battalion and all the other regiments of the army. One really wants to meet those people in training, to get to know them, to enhance mutual understanding. This is especially important for the Fire Support Team, or FST. The FST are the group that control the indirect fire – the mortars and the artillery as well as the drones, helicopters and other aircraft. One can go on any number of video-hosting web sites and see the devastating effect of the arsenal that they control. But they had been taken for a different exercise. We had met for three days of the exercise in Norfolk and I got ever more anxious to bring them into the team. Same detail for the troop of engineers.

In the event there were only three individuals who stayed with us for those two weeks who we would eventually see three months later in Afghanistan. Two signallers who would help with operations room radio duties and Lance Corporal Michael Pritchard of the Royal Military Police. The Military Police are normally regarded with huge suspicion by Riflemen of all ranks. In Helmand every company has two police attachments and they need to be integrated along with everyone else. 'Pritch', as he became universally known, won the respect of the Riflemen of A Company very quickly during these two weeks in July by doing everything that they did and his job on top of that. We could not know in late July that he had barely five months to live.

Early in the second week of the exercise, having done just one operation, my patience was wearing a little thin. The most exciting thing to have happed since the IED factory operation was that Colour Serjeant Tim Lush had almost blown himself up with the army-issued improvised explosive device that is the 'Puffing Billy' or M67 Immersion Heater, to give it its proper name. Lighting these things is an art: too little fuel and it won't start, too much and it goes bang. Colour Lush overfilled just a little. The bang caused all the sentries to give the signal for indirect fire and the ops room geared up for an incident. Amongst the shouting a blackened face with a strong smell of singed eyebrow appeared in the ops room telling everyone to calm down. By the time we had spent a few months in Afghanistan, where all our washing water was heated by a Puffing Billy, we were pretty irritated by how similar the explosion sounded to a genuine IED. Anyway, exploding heaters aside, after some discussion I was allowed to go and see the 'Enemy' commander and start running incidents against the patrol base to liven things up. We discussed the type of incidents we wanted and I let the enemy have a free hand for a day or two. I wanted to see how many incidents we could handle simultaneously. I cannot remember how many we got to, but it was definitely single figures, when Ben emerged from the ops room saying that the signallers were frazzled and we needed to turn down the heat a bit. In Afghanistan we got up to forty incidents in one day, something we would have dismissed as totally impossible and utterly unrealistic in July. As Ben would come to say in our evening meeting, to a progressively ironic groan, 'just another quiet day in the Inkerman AO'.

The other little pleasure we had was a visit from the CO of 4 Rifles and the brigade commander of 1 Mechanised Brigade, who were our chain of command for everything outside of the operation. Sending an independent company to another brigade is a bit like sending your child to a school friend for tea unsupervised. At the end you want to know how they have behaved. You might ask the child how they have behaved; you might ask the child's friend; and then you ask the other parent to find out the truth. And then on the way home in the car you either praise or castigate the child on their performance. So it was with some trepidation that I welcomed them both to my crowded abode. They stayed for about an hour. A popular captain in 4 Rifles had been badly injured by an IED explosion in Helmand and the CO came bearing news that he was still very much fighting for his life, despite the excellent attention of the staff in Selly Oak. We had rather presumed he was well on the way to recovery, which thankfully came in the end, but at the expense of a second leg. The news from the brigadier was good. He even told me I had the opportunity to command the best company in Afghanistan. This was high praise and I shared it with the company, trying my utmost to keep a lid on anything that might provoke a sense of complacency, because as I kept on saying, to anyone who would listen 'you are only as good as your last patrol' and that, for a couple of members of the company, had not gone particularly well.

*  *  *  *  *

I contend and have for some time that there are two candidates for 'hardest job in the army'. This does not include 'army wife', which is the clear winner. They are lance corporal and second lieutenant.

Lance corporal is one of the hardest ranks to gain, but probably the easiest to lose. The first step on the promotion ladder for a soldier is entirely in the gift of the Commanding Officer. What he gives with one hand he can take away with the other. Behaviour that may be tolerated one day in a Rifleman is suddenly no longer tolerated because of the responsibility that a lance corporal has for the discipline and administration of what are, by and large, his peer group. It is also the first exposure to the privilege and responsibility of leadership, which at lance corporal level comes with rather more responsibility than it does privilege.

Its rival in this competition is second lieutenant. The job of taking command of a platoon, especially on operations, is huge. It is the only job in the army where the man who is nominally your second in command is older, more experienced and more professionally qualified to do the job you are doing. The only thing that marks you out over him are your 'personal qualities', which somehow add up to result in you being given the leadership role. Into that add a generous dose of inexperience in life and tactics, stir with a spade full of confidence, enthusiasm and a bundle of theory, and it is a potentially lethal cocktail. Moreover, as a junior officer you can never get to know the men under your command too well. Finding out the pressures in their lives, and learning what motivates each individual gives one leverage in command. On arrival one knows nothing of them, and even when you live with thirty people day in day out for six months what they come up with can sometimes surprise or even astonish. When it comes to command of Riflemen, the only thing that isn't a surprise is the surprise.

My own experience of this was in Bosnia in 1998. I arrived in B Company 2nd Battalion The Royal Green Jackets to command 7 Platoon in February 1998.

We deployed to Bosnia six weeks later. I had conducted meet and greet interviews with all members of the platoon on arrival, but it wasn't until we were in Gornjie Vakuf that I had a chance to really sit down with each of them. My stock question at the end of the interview was, 'Is there anything that we haven't covered that you think I ought to know?' Four months later at a Platoon House in Prozor a young Rifleman was on guard and I went out to have a chat. In the sentry post was a picture of a small baby. The conversation ran something like this:

'Who's the baby? Nephew, niece, brother or sister?'

'Nah Boss, she's mine.'

'Really?' trying to keep the shock from my tone, 'When was she born?'

'Just before we came away.'

'Right, so how is she?'

The pleasantries of the conversation continued for about five minutes before I could hold back no longer.

'Rifleman Smith, when we had that chat in GV and I said was there anything else I needed to know, this was one of those things. Is she on your next of kin form? Are you paying maintenance? If she was ill would you be asking for compassionate leave? None of these things can I help you with, unless you tell me.' By now I had a considerably exasperated tone.

From one perspective it looks like lack of trust on the part of the Riflemen. From another, why should he tell, to all intents and purposes a complete stranger, the intimate details of the results of a passing-out parade fumble? On the upper side of the chain of command in 1998, to make matters worse for the young Second Lieutenant Streatfeild, there was equal initial distrust. On my arrival in Paderborn B Company had gone straight on exercise. I had completed the officer training course at the Royal Military Academy Sandhurst, the Platoon Commanders' Battle Course at the Infantry Battle School in Warminster, swiftly followed by the Armoured Infantry Platoon Commanders' Course, tactics with vehicles being somewhat different to tactics on foot. Eighteen months of military training, after which I felt like I knew what I was doing. I finally had my own platoon, on exercise, and was sitting in my first set of orders. Harry 'Wank Duaarrrch' Emk, the company commander, finished his orders, looked straight past me at my platoon sergeant and said 'Sergeant Healy, any questions?'

I tried not to let my disappointment or my inner confusion show. Three months later, on a company operation in Bosnia, as Sergeant Healy and I went to yet another Orders Group together, I saw that same look of horror cross *his* face as Harry leaned out of the door and said. 'It's alright Sergeant Healy, you can go and get the platoon sorted out. Mr Streatfeild can handle this one.' It took time, but when it happened it was an unequivocal signal that as far as the OC was concerned I had the con. As far as Sergeant Healy was concerned that did not come until a little while later, and only after I made an unequivocally correct tactical call when he had thought otherwise. All through that period I learned new lessons every day about how reliant I was on him and on the section commanders for their professional judgement and also for advice on the man-management of the Riflemen. The long and short of it is that mutual trust develops through experience, and most importantly shared experience. As a newly arrived second lieutenant you have neither, which makes things very difficult.

*     *     *     *     *

Corporal Penk and the men of 3 Platoon returned from a patrol. It was sometime in the middle of the night. As they cleared their weapons to make them safe a blank round was fired. The standard procedure is for the weapon to be removed immediately from the soldier and checked by an armourer to ensure no mechanical failure and only then, if it is a failure of drill on the part of the soldier, does he get charged for negligence. In Helmand, as in all other places, the procedure is to use a qualified individual to check that the weapon is safely unloaded and it was this procedure that should have been in place that night. Tom, who had only recently arrived as the 3 Platoon Commander, was the 'senior' officer present. No one had been checking the drill and the weapon had not been removed. Corporal Penk said he had fired the shot deliberately after a problem with the extractor had left a round in the breech. He said he had rectified the mechanical fault – a sticky extractor. To a platoon commander faced with a relatively senior corporal this might sound very plausible. To an OC it sounded highly implausible and my hunch was that it was deceitful.

Corporal Penk and his young family stood to lose a month's wages if a negligent discharge of a round was proved. As an experienced man, my guess was that faced with that, and the personal and professional shame, he had likely chosen a story that shifted the blame on to the person supposed to be doing the checking, but kept some for himself: he could be blamed for an error of judgement in discharging the round deliberately, but would not face formal administrative action and a fine. I seethed internally. Tom got a long chat. Fairly friendly, but with more than a few pointers as to how things might have been done differently. Corporal Penk got the full version of the lecture from me and then from Pat Hyde but stayed resolute in his denial. I had the weapon checked to confirm there was no problem with the extractor. I could never have proved it had never been rectified because there was nothing wrong with it in the first place. I more than suspect, however, that anything I or the CSM said or did to Corporal Penk would never have compared, in the slightest, to the wrath of Mrs Penk if he had lost a month's wages. He just used all his professional and life experience to make sure he never had to face that fury.

As the training concluded and the tour commenced, the resolute Corporal Penk received ever-greater praise from those who worked with him. For me, however, there was always the cloud that cast the shadow. The honesty and integrity of subordinates and superiors is something that really, really matters. That is not to say I don't like or admire people who can manipulate or bend the system to get what they want, it's just that when I ask them a question I want an honest answer, however difficult that may be to deal with. Trust and the truth that underpins it is the most precious commodity. It means that one can underwrite the honest mistakes of subordinates and superiors alike. Either by the support you give for the chain of command by passing on orders without excuses, or shouldering responsibility for situations that turn out badly.

*   *   *   *   *

Sometime near the start of the exercise I said to Graeme, my fellow 'independent' company commander from B Company 1 Scots, 'Not good news from Wishtan.'

'I don't need to think about it for too long before it gives me the heebie-jeebies' he replied.

2 Rifles had just suffered their worst day. Five had been killed and several of the commanders, including the company commander, had been wounded. At that moment I would not have swapped with Graeme for all the tea in China. It was hard not to cover my own sense of relief that I thought we would face a more limited version of that particular threat. In the event B Company 1 Scots did a fantastic job in overcoming the threat both physical and psychological, testament to the continued resilience of the 'jock' and the leadership of Graeme and his team.

The training season was drawing to a close. One last serial to complete. The Combined Arms Live Firing Exercise, or 'CALFEX' in the lexicon. By now the company were tired. Three weeks' leave beckoned in the second week of August, and all we wanted was to pack up and go. Bizarrely, the brigade staff had conspired to put us under the control of the Royal Welsh Battlegroup for this phase of the training. In all I worked, as we would in Afghanistan, with what would become my real HQ for only two weeks in the whole of six months. Even then we had only conducted two missions of any significance in which we could get used to each other's foibles. A serious error. I was uneasy about it then and campaigned to do the CALFEX with 3 Rifles, not least because we would get away on leave a week earlier, which many had planned for. Having booked holidays I had to release half a dozen who had paid for flights to be with their families. This included both a platoon commander and a platoon serjeant.

I consoled myself that this was good practice for R and R, stepping people up into unfamiliar roles, but the limited work we had done with the Battlegroup Headquarters was to prove a headache when we got to Helmand. I should add that the HQ, fully formed, includes a number of cells. For combined arms live firing the most important is the relationship between the fire support team and the Royal Artillery battery commander with his fire support cell. In our case we had a fire support team from the 4/73 (Sphinx) Special Op Battery, originally from 5 Regiment Royal Artillery, who were now attached to the Chestnut Troop of 1st Regiment Royal Horse Artillery, and of this group only the fire support team were on the exercise. In short, it was a bit of a muddle.

I had done less than a week of training with my fire support team and here we were just about to go through a mandatory exercise reporting to people whom we would never see again. Both Frank Ledwidge and Rory Stewart have written long and hard about the impact of military culture on operations at the strategic level. At the tactical and operational levels it is worse. 'Just crack on' is the cause, symptom and cure of a mountain of problems bestowed on Tommy Atkins. The muddle that faced us at the start of this exercise was just another example of it.

Anyone who has been to Otterburn in August knows one thing. Take your mosquito repellent. The slightest sight of soft skin and the beasts are poking in their proboscis. The military repellent is industrial strength and, when added to cam cream and a good sweat, causes untold agony as the rivulets run into your eyes. We also had our issued protective glasses for the first time. I was more than keen that we operated with these on at all times. It wasn't only me. The enforcement of the wearing of protective equipment was reaching a crescendo across the army. Examples of blinded soldiers and those who had had their sight saved by protective specs were regular features of briefings. That and moulded hearing protection were absolutely to be worn. When an IED goes off it badly injures or kills the person who steps on it, but the fragments that get thrown out can blind and the overpressure from the blast can deafen. One casualty is inevitable, but can turn into four or five very easily. This risk can be mitigated by hearing and eye protection. Unfortunately it is not that easy. The moulded ear protection is painful to wear and the microphone system contained in it makes you sound as though you are speaking from inside a tank of water. If you go out at dawn, as you start to sweat in the cool air the glasses steam up. The sweaty repellent-laden rivulets run over the Perspex. In the heat of battle, stopping to give your specs a quick wipe is often not an option; it is another Hobson's choice. For the CALFEX in Otterburn I was utterly determined at least to practise with these items. I encouraged suggestions as to how they might be improved. Some glued foam over the top to create a barrier from the sweat or pulled them forward to increase air flow to prevent fogging. An easily accessible rag on a string became part and parcel of company standard operating procedures.

The highlight of the CALFEX was the Company attack. Again the limited Vallons meant Helmand tactics had to be played rather than trained. I went to see the Range Conducting Officer (RCO). I was all set for a bit of an argument.

I had heard what the attack involved and it sounded to me far too much like a traditional company attack. Fighting the Soviets on the North German Plain rather than insurgents in Afghanistan. First on the list was to be the targetry. Were there civilian targets so we could practise positive identification of targets? Were there realistic engagement distances? How close were the artillery, mortars, and heavy machine-guns going to be allowed to fire in support of the troops? How low would the aircraft and helicopters be allowed to come to really show the company what kind of fire support we could draw on if they really got in the shit? I was working myself up into righteous indignation as I drove to the range. Standing there to greet me as the RCO was Colour Serjeant Tom Platt. Platty, the ginger platypus, Plat man or any number of less repeatable names, had been a corporal and then a sergeant in 2 RGJ when I was but a whippersnapper. He was someone I did not know that well, although I knew that I would get an honest assessment of what lay ahead. 'Well, to be honest boss, it's wank.' Great, I thought. He then explained in some detail why.

Him 'For a start it is a company attack over 3 kilometres from first contact.'

Me (inner voice) 'Holy shit it's going to be a lick.'

Him 'Brigadier wanted it like that. Wanted a real tester.'

Me, sardonically 'nothing like ending on a high…'

Him 'Most of the companies we've had through have had to miss bits out just to reach the end.'

Me 'Bet that makes them feel good.'

Him 'Not really, but we have to get them to the bit where they can fire the mortars. Not that you can see them. Safety means they're so far off to a flank the blokes won't even know it's happening.'

Within two weeks of taking over in Inkerman 2 Platoon got isolated in the open and the smoke from the mortars dropped around them. No one was hurt, but I doubt it would have happened if we had been given a chance to train with all of the people who supported us. The Chestnut Troop and 3 Rifles mortars fired smoke and illumination rounds almost every day in support of operations that we undertook in Helmand; they helped guard the base; some even came out on patrol. It is a great shame that we never got to train with them before we left. I don't need to labour the point, but it was a disappointing way to finish – saved only by fortuitous coincidence.

Platty took a very Green Jacket approach to the range – everything necessary and nothing that was not. It meant we were given a realistic view of the firepower of the fire support group; Freddie and his crews on the heavy machine-guns. He was ably assisted from the skies by an Apache helicopter flown by another ex-Green Jacket called Tom. Tom had been the in the 2 RGJ Battalion Headquarters at the same time as me but then transferred to the Army Air Corps. After we finished the attack completely, he landed the aircraft at the end of the range and allowed the Riflemen to crawl all over it. We then then had a company photograph with the Apache hovering behind. This just about made the whole trip worth it. There is nothing more comforting in Helmand than the sound of an Apache coming overhead. As an infantry soldier burdened by kit and having to move tortoise-like toward or away from the enemy, the presence of an Apache means the insurgents lie low. It fixes them in place so that one can either manoeuvre against them or withdraw. It was great to get a first-hand brief from the guy who had just supported the attack and get a Gucci little company photograph to boot.

The last training the Company did was a final fitness test, the Advanced Combat Fitness Test Part Two (ACFT2). It is conducted over two days. And took place after summer leave.

Day one: 20km endurance march over varied terrain, at least 6km off road; must be completed in three hours and thirty minutes; 30kg load to be carried.
Day two: 20km endurance march over varied terrain; at least 6km off road; must be completed in three hours; 20Kg load to be carried.

This is the longest, hardest fitness test the regular army has to offer. By the time we got to it I thought I was quite fit. The route chosen was fourteen kilometres off road and over some of the largest lumps on Salisbury Plain. As we climbed the last big hill on the second day, from the NN crossing to the radio mast just outside Bulford for the real connoisseurs, I was forced to have a quiet word with myself. Through the lactic acid burn and with the whispered encouragement of the voice in my head I kept pace with my platoon commanders despite giving them ten years and twice as many pounds. Rescued by commander's legs. Still, I was extremely happy with the results: 95 per cent passed. All those who did not had at least passed the Basic Combat Fitness test that formed the first half of the first day. The reason I was so happy was that the test is not really physical. It is more a test of individual and collective will. There was no better example of this than at the end the second day. One of the Riflemen, Carlo Apolis, was there at the end walking like John Wayne. Having chosen the wrong underwear he had marched until he was raw and bleeding; his blood stained the crotch of his combats to prove it. That kind of determination to finish, to go on to the bitter end, is a very precious commodity. Despite the tiredness, the majority had two weeks to recover. But the recovery of a twenty-year-old Rifleman is pretty rapid, while that of a thirty-six-year-old major is less so, but I consoled myself in a long bath that we were in the best possible shape, physically and mentally, to deal with what was coming. We left the period of training as well trained as it was possible to be. It is a paradox that this should be better trained than any of our predecessors, but barely enough for what was to follow.

## Chapter 4

# Leave, Leaving, Left

As summer leave started we had eight weeks to go before the tour. I had two things in mind for summer leave; fitness and family time. Those who support the families in the build-up to a tour reckon that, with about six weeks to go, whichever partner is going on the tour is already mentally there. The tour is so imminent that the mind of the person going puts up self-protecting mental barriers in preparation for separation. Couples often go through a very similar set of emotions to those that surround divorce and some even go through a form of grief. In any event it is cruel and unusual punishment. You are caught in the paradox of wishing to draw out every second you have and at the same time wishing it were all over. You want to see everyone and see no one. Those who you do see fall into a number of categories, the worst of which by far is what I came to call 'dead man walking' syndrome. The path to leaving is a rocky one. On a personal level it is difficult to know what is going to get to you and what isn't. One aunt told me that my deceased grandmother would be very proud, which put a lump in my throat for an hour. My godfather, a priest, offered his blessing, which also completely turned me over. There were others who I thought might be difficult but turned out to be rather more straightforward. Another aunt who was very ill and whom I never saw again was an easy parting. It was almost as if we both knew the next six months might be quite tricky and that was something we shared as we offered each other goodbyes. But conversations with people who seem to fully expect never to see you again are not easy, happy or distracting. In the face of unrelenting pessimism the barriers go up.

We were lucky with the weather that summer. Having enjoyed only two days of rain during the whole of the training period and generally sweated in all parts of the UK, in August for most of the of the country the weather broke. Except, that is, in East Anglia. Planning six months ahead, we had thought in February that it would be a good idea to go to Southwold in Suffolk with another family in August. One of my oldest friends and his wife had some friends who thoroughly recommended it: a picturesque village, good pubs, nice beach, an almost quintessentially British seaside holiday. We had umm'd and ahh'd about going with friends, eventually deciding that at least we could get a couple of nights out together by sharing the babysitting. It would give the kids someone to play with and generally make the whole thing a bit more distracting.

Moreover, having lived, breathed, eaten and slept army and Afghanistan for four months, military stuff would be the last thing I wanted to talk about and the company of non-military friends is the only way to achieve that.

So it was off to Southwold for two weeks. The days on that holiday merge for me into one. The routine took the form of an early start; both sets of children were early risers. One parent was selected/forced to do the early shift from 0530 to whenever the rest got up, kicking off with whichever DVD was the unhappy compromise between Emily and Billy, our friends' eldest. Emily had cultivated an ally in Digby, Billy's younger brother, so usually by force majeure it was *Dora the Explorer* rather than *Power Rangers* that was chosen. Henry, who had his third birthday during that holiday, was too young and too disinterested to get a vote.

I have strong memories of both Henry and Emily in Southwold. Emily had grown from toddler to girl but something was up with Henry. Until the age of two and a half he had made good progress, but in the previous six months his language had not improved. He still only had a few one-word indicators of what he wanted. Despite a couple of attempts we had not been able to potty train him and Rachel was beginning to get concerned. I was much more blasé. All kids had a little plateau. Emily had had a year where she did not make much progress but was now chatting merrily away. Henry was quite withdrawn. He did not like being around Billy and Digby. He was at his happiest rolling down a sand dune or swimming in the sea and I was quite happy to indulge him in this. After all, kids, as I had often been told by my mother, are barometers of their parents and this was a particularly high-pressure time. I was sure that however hard we were trying to have a good holiday they could not help but pick up the signals that something was afoot.

On the second day we were there it was brought home to me just how tense things were. The end of the day was always signalled by kids' tea at five-thirty, after which I had agreed with Rachel that come what may I needed to take some physical exercise. The first night I ran along a near-deserted beach in the twilight. Day two I decided on a circuit on the beach. Thirty-metre shuttles in the soft sand, followed by a series of press-ups, sit-ups, star-jumps and the like. There were one or two other holiday makers taking an evening stroll who clearly thought I was quite mad. As I put myself face down in the sand for the first time I felt grit grate under my wedding ring. So I popped the ring off and placed it carefully on the towel. Forty-five minutes later, hot and tired, I finished the physical jerks and went to pick up the towel. No ring. Shit. I looked carefully under where the towel had been. No ring. Bugger. I cast gently around, trying not to dig up the sand for fear of burying it forever. I looked up to see if any of the passers-by had come close to the lunatic running up and down. No. Shit, shit, shit. This did not auger well. I spent twenty minutes looking and by now it could be anywhere as my search in the last five had become increasingly desperate. Nothing for it but to go back and 'fess up. I got back to the cottage by the sea five minutes later to explain what had happened. I thought a matter-of-fact tone would best convey an 'I'm not worried I can always get another one' kind of sentiment. The tone I should have used was a 'Help! I've lost my wedding ring and I need your help to move heaven and a good deal of sand until I find it.' Rachel and I set off back to the beach laden with sieves and spades. I think Rachel would have been ordering arc lights if there had been any reception on the mobile. The five minutes to my gym area of the beach were punctuated with a fair number of 'Icantbelieveits' and 'Whydidn'tyoujusts'. Topped off by the unanswerable, 'This is not a good sign.' The excavation began. After two minutes with no joy I was just beginning to think needle and haystack and how much was it going to cost me in time, attention and cold hard cash to get anywhere near making up for this faux pas, when Rachel found the ring. Clearly I had not looked carefully enough in the first place, a 'daddy look' not a 'mummy look' as Emily still calls it. I still had a major amount of making up to do, but the crisis had been averted. Hindsight makes this event seem amusing, vaguely ridiculous. At the time it could not have been more serious. It was as though the tea leaves had been swirled and the marriage would end. I have never been superstitious, but as the tour got closer and when death travelled with us, ritual, superstition and religion played ever greater parts in all our lives.

We had several visits from both family and friends while in Southwold. My brother and sister appeared. My brother took me out for a run. He is an actor and takes his personal fitness seriously. As we ran I pushed him satisfactorily hard for the last two miles despite giving him two years and at least two stone in handicap advantage. Post-run rehydration was followed by a certain amount of dehydration. Adnam's ale is brewed a couple of miles from Southwold and is as close to what I think of as a proper pint of bitter as you can get, topped only by Larkins, which is a local gift from my home village of Chiddingstone, a gift that keeps on giving for at least twenty-four hours after the last pint is drunk. I reckoned that a few extra drinks before we went would be more than compensated for by seven months dry. This is the ultimate form of binge drinking. The army has tried hard to shed the drinking culture in recent years, I have to say to little effect. A platoon night out is generally accompanied by the recommended weekly intake of units of alcohol. Drink is not commonly served at lunch any more, unless the mess is entertaining guests, but a regimental dinner in all messes, corporals', sergeants' and officers', will go on till dawn. My own view is that in an age when puritans are forever advising us on the dangers of these things, there is less and less attention paid to the social benefits: the opportunity to share a problem and then forget about it for a while. All things in moderation, including moderation. In the evenings of that summer, as my thoughts turned to the days ahead, the darker ones were dispersed and defrayed by a drink, or two.

So the start of each day began a little more slowly than it might have done, but after a good breakfast the important things were achieved. A trip to the pier, fish and chips on the way to go crabbing in Walberswick, pub lunches or sandy sandwiches on the beach. Weather that continued to do us proud by way of being just hot enough to sunbathe without being roasted, and as the rest of the country got wet we stayed dry. All this sounds pretty idyllic. At any other time and place it would have been, just not with eight, then seven, weeks to go. There were moments when our sharing of the house became oppressive. Generating quality family time became difficult until a whispered imperative made it so. The internal conflicts of trying to generate a sense of normalcy versus feeling anything but normal are subjugated by a desire not to argue or discuss difficult topics because it might overshadow everything else. It becomes increasingly important to be making the most of the time, to be doing something, to be having fun. The trip to the maize maze close to Southwold was fun, until we ended up at the far end rather too close to lunch. Finding our way back with hungry children became an exercise in restraint as well as navigation. Much like being in a maize field in Afghanistan. Some people like to think that being in the army is like being a breed apart, that because of what we go through we are not like others. I do not subscribe to this. I do not believe we are different. I do think, however, that an operational tour, especially one that is prospectively dangerous and difficult, applies a magnifying glass to the emotions we all feel at various times in our lives. Coping with this is indeed difficult, and in my experience has led to the break-up of relationships both casual and married at a rate that is far higher than in 'normal' life. This effect works on two planes: it not only magnifies the height of the highs and the depth of the lows, but it also squeezes them into a very short space of time, which reduces the ability to contextualise, rationalise and resolve. It is a quart of emotional vodka in a pint pot to down in one. Enough of the amateur psychology, you just have to 'crack on' through.

By the end of leave there were six weeks to go until we left, the date now confirmed for 4 October. We made our way back to Bulford. I completed my fifteenth PE session in three weeks, something of a personal record for a period on 'holiday', and went back to work. Over the last weekend of my leave Rachel was searching on the internet, plugging in some child development symptoms. Over the course of the three weeks, despite our best efforts, we had given up on potty training Henry. He had taken to disappearing down the Southwold promenade and peeing on the veranda of unoccupied beach huts. Amusing if you are not a worried parent. He had hated his third birthday. Rachel printed a list of symptoms.

'You know, he might have autism.'

'No way.'

We read through the list. My view was that it was far too early to tell. Our experience with Emily was that it took her a while to get going but she was now a very happy nearly five year old who was meeting all her milestones. She was just about to have her first proper day at big school and was very much looking forward to it. Only time would tell and besides there were other things to worry about. I had to get the company fit and ready to go. I was already there.

*   *   *   *   *

In May 2009 I went to a play that my brother was in at the Bush theatre. Also there that night was an old friend of his who worked at the BBC on the *Today* programme on Radio 4. I knew from my time in the MoD PR department, which sat next door to the 'News' department, just what kind of sentiment *Today* provoked on the news desks. It generally wasn't very pretty. So after yet another bravura performance from bro – no bias, durch – we headed for after-show drinks. Afghanistan came up. The Welsh Guards were beginning to come under pressure and my complaint to John was that the news programmes seemed to report only death or glory and not much in between. His very frank assessment was that anything else wasn't really newsworthy. This was honest, if slightly frustrating. I pressed my case that the military was caught in a Catch 22 of not being able to explain what we do day to day because we were either being cast as heroes or corpses, neither of which got near the truth for the vast majority.

Anyway at one point during this conversation I said that I was going to Afghanistan in six months and that I would do a blog for *Today* if he wanted. The answer in May was 'Thanks but no thanks. It's just not the kind of thing we're into.'

That summer, as the controversy over army equipment and casualties grew, I got a phone call sometime in July. John and the team had been kicking around a few ideas in the office looking for a different angle on Afghanistan and John had a remembered the brother of a friend who was going in the next couple of months who had said at one point that he would do a blog. By this time I was far more sanguine about the whole thing. I knew that the next months were not going to be easy. I got in touch with my commanding officers who put a caveat on that if I did the blog there must be no deadlines. There would be other, more pressing deadlines. Moreover, I needed to get it cleared in London.

I phoned my successor in the PR department. I was keen from the outset that the MoD did not see this as a 'news' item, although I had my suspicions that the director of the News desk in the MoD would take a different view. Anything on the *Today* programme is news. After some deliberation the MoD agreed, but any report I did would be filed in the same way as the journalists in theatre, through the media team in the Task Force Headquarters (TFHQ). A meeting was arranged with John from the BBC and Bob from the MoD on the neutral ground of Wagamama on the South Bank. The BBC had some concerns as well. I think one of them was that they feared they would be getting pure propaganda.

Anyway, all this left the way clear for a preliminary agreement. I would do five pieces, two before I left and three on arrival, and then we would see how things were going. This had advantages all round. It gave the BBC and the MoD an opportunity to test audience reaction and see what kind of content I would put in without having to commit to the long term. For my part I was glad there would be no deadlines and I could dip my toe before deciding whether to take the plunge. My previous experience of op tours was that things were very busy at the start, slowed down a touch as you found a rhythm, but then speeded up dramatically towards the end. I just had no idea how this one was going to turn out, so I was happy enough to have an initial limit.

What I did not say at the time was that there were other reasons why I was hopeful it would work out. For a start, one of the things on the company commander's list of things to do on operations is to keep the families of those abroad informed about what is going on. This generally means that a couple of newsletters get produced in the first weeks and months and then the thing dies as R and R kicks in and news filters back in different ways. At least the blog would keep the families informed. If I ever had an idea about the material that would go on the blog it was that it would consist of the things I would be happy to tell my family. This book will relate some of the more gruesome aspects of life there, but a blog was not the place for such tales. Another motivation for the blog was to explain in reasonable terms what it is like to go on operations. To deal with some of the myths and explain in a little more depth some of the activities we undertake, why we do them, what counts for success and how we cope on tour. The final reason for doing it was that I knew, if it was done well, that it would give us public recognition for what we were doing.

Public recognition is absolutely not what we do operations for. But there is a paradox that one of the most damaging psychological wounds for a soldier is not to have his effort publicly recognised. Much of what one reads about post-traumatic stress disorder after Vietnam is about the lack of the ticker-tape parade, no victory march, nothing to point to say that's what we did, that's why we did it and we have a lot to be proud of and have made you proud of us. It's not that we want it; it is a question of psychological need. I wanted something that we could all point to and say, 'that explains it pretty well'. Moreover I could not see us getting recognition from anywhere else. As an independent rifle company you sometimes don't get the attention of any visiting press, and I didn't see why 3 Rifles would make an exception for us. If anything having a 4 Rifles tag would make matters worse. In the fight up the greasy pole commanding officers are fairly protective of the reputation of their battalions. They are charged with enhancing it. There was no way our new stepmother would want Cinders stealing the limelight from her ugly sisters.

There are drawbacks to creating a public profile in this way. The army is innately suspicious of those who 'do media'. The army is in the business of doing, not talking about it. Unfortunately, on an operation where winning hearts and minds is the key, 'doing' is not nearly enough. It needs the art of persuasion. 'Politics with an admixture of other means'. Yet the culture is anti-political, albeit political in the extreme. It is a paradox yet to be resolved. If that is true in the upper echelons, it is equally correct at the tactical level. The information operation in Sangin in 2009/10 was lamentable. Pamphlets and posters for a population who could not read. No radio. We could have broadcast on ICOM, the local walkie-talkie system used by the insurgents and civilian population alike, except we were not allowed. A way of getting the message to the people without getting shot at or blown up in the process might have been a useful addition to our armoury.

Anyway.

In September 2009 I trotted off to Salisbury to BBC Radio Wiltshire to record two audio blogs. The first outlined my hopes and fears and the second covered the training we had undertaken.

It's finally here, day one on Operation Herrick. It's been some time coming as I was first told that A Company would be going to Afghanistan in early January. A Company is usually part of 4 Rifles. For this tour we are under command of another Rifles battalion, 3 Rifles. We are to form part of Battlegroup North in Helmand which is based around Sangin. A Company is over one hundred strong and with attachments from other branches of the army is considerably more than that. We have been training together since Easter. As I look back it seems like an incredibly long period of training for the mission we are going to undertake. That said I've never heard anyone in my position say we were too well trained for the task.

The training has many aspects. Everyone going to Afghanistan needs to know how to operate safely. They need to know enough about the culture to avoid inadvertent offence. We learn a bit of Pashtu to be able to break the ice and give basic instructions. We all do first aid training and the majority of the company are trained to a more advanced level. And of course there is the requirement to keep people physically fit and healthy. The collective training has been a tour of all the most delightful parts of Britain. Kent, Northumbria, Norfolk, Wiltshire and Wales - twice.

We were the second group through the new Afghan village complex in Norfolk. At times on Army training areas it is hard to replicate a civilian population; this however was about as realistic as it gets, manure and straw with a number of the Afghan diaspora. I got put through my paces in a post-mission Shura trying to convince the local population that we had done something that would increase their security. Not an easy sell.

I also found it amazing how much of Norfolk is irrigated in the same way as the valley of the River Helmand. Good practice manoeuvring around the ditches, wet feet, deep mud and not much commander's dignity. After the bulk of the training was complete we were able to take a couple of weeks' leave. Whilst the training is vital there is nothing as dangerous as fatigue. Tired minds and bodies are prone to bad decision-making. We have had the chance post leave to do some refresher training and get the administration of the company in order. We will get our final training top-up on arrival in Afghanistan just to get the latest from the guys who are already there. Then we'll be good to go.

I was upbeat and positive. I did genuinely believe we were as well trained as we could be. It had been agreed by all involved that this would be broadcast once I was there. The time was coming soon. There was less and less to do before departure. I was asked to summarise my hopes and fears for the tour:

Every father has hopes and fears. It is part of having children. I am no different from every other father in the land in that respect. My greatest desire in this regard has crystallised round the hope that I will be able to take my son to the first day of an Ashes Test at Lord's. My greatest fear is that I will not be there to go with him. This fear may be no different from other parents', but it is perhaps brought into sharper focus by the prospect of six months in the Upper Sangin Valley. On a professional level it is rather different. We don't generally deal in fears. We harden our hearts against the prospect of some very difficult decisions.

My personal hopes and fears are wrapped into the same moment. Making the right decision. Through training, experience, character and enough thought I hope I make good decisions. I will spend a good deal of time planning and conducting operations. During that process and over the course of my tour there will be plenty of decisions to make. Most of the time the result of a bad decision will be rectifiable, yet in my profession and very obviously in Afghanistan it is sometimes about life and death. It is an incredible privilege to command a company of Riflemen and all the soldiers and officers who will be part of the company group. I have got to know some of them and their families extremely well. I know from friends and colleagues that the worst moments of their professional lives have been in the moments of grief following the death of a soldier for whom they feel totally responsible. I hope that I can face that with stoicism and sensitivity. It is easy to get fatalistic about operations in Afghanistan but there are companies in battlegroups that all come back. I hope we all come home. The summer has been sobering in that regard and the families and comrades of those serving in Afghanistan this summer have barely been away from my thoughts. There will be many factors involved but I certainly feel that the decisions I make and have made during training will play their part. It is a good pressure if used properly. My final hope is that the company group can do a difficult job in the right way. I hope we can understand, persuade and influence as well as clear, secure and protect. I hope we can hold and build on ground that we clear of insurgents. I have no doubt that this is not just a six-month project, but I hope we can make a positive difference.

This was my public face – I still agree with all of the sentiments therein, but I omitted the other half of the story. It was the truth, just not the whole truth and nothing but the truth. My misgivings were all too apparent to those who knew me well. My brother Geoffrey and sister Daisy had to endure the sight, on the two occasions when the dark thoughts could not be pushed aside, of their eldest brother weeping and raging over the thought that there was a reasonable chance that I had just six weeks left with my wife and children, and fearing that the 'cause' for which I was just about to endanger myself was tenuous at best and at worst pure folly. I cannot print the list of the accused, but I suspect that history will not be kind to those who dreamed up the idea that we could be in Helmand with 9,500 troops, deep in the Pashtun tribal lands, to get our third kicking in as many centuries. Worse, the policy made the streets of Britain even more dangerous as our presence in Afghanistan inspired jihad in communities at home. However, now as then I will suppress the rant.

In the weeks running up to departure the military does checks and checks and checks. Kit gets packed and repacked. At the beginning of September the 'comfort boxes' had been loaded. The little extras that we thought might never reach us, but if they did would make winter bearable. Blankets, winter boots and duvets were popular. Then there are the 'G1' checks. Medical records, passports, insurance, next of kin forms. And as people came back from courses these were done again and again for completeness.

When I took over A Company I had asked my predecessor what was the one thing that he would have changed about his time taking the company to Iraq. He took me through a story of a man who had been killed; he had died without writing a will. He had signed before he left to say that he had one. He said that if he had the chance again he would make the whole company bring their wills to him. This of course is entirely against the law. Executors and lawyers read wills, not work colleagues. But it was still good advice. Young men think they are immortal. That's why they make good soldiers. It doesn't make them very good about preparing for the worst-case scenario. In addition to a will I wanted to see insurance. The insurance that most people use in the army is PAX insurance. It works on a points scale up to fifteen points, or the maximum pay-out, for life and personal injury insurance. And we were to be 'PAXed to the max'. There are, of course, other insurance providers! And there were some who went with them. Partly I think in some cases for the bravado of saying they did not have PAX. Whatever. After Mark's experience I was going to make sure we all had a will and some insurance.

The other piece of kit that you get issued in the run up to leaving is your 'dog tags'. These two pieces of metal with your name, number, blood group and religion are the only formal piece of identification that you carry. The 'dog tags' make you feel like a soldier. A little bit of your own identity goes and in its place is a sense of being part of the whole. They take some getting used to wearing. The chain is very breakable and hirsute types are often subject to a random deforestation of chest hair. More disturbing was that during the final weeks before leaving the army began a programme of swabbing for DNA. It was a voluntary process and caused much suspicion among the Riflemen. It was not that they baulked at the idea of being blown to smithereens, making formal identification impossible. No, they feared it could link them to scenes of crime! It took all our persuading that this was not the case, but still the cookhouse rumour persisted. Luckily we never needed it in Afghanistan, but the take-up had been minimal.

There had also been much chat in the company about last letters. Rachel and I had had a number of unsatisfactory conversations about what should happen if the worst happened. The memory of Rupert Thorneloe was still very fresh. If it could happen to him and to Sean Birchall it could happen to me. The fickle finger of fate was always lurking. I decided over the summer that I *had* to write a last letter. I got to the point of sitting at my desk late one evening. I only ever got as far as 'Dear Rachel'. I have no idea from that day to this why I could not write it. There was a much-publicised example of the hurt that it caused not to have one, and an equally well-publicised example of one that had been written that gave comfort to all who read it. But I could not. We had talked. I had thought about doing a video message. Even reading a dozen or so children's stories on video so they could be read at bedtime while I was away nearly did me in. Not that one can get too emotional about the *Enormous Crocodile* or *Chicken Licken*, but when it came to ' Happy Christmas to all, and to all a good night' I could barely get the words out. I promised myself I would find it easier to do in Afghanistan. Plenty of time in Camp Bastion to get something down.

I had gone so far as to say that I did not want a military funeral. I wanted to be buried in Chiddingstone alongside a good number of relatives. 'You can play *High on a hill* to represent the military part of my life,' I said, or something along those lines. I primed my brother Geoffrey with the knowledge that there would be pressure to have senior military representatives there, but it was categorically my wish that they did not come. They would not be welcome – at least by me. I had never seen the army as my vocation: a brilliant job, yes, but never my life. My experience is that those who do tend to see conflict as an end in itself. General Mike Jackson's eternal regret is that he didn't fight a conventional war, but most who fought in the First or Second World Wars never wanted to see the like again. If I wanted to get even vaguely philosophical about it I would say that I am a citizen first and foremost, and I had a notion that I wished to be returned to the village where I grew up as a citizen rather than a military officer. This may seem rather contrary. Most want to be buried with military honours.

I have been to more military funerals than I care to think about. They are powerful, emotional affairs. An army chaplain, ranks of red tabs, *I vow to thee my country*, bugles, a volley at the graveside, flag folding and a Rifles cap. Good for some, not for me. First rule of leadership applies; know yourself. As it turned out I never wrote the letter, made the video or had the funeral. I even thought of making a random recording on the dictaphone I used for the blogs. But whenever I got close to doing it, something else always got in the way. It is pretty much the only time that I have not been able to do something that I have asked others to do. I was perhaps prepared to do it. Tried and failed. Thank God it never came to anyone searching for what might be there, but was not.

'Don't go' said Emily. It was eight o'clock in the evening on 3 October 2009 and she was falling asleep. Her tears wet my cheeks as I kissed her. Henry was easier. Easier for him as well. Must be a man thing. He had no concept of what was coming and just as well. My kit, packed and ready in the spare room for two days, had been taken into the camp ready for transport to Brize Norton. We had done all the things that we wanted to do on that 'last day'. A family day. A long walk. A Saturday roast. As I came downstairs, my wife asked 'How was that?'

'Pretty shit, to be honest, but it's done.'

That night we watched *Slumdog Millionaire*. Nothing more left to say. Had a shower. Went to bed. Got up at the unearthly hour of three o'clock in the morning ready to walk down the hill to the bus that was leaving at 0400. We had planned it like this. Worked out how we would want to spend the last few hours. No point in wasting them. Somehow they seem more important than any other, such is the imminence of parting. And contra to the bard's best sentiment, parting is not such sweet sorrow. It stinks. As I kissed Rachel goodbye I could see and feel the emotion clambering up her throat, held in the quiver of lips and the well of tears.

'Better go.' I said. 'Shouldn't be late for my own parade.' Or some other appalling attempt at diffusing the intensity.

I was out of 7 Nelson Close and down the road, numbing fast.

At eight o'clock that morning the advance party, ten of us, including all the platoon commanders, from A Company 4 Rifles, were told we had not been allocated seats on the plane. We could either go to a hotel or back to Bulford. No plan survives contact with the enemy. And more often than not, a leaving plan does not survive contact with the RAF.

I called Rachel. I explained the situation and said that I had decided – she did not get a choice for once – that I would come back home rather than spend a day wondering what they were all up to. So I crashed back through the door at 1030 to the confused delight of Emily and went to bed for a couple of hours. We spent the rest of the day doing exactly what we had planned for Rachel for her first day alone with the children. We went to lunch with some cousins who lived close by. 'Nice surprise,' said Simon. 'Not really,' I replied. If you want to really play with someone's emotions, get them into a situation where they have to say goodbye to their children for six months twice in twenty-four hours. As I say – cruel and unusual punishment. Yes, I could have stayed in the hotel. But I know I would never have forgiven myself if anything had happened, not necessarily to me but especially to them, if I had stayed away that day.

So as I put them to bed again that night, Emily was, if anything, more emotional than she had been the previous night. Perhaps it had taken her a while to work out a question that would be incredibly difficult to answer.

'Do you have to go?'

Yes, I have to go. Or do I? In what context are you talking? I am a volunteer. If I didn't want to go I could have resigned. In some senses I want to go. I want to put myself to the test. I have a responsibility to those I command. I have a responsibility to the country that pays me to do this job. Of course I have to go. But what about my family? Aren't you risking a lot for very little? Risking your life, the lives of your men and for what? Isn't this all incredibly selfish? Professional pride getting in the way of innocent lives? It's alright for you volunteers. And those who knew they were taking on a soldier. But not the kids. They never asked for this.

No use thinking about this now.

'Yes, I have to go.'

'Bye.' Kiss. Choke. Cough. Breathe.

Rachel and I watched *Angels and Demons* that night. Tom Hanks's finest hour – durch. Shower. Bed. 0300. Kiss. Door. Bus. Airport. Plane. Stupid relief that I was actually flying. Sleep, for almost eight hours straight, exhausted by suppressed emotion.

\*   \*   \*   \*   \*

One doesn't touch down in Afghanistan, one plummets. Body armour and helmets on in the darkness, you drop through the protected hole in the sky, steepling onto the runway. Then out into a pleasantly cool but dust-filled breeze onto an un-air-conditioned bus, unwashed and feeling fresh as a fart.

'Sirs, Gents 'scuse rank.' Names. More names. 'Street-filed', 'Here'. Off the bus. Into the queue. Welcome to Afghanistan.

*Chapter 5*

# Heeellloooo Hellllmand

All organisations have their own lingo, but the army does acronyms like no other organisation I have encountered. There are three, four and five-letter abbreviations for everything. The preliminary period spent in Camp Bastion is known as RSOI: 'Reception, Staging and Onward Integration'. RSOI: an acronym to be proud of. We came into Camp Bastion late at night. The cool, dust-filled breeze had even felt mildly refreshing after an hour cooped up in the darkness of the tactical flight in. In the middle of the night the glare of the floodlights illuminates the dust giving the camp a fluorescent halo. When I came in on the recce even in the middle of the night it was almost unbearably hot for someone acclimatized to Britain's BBQ summer. This time there were many favourable comments amongst the party, their last tour having been in the heat of an Iraq summer which combined intolerably high humidity with soaring temperatures.

After a late start the briefs began. Being un-acclimatised meant that we did little physical activity, as our bodies slowly accustomed to the midday heat, which was still in the upper thirties. The time was filled with the latest intelligence briefs and a myriad of other subjects, twenty-one in all. Reminders of subjects briefed during training, but now with a much greater urgency. The package continued over a number of days. The time passed quickly because the days were full, starting early and finishing late.

We got the sharpest of reminders of what we faced with a day on IED (Improvised Explosive Device) training. The sharpest of reminders about IEDs was in fact a device on the range itself, which killed one of the party that had flown in with us. Some of the 3 Rifles Battlegroup were on the range when a soldier from the 1st Battalion of the Coldstream Guards was hit by an IED. We were with the mortar platoon of that battalion undergoing Vallon training when a grim-faced officer turned up. There was an awful lot of 'Ohmygodnotalready'. But it concentrated the minds of all those present on the drills that we were refreshing with the help of those who had done it for six months.

So we carried out the drills in the midday sun until we were totally confident with the latest equipment, tactics and procedures. 3 Rifles were taking over from 2 Rifles in Sangin and I knew many of them well, 2 Rifles having previously been a Green Jacket battalion, and some of them were already in Camp Bastion.

The Riflemen from 2 Rifles coming through were upbeat. I clearly drew comfort from that at the time. I remember being similarly optimistic at the end of our tour. The company I was taking over from was still in place but I met Karl, another company commander, who had worked in the MoD at the same time as me and had lived on the same housing estate, or 'patch' in military parlance. We had served in the same battalion in Bosnia in 1998. His view was that you had to keep the insurgents guessing. Get over the IEDs in whatever helicopters you could get hold of and disrupt the insurgents to keep them away from the bulk of the population. He flew back to the UK that evening via twenty-four hours in Cyprus to his wife, daughter, and young son. I was envious.

The death of the soldier on the range was our first exposure to Operation Minimise. This set of protocols limits access to internet and satellite phones to give time for the next of kin to be informed. We were to become all too familiar with a state of electronic lockdown. It was, however, heartening to hear of the progress made and opportunities for future progress at first hand. Better news from those who had been on the ground rather than those who had been reporting it. Undoubtedly their story was one of bad days as well as good days, but it was certainly in better balance than I had previously thought.

I published my first blog during this compulsory rest period as part of acclimatisation.

> And that is what Bastion was like. Arid, hot and dusty. The smell of a portaloo in the midday sun and the taste of the best food anywhere I have been on operations. An unlikely combination of emotions: happiness of those going out after a hard job well done; tinged with grief, relief and the anticipation of seeing friends and relatives. For those coming in it is the desire to get on with the job in hand, determination, with anticipation and a few pre-match nerves. Whilst all around the mechanics of the vast operation to get the units changed over continues. The helicopter noise is continuous, providing the drumbeat of the operation. Whilst I understand the value of our stay here I want to be in the Forward Operating Base. I want to continue, together with the Afghans, to try for a safer future in Sangin. I have to be careful what I wish for but right now, I and the rest of A Company are living on the verge of and in anticipation of that challenge.

I am mildly ashamed of the motherhood and apple pie sentiment that I wanted to continue with the Afghans to try for a safer future in Sangin. It is a curious paradox that while the statement remains as true now as it did then, it sounds so simple and yet it has proved impossible. It hints at the crunch question. One that I was never prepared to answer even though I was asked many times. Was it worth it?

The other bit of this blog that rather sticks is my first attempt to capture the smells, sights and feelings that are rarely reported. Back in the UK I had been given two bits of advice from the BBC about the blogs. Keep the sentences short and describe what is happening through all your senses. Some, mainly my brothers, thought I was getting help. Top of the list of suspects were MoD propagandists. Propaganda in the true rather than pejorative sense of the word. And I did indeed get some advice from the MoD; the only 'help' they gave me was a list, by month, of communication themes. 'It would be helpful,' said Bob 'if you could at least talk about something to do with the theme.' This was absolutely no bother. They were things like 'working with allies', 'Honour and sacrifice' and so broad that it was easy to incorporate something. The RSOI blog was the first to go through the Media group in Lashkagar. I was nervous about this process. As it turned out I needn't have been. Over the next seven months they never changed a word, not one. I still think that is to their credit. It may also be because the bulk of what the censor changes in journalists' copy is based on security issues and I, very definitely, had no wish to risk the security of those on the operation or who would come after.

I did the rounds in Camp Bastion again. I had a visit to the 4 Rifles Headquarters. One of my old platoon commanders from R Company 2 RGJ, now serving with B Company 4 Rifles, came in from across the desert with his fire support group. With his hair long and matted, the well fed and watered look of the officers' mess had given way to hollow cheeks. The B Company serjeant major was there as well. His face was chicken-pocked by a rash caused by the fragmentation of an IED. If he hadn't been wearing his specs he would surely have been blinded. One for the rest of the party to come and see, just to ram the point home about wearing those specs. The RSM, having been in Bastion for the best part of five months, was going up the tent wall. I remember seeing with some amusement what purported to be the fifth version of the plan for the 4 Rifles medals parade. I gathered from him that there were likely to be several more. R Company had just gone back after four months and B Company had been extended to six months having not had R and R. It was not an easy time. I asked the QM whether we could keep some of the radios 4 Rifles had brought in to theatre. It was a bit of a punt, but I was already worried that we were going to be twice the number of our predecessors and it would be useful to have enough. He said the plan was to get them from B Company when they came back. It would never happen and was a source of great frustration.

The strangest thing about the RSOI period is the look of the soldiers in Camp Bastion. Those coming in are pasty white but stocky. Their desert uniforms are clean, and in some cases still bearing the creases from the packet. Those going out are in an altogether different state. The camouflage is bleached by dust, sweat and sun. They are whippet thin. Some have shaven heads, but most have hair over their collar. Then there are the eyes. It is a look almost impossible to capture. The conflict of relief at being out of danger while friends are still on the front line; for some the look of people who have seen things that mean nothing will ever be the same again; some defiant, almost the, 'What are you looking at?' look of the nightclub queue. Excitement, the pure excitement of getting off the phone being able to say 'I'll see you on Wednesday', then walking past the man who is thinking 'I'll see them in February. Insh'Allah.' Those coming in rushing everywhere, those going out in an altogether more relaxed frame of mind. In the cookhouse, which serves some of the best meals I have had on ops, those coming in pick nervously at their plate. Those going out pile the plate high with solid food for the first time in months. On my recce, Iain, my predecessor in Inkerman, had complained bitterly that they had not received fresh rations for sixty days. To go from that to a cookhouse replete with steak and ice-cream feels like all your Christmasses have come at once. Because of the numbers coming in and out the whole time the whole thing is conducted to the metronomic thump of helicopter rotor blades cutting through the sky incessantly. Mercifully, during this period, not landing too often by the hospital. After a couple of days of this I was restless. Just let us get on with it. The anticipation is infinitely worse than the reality. We flew on day seven.

\* \* \* \* \*

At the end of a challenging week it was a pleasure to lift off from Camp Bastion and see the jagged horizon free from dust. The noise of the helicopter rendered conversation impossible so I was left with my thoughts for half an hour as the helicopter flew high over the desert. The helicopter, packed with men, materiel and post, banked steeply and plunged into the landing site at the Forward Operating Base. The quad bikes buzzed around disembowelling the 'bird'. Fully kitted and armed we made our way into the gates to unload our weapons and greet the smiling faces. Iain and other members of B Company smiled broadly, as I did six months later; always good to meet the relief.

As afternoon turned to night the temperature was notably cooler than in Bastion, with a top end of the low thirties, and certainly not as dusty. The moon was not up and the night was black but the stars were an astronomer's dream. As far back as April I was determined that we would try our best to have a rancour-free hand over. That generally means keeping your mouth shut about what you see in front of you that to you is glaring, but to those who have lived with it for a while, and knew how bad it was before, it has become totally normal. I did not want to sound a single note of criticism. B Company had been given a tough job. One for which they seemed to me to be woefully under resourced. But I became seriously impressed with the fortitude of the young men of B Company in the short time of the handover. In the dark of the night I followed a pair of them along a path in the Forward Operating Base. 'I am going to miss it,' confided one to another, almost guiltily. I was not going to criticise them because soldiers do what they're told. They do not, as some would have it, get up every day to let you down – I have long believed in Napoleon's maxim that there are no bad soldiers, only bad officers. Nothing in my military career would suggest otherwise. In the two platoons and three companies I have been lucky enough to command I often caught sight of my own reflection. Sometimes it just isn't as pretty as one would like, same as the mirror.

The patrol in July that had been completed on my arrival on the recce was the last in which B Company HQ had deployed on the ground. They were getting hit with small arms fire if they went further than 400 metres. They simply did not have the number of force elements required to fix the enemy in place and get another lot to move to outflank them. Having a lightly protected group out on the ground doing all of the command and control was inviting disaster when there was a well-protected base less than half a kilometre away. So they went out in platoon strength, going early and getting as far as they could before occupying a temporary defensive position and waiting for the enemy to come and attack. When the enemy had given their positions away they used bombs from the air, Apache helicopters, artillery, mortars and guided Javelin missiles to try and inflict casualties. There is a video of 6 Platoon B Company 2 Rifles on YouTube that shows exactly what I'm talking about. The total number of high-explosive mortar bombs and artillery rounds fired from Inkerman in the summer of 2009 was in excess of 10,000. Fifty-five a day for every day of their tour.

While this was going on there were two other major tactical things happening in the Inkerman area of operations. Firstly there was a real fight on to resupply the base. The resupplies conducted by the Combat Logistics Patrol (CLP) brought materiel up to Sangin through the desert from Camp Bastion. Inkerman was at the end of the line, the most remote base in Helmand to be resupplied by road. Kajaki to the north received everything exclusively by helicopter. As a result it had a rather more comfortable existence – at least in terms of fresh rations and the timeliness of the mail. The resupply patrol, once in Sangin, had used the only major route. The 611. Known pretty much exclusively as the 'six one one'. It has sometimes been called more prosaic names. Given that it runs up the Helmand valley it slithers through some of the most contested areas since operations began in Helmand this time around.

By the time thirty-odd vehicles rocked up in southern Sangin the patrol had taken thirty-six hours to get across the desert. The issue for those in Sangin was that when the Taliban identified the convoy was on its way this was the signal for the insurgents in Sangin to prepare a welcoming committee. That committee could only be stopped from doing its work by deploying to secure the route as the logistics patrol set off. The route had to be picketed. That meant takeover compounds every 500 metres down the road between Inkerman and Sangin. The array of targets static for so long was too good for the enemy not to have a go at. A and B Company 2 Rifles had fought for over two days to keep the road open. They had conducted a high threat clearance of the road. A high threat clearance is a bomb disposal team sweeping a four-kilometre path to make sure it is clear of IEDs. Some of this had taken place at night with the mortars firing illumination. The whole thing had not been a happy experience. Whilst traversing the 'cleared' route a B Company vehicle had been blown up. No fatalities but some very serious injuries ensued. The company had been out for fifty-two hours and taken some pretty nasty casualties to sustain them and then us for a month.

Such was the cost to limb, if not life on that occasion, that an alternative route had to be found. There was a dog-leg route east in the desert that could be taken, through the wadi past Wishtan and then north. We would still have to search the last 2km and picket the route, but it looked a safer proposition. It would be the last operation that B Company commanded before handover. We would help do the operation with B Company commanders. Iain was still 'in command', but it was a very useful opportunity to see how things ran.

On the other side of the compound wall the Taliban had been doing their own thinking about how to defeat us. The tactic they had come up with was 'neutralisation'. The tactic is a bit like that of an anaconda. Get the prey in your grip and then slowly squeeze the life out of it. The squeeze was being applied by IEDs. B Company had only had three IEDs at the time I went on my recce in July. By 10 October when we arrived in Inkerman they had experienced thirty, mostly finds but including one killed and several life-changing injuries. One man had been saved despite the loss of two legs and an arm. Crucial in saving the Rifleman's life was a young interpreter, Adam, who had been in Sangin for three years. He knew our medical drills as well as we did. During the handover he was given a bonus payment in lieu of other possible awards. He was away for the first month of our tour getting stones removed from his back that had embedded when he was close to another IED strike. He came back to us later on and thank goodness he did.

The results of this tactic of squeeze were brought home to me on my first patrol. We set off for the local village early in the morning. B Company had just got some ladders so we took a direct route through the agricultural compounds. This would hopefully avoid the IEDs that they were sure were being laid in Sareagar. The village was eerily quiet. The only people we saw on the streets looked in a bit of a hurry. It tended to be groups of women dressed in black. We stopped by the local motorbike garage. A few old men lay on their blankets by the side of the road. Greetings were exchanged. 'Salaam Alaikum' 'Alaikum salaam'. We knocked on a few doors. When one finally answered we gave a few minutes for the women of the house to move into a room and then we spent an hour or so chatting to a farmer who seemed to me to be relaxed and friendly. I kept the conversation as neutral as possible, the things that farmers across the world like to talk about. The weather, the state of the harvest, the price they could get at market. He was happy to talk. There was even an attempt at humour. He thought I looked big and strong and might help him bring in his crop. The Afghans have strong sense of the ridiculous. Looking back I can now see this as him pulling my leg... as if we were going to do anything as useful as help bring in the crop! I should have called his bluff. We went back via a different route. We passed an alleyway that had a very obvious piece of ground sign indicating the route had IEDs laid. A stone completely out of place in the middle of the track. Once pointed out it is blindingly obvious. There are often different markings for different types of IED attack. But a stone is a stone and on rough stone tracks spotting the out of place stone is damnably problematic for those of us for whom stone tracks are mostly consigned to history.

As we came into the last leg of the patrol we passed a man lying on his mat. I was with a B Company Platoon Commander. We stopped to chat. During the conversation he indicated that there were IEDs in the area. He gesticulated to a general area between us and the Base now well in view. Try as we might we could not establish exactly where. I am sure if we had better language skills that we would have been able to get a better idea. Every language has what appears to be a generalisation for distance and location that can be interpreted quite specifically if one knows the local idiom. We set off across his ploughed field just to be sure. The base was five minutes away. The section 100 metres to my left was about 300 metres from base, they had a section 100 metres ahead of them. An almost classic platoon patrol formation trying to get breadth and depth from every angle. Bang! Not a big bang but I felt the blast wave a second later. It took what felt like several seconds to compute what I had actually seen. The object ten foot in the air had actually been a man, looking for all the world like a rag doll spun randomly. 'Contact IED get down.' We hit the dusty deck. The radio cracked into life, the B Company Platoon Commander ahead of me taking control of the situation with well-practised authority.

There are three things that are happening pretty much simultaneously in this type of situation. There are a group trying to treat the casualty to stop any catastrophic bleeding. There are another group who are in the headquarters who are desperate to feed the information about the casualty up the chain to get the helicopter on its way. And then there is everyone else on the ground, who need to be watching like hawks for the follow-up attack but have a tendency to be asking irrelevant questions about the casualty or trying to see what is going on.

The guys from B Company were straight into all of these but it was only us, the new boys, who glanced over their shoulders to see what was going on. B Company knew better. I closed up with the section I was with into an all-round defensive posture. Another device had been found close to the casualty; he had received initial treatment and was ready to move. The first few steps from lying down to a position to protect the incident were nervous ones to say the least.

The injured Rifleman was brought past our position. 'Carried off on a stretcher' does no justice to how difficult it is to get a casualty away. With a rigid stretcher you need at least four men. They are already carrying fifty-five kilograms each on average. Add their share of a seventy to eighty kilogram man and they are each carrying their own bodyweight. Imagine picking yourself up; now run 100 metres; now run 400 or further still to the helicopter away from the incident. The four others in the section are carrying the injured man's kit. The ground ahead of the stretcher needs a double-width path swept ahead of it. You rapidly run out of manpower and those that are left are as loaded with kit as to make speed a real problem. Luckily our proximity to the Forward Operating Base meant that a vehicle came out and the casualty was whisked away in short order.

Being close to an IED explosion had nothing to recommend it. A member of 2 Rifles lay very seriously ill in Selly Oak Hospital as a result. The cliché is true: time slows; fear, adrenaline and then training kick in almost simultaneously. Watching the lads from 2 Rifles go to work for one of their own was inspirational. The rapid effective treatment, a lung-bursting stretcher-carry and a slick handover to the doctor in the vehicle, and he was away as quickly as possible to the best trauma facility in the world, giving him the greatest chance.

A group of the advanced party, including Jodie our medic, had arrived whilst we were on patrol. The flight also included the Commanding Officers of both 2 Rifles and 3 Rifles. Jodie found herself covered to the elbows in blood within an hour of arrival. I had often wondered how Jodie was going to cope with operations, especially in Afghanistan. She had been to Iraq but I had not found out details of what she had done there. She had proved a capable administrator in camp. She had completed all the mandatory fitness. Just to complete the cliché of my prejudice she was five foot two, very blond and very Welsh. The doctor, Captain Collette Davey, came up to me afterwards and said in tones that mirrored my surprise, that Jodie had been really good. Just got stuck in and clearly really knew what she was up to. During her combat medical training Collette had been told a story about a young medic who on her first tour in Iraq had retrieved multiple body parts from the inside of a vehicle. Cleaned up and never flinched. It later transpired it had been Jodie. I should never have doubted her. Between them, Jodie, Collette the doctor and Corporal Hayley Wright set about showing why life on the frontline should not be the exclusive preserve of the male soldier. Below is a summary I sent to the Adjutant Generals Corp Headquarters when Hayley Wright was posted two-thirds of the way through the tour, written in the rather brusque style beloved of the military:

Corporal Wright served with A Company 4 Rifles from July 09 to February 10. Corporal Wright is a mother. Her son spent the tour with her parents in Scotland. A Company is an independent rifle company under command of 3 Rifles based in Forward Operating Base Inkerman on Op Herrick 11. The Inkerman AO is the most kinetic area of operations on Op Herrick 11. Corporal Wright took over responsibility as the senior company clerk towards the end of the Pre Deployment Training period. During September she was responsible for the management of the MCCP (Documentation and pre deployment administration) process. 3 Rifles are based in Edinburgh and A Company in Bulford. The remainder of 4 Rifles were deployed on Op Herrick 10. She achieved the necessary clerical support and administration to the Company without the supervision or support of her detachment commander who was deployed. The fact that the Company deployed in very good order was largely down to her diligence. This meant the Company was in the strongest position possible to launch onto operations. All Riflemen who have been injured have had 15 units of PAX. She spent a long time ensuring that was so.

Whilst deployed on Op Herrick 11 Corporal Wright volunteered to assist with the most demanding tasks. She was the Barma woman for the CSM's group on a Company patrol into the Green Zone. She commanded VCPs outside Forward Operating Base INKERMAN. When A Company began to emplace Patrol Bases along the 611 a 6km route from Inkerman to Sangin Corporal Wright volunteered to be a Mastiff vehicle commander. She commanded the lead Mastiff. On three occasions there were IED strikes onto the vehicle she commanded. She was involved in three casevacs of members of the company who were seriously injured and in two cases mortally wounded. When required on the company command radio net she was clear, concise and confident; reporting the situation when the CSM was on the ground. Corporal Wright did not flinch from going back out again. She has demonstrated the highest standards of selfless commitment and physical courage. Her contribution went far beyond that expected of her rank and position. Her contribution to the combat effectiveness of A Company 4 Rifles is worthy of recognition.

The absolute equal of her male peers.

As the Rifleman was evacuated I went to have a chat with the CO of 3 Rifles. 'Well that was interesting. So much for no IED's and a clean fight.'

Handovers can be fractious affairs, mainly because as equipment is assiduously accounted for by quantity and serial number, and differences in tactics are discussed in detail, the fact that what has been taught in training has been adapted by six months of practice by the in-place unit can lead to petty arguments. There was none of that this time. I was lucky to be bringing more troops, so Iain was constantly caveating his advice with what was, by the end, a well-worn refrain. 'If I had four platoons I would…' It was certain to give us greater flexibility. They were a fund of information; moreover, they had taken great personal risk at the end of a long tour to give us the best start.

But there was still the question of the logistic patrol before I finally got my hands on Inkerman. The bomb disposal team who came up to deal with the route out to the desert was headed up by Staff Sergeant Oz Schmid. Everything that has been written about Oz Schmid subsequently chimes with my experience. On the two days' worth of clearance that he undertook in support of bringing in the patrol he defused eight devices. It was all done with the kind of cheerful bonhomie and thorough professionalism that gives one great confidence. He was one of at least eight different bomb disposal teams that the Company worked with. We were lucky that he was the first. Later on in the tour coming to this part of Sangin was nobody's idea of fun, least of all the counter IED teams'. He confirmed that the IEDs he had found still had enough metal in for the Vallon to be effective, something to give us confidence given the chat about low and no metal content devices. The issue was that these devices had been placed very close to the Forward Operating Base. It took us a while to work out just how much the insurgents had changed tactics and it had been the B Company method of operating that had saved them from more IED strikes. It's just as well I didn't know how tight the squeeze really was, because we were about to do something ten days later that no one could have prepared me for and if I had known that we were going to be walking through a dispersed minefield to do it I would never have allowed it. By 19 October the supply train had come and gone with no insurgent activity and we were able to start the process of really getting to know the area. So the next day, as Iain and I shook hands in front of the map and then under a flag, he formally handing over responsibility to me and my men and women, I hoped we could match their effort.

# Chapter 6

# How on earth did I end up here and what the hell am I going to do about it?

In the three days from 16 to 19 October I had some serious thinking to do. Iain and I had very little left to hand over, and after ten days I was getting agitated watching him exercise the last vestiges of his operational command. So aside from when decisions had to be made I hid in plain view and wrote the set of orders that I would give immediately on his departure. I had seen the surrounding countryside, and courtesy of exhaustive briefings was now armed with all the knowledge I could absorb from B Company to set us off. I knew that getting into it was going to involve a good deal of danger. I emailed CO 3 Rifles. I wish I still had that email, but it is lost in the military ether. The basic tenor was; how the hell did we end up here? We enjoyed a brief exchange that highlighted the fault line in most military minds that it was the politicians and the civil servants who messed this one up. I was not so sure. I felt very, very isolated. Not that I couldn't defend the base – I had more than enough to do that, but to my North, my East and my South spread miles and miles of ungoverned space. I was reminded of a small band of indomitable Gauls sitting in North West France with nothing other than magic potion to hold back the invaders. Except paradoxically in this situation we were supposed to be playing the part of the Roman legions. So how *did* we end up here?

Inkerman was founded in June 2007 by the Grenadier Guards, named so for the most obvious of reasons, if you are a Grenadier. When the 3rd Battalion of that Regiment was placed in suspended animation on 31 March 1961, Her Majesty The Queen directed that a composite company should be formed from all ranks of the 3rd Battalion The Grenadier Guards and should become the Left Flank Company of the 2nd Battalion in order to keep alive the traditions of the 3rd Battalion. Her Majesty directed that this new Company should be known as The Inkerman Company.

But what was it for, what purpose did it serve? The answer was simple – to relieve the pressure on central Sangin. Simply put, take the fight elsewhere.

Hindsight is great but the Brigadier commanding British troops in Helmand at the time in an interview said that his troops took the fight, daily, to the enemy. He also said that the Taliban had a near limitless supply of manpower. Therefore, ironically, by his own logic and understanding Inkerman simply presented an opportunity for the Taliban to fight ISAF four miles away *and* in central Sangin. Another example of what Rory Stewart has highlighted as the problem of the insurgency following the military, not the other way around. The view of Brigadier James Cowan, now installed as the new commander of the Helmand Task Force, was that bases should be placed not to take the fight to the enemy, but to protect the population. The Grenadiers did also put in Patrol Base Blenheim and Patrol Base Downes in 2007 between Inkerman and Sangin on the 611, of which only Blenheim survived and was no longer in the Inkerman area of operations.

If we were in Inkerman to protect Sangin, why were we in Sangin? There are two schools of thought; among those who were there in 2006 there are a number of versions, but the most credible insists that we went there at the request of the then Governor of Helmand, Governor Daoud. A request he made when British troops arrived in force in spring 2006. The plan that 16 Air Assault Brigade flew to Helmand with did not include the occupation of the northern towns Now Zad, Musa Quala, Geresk and Sangin, but Daoud insisted that the Taliban could not be seen to hold sway over these places now the British were in Helmand.

So Sangin needed ISAF presence for political reasons. But the military equipment to back the best of political reasons did not exist and consequently 3 Para came under enormous pressure in the Platoon Houses across the towns of northern Helmand. None more so than in Sangin, where to defeat the attacks on Forward Operating Base Jackson, named after a fatality from 3 Para, ISAF planes pounded the local area, including the market, into a rubble. Furthermore, in supporting the local police British troops found themselves on the wrong side, the population hating the police and their narcotics baron paymasters more than the Taliban. There is also a charge of military adventurism that has been levelled at Brigadier Ed Butler and Colonel Stuart Tootal, both now retired. Perhaps they were just applying a good military maxim courtesy of Field Marshal Bill Slim: when faced with two evenly-matched courses of action – choose the bold one. The bold course of action was not backed with enough men or materiel to be able to do the job, and as a consequence paratroopers in Sangin were pinned into the Alamo. Whatever the plan, and I make no judgement on it, that was the result.

Sangin is a town of roughly, because no one really knows the true figure, twenty thousand. In the UK that's Towcester, Strabane, St Andrews or Colwyn Bay: of local rather than regional importance. But Sangin does have international importance. The real importance of Sangin and its district is the amount of money generated through the narcotics trade. Sangin has been called the heroin capital of the world. Sandy Gall (*War against the Taliban*) does a great job of unpicking the various machinations that led to the deployment to Sangin in 2006. The complexities are manifold. In the event the political judgement was not backed with resources. Daoud may have had the interests of good governance and the resistance to the Taliban as motivating factors, but I would be happily surprised if control or at least influence of the narcotics trade had nothing to do with it. We will never know.

So if we had to be in Sangin because we were supporting the governor of Helmand, why were we in Helmand? Helmand has a population of, again who knows?, but no more than two million. To understand why we were in Helmand one probably needs to go back to 9/11. The Taliban had provided the greenhouse for the terror visited on New York and paid a high price in late 2001. But as the US turned away from Afghanistan and towards Iraq the Taliban grew strong again, with the help of Pakistan. The heinous complexity of the Afghan-Pakistan relationship finds its origins in the 'great game' played between Russia, Britain in India and Afghanistan during the nineteenth century. But to my simple military mind all one needs to know is that in the best traditions of the British Empire, a civil servant called Mortimer Durand drew a line, a fairly straight line, through the Pashtun tribal heartlands that now straddle the border between Afghanistan and Pakistan. More correctly, it was established after an 1893 agreement between Mortimer Durand of British India and Afghan Amir Abdur Rahman Khan for fixing the limit of their respective spheres of influence. Mortimer Durand was the Foreign Secretary of colonial British India at the time. The single-page Durand Line Agreement, which contains seven short articles, was signed by Durand and Abdur Rahman Khan, agreeing not to exercise interference beyond the frontier Durand Line. On one side was India, on the other was Afghanistan. After half a century of the great game it had the neat effect of protecting India from Russian influence and the Afghans from British influence. All achieved by knowing they could never really govern the Pashtun heartlands that run from the Northwest Frontier, now in Pakistan rather than India, to Helmand. And now it is alleged that Pakistan fosters the Taliban to weaken Afghanistan to prevent the worst possible outcome, an Indian-Afghan pact.

So with assistance from an Iraqi distraction and a helpful neighbour, by 2004 the Taliban were back and getting stronger in the south. With regime change complete in Iraq in late 2004, and without the benefit of foreseeing an Iraqi insurgency, in a meeting in Istanbul Tony Blair agreed that Britain would lead the NATO expansion across the rest of Afghanistan. The view then was that there would be no trouble. When the military recce was done we knew there would be trouble if we did not deliver the promised level of security and development. Elders in all the northern towns said so. The advance party in

Helmand in early 2006 was under no illusions. One of my former Commanding Officers, Henry Worsley, (mis)quoted in the *Telegraph*, said we would be 'stirring up a hornet's nest'. The truth was that the Taliban had been passive in Helmand and therefore we were lulled into thinking this deployment would be straightforward. Therefore it didn't matter that we had Helmand and the Canadians had Kandahar and the rest of Afghanistan became a NATO patchwork. But of course it did matter, it mattered very much that the British were coming to Helmand, because the people to whom it really mattered were the Pashtun population. What mattered so much can be captured in a word – Maiwand.

The former chief of the defence staff has called it the 'whole Maiwand thing'. Maiwand is thirty-three miles south of Inkerman just over the border in Kandahar Province. On 27 July 1880 the British were routed there. Of the 2,467 British troops engaged, the force lost twenty-one officers and 948 soldiers killed. One of the antecedent regiments of the Rifles, the 66th (Berkshire) Regiment was annihilated, losing over sixty per cent of its manpower. Kipling captured it thus in his poem *That Day*:

It got beyond all orders an' it got beyond all 'ope;
It got to shammin' wounded an' retirin' from the 'alt.
'Ole companies was lookin' for the nearest road to slope;
It were just a bloomin' knock-out—an' our fault!

Now there ain't no chorus 'ere to give,
Nor there ain't no band to play;
An' I wish I was dead 'fore I done what I did,
Or seen what I seed that day!

We was sick o' bein' punished, an' we let 'em know it, too;
An' a company-commander up an' 'it us with a sword,
An' some one shouted ''Ook it!' an' it come to sove-ki-poo,
An' we chucked our rifles from us—O my Gawd!

Now there ain't no chorus 'ere to give,
Nor there ain't no band to play;
An' I wish I was dead 'fore I done what I did,
Or seen what I seed that day!

There was thirty dead an' wounded on the ground we wouldn't keep—
No, there wasn't more than twenty when the front begun to go;
But, Christ! along the line o' flight they cut us up like sheep,
An' that was all we gained by doin' so.

Now there ain't no chorus 'ere to give,
Nor there ain't no band to play;
An' I wish I was dead 'fore I done what I did,
Or seen what I seed that day!

I 'eard the knives be'ind me, but I dursn't face my man,
Nor I don't know where I went to, 'cause I didn't 'alt to see,
Till I 'eard a beggar squealin' out for quarter as 'e ran,
An' I thought I knew the voice an'—it was me!

Now there ain't no chorus 'ere to give,
Nor there ain't no band to play;
An' I wish I was dead 'fore I done what I did,
Or seen what I seed that day!

We was 'idin' under bedsteads more than 'arf a march away;
We was lyin' up like rabbits all about the countryside;
An' the major cursed 'is Maker 'cause 'e lived to see that day,
An' the colonel broke 'is sword acrost, an' cried.

Now there ain't no chorus 'ere to give,
Nor there ain't no band to play;
An' I wish I was dead 'fore I done what I did,
Or seen what I seed that day!

We was rotten 'fore we started—we was never disciplined;
We made it out a favour if an order was obeyed;
Yes, every little drummer 'ad 'is rights an' wrongs to mind,
So we had to pay for teachin'—an' we paid!

Now there ain't no chorus 'ere to give,
Nor there ain't no band to play;
An' I wish I was dead 'fore I done what I did,
Or seen what I seed that day!

The papers 'id it 'andsome, but you know the Army knows;
We was put to groomin' camels till the regiments withdrew,
An' they gave us each a medal for subduin' England's foes,
An' I 'ope you like my song—because it's true!

An' there ain't no chorus 'ere to give,
Nor there ain't no band to play;
But I wish I was dead 'fore I done what I did,
Or seen what I seed that day!

In a country where revenge is a matter of honour and honour is the most important thing in life we were back for only one thing; to avenge our dead and restore our honour. It is no wonder that when we backed the police in the northern towns in 2006 the population saw us as part of the problem, not the solution. So Helmand was not a great choice. I have alluded already to why we were in Afghanistan, so I will call a halt to the history there. More importantly, on 18 October 2009 I had to pass on all I knew about the situation we were in, whatever had happened previously, and then come up with a plan, Canute-like, to turn the tide of history.

*   *   *   *   *

At the top of my sheet I started with a quote which I thought summed up ISAF activity up to that point in our area as much as any other.

> A military force, culturally programmed to respond conventionally (and predictably) to insurgent attacks, is akin to the bull that repeatedly charges a matador's cape – only to tire and eventually be defeated by a much weaker opponent. This is predictable – the bull does what comes naturally. While a conventional approach is instinctive, that behaviour is self-defeating. *COMISAF (General McCrystal), summer 2009*

I started with what I had been told of the enemy.

The different tiers of Taliban that exist in Helmand Province are as follows: Tier one Taliban represent the command element. They are motivated by ideology, the desire for power, status and increased financial standing. Sitting above this tier is the Quetta Shura, which issues direction to different commanders within Pakistan and Afghanistan. Many of the tier one commanders are able to act independently of the Quetta Shura because of their access to finance from the narcotics industry. This also ensures that the 'narco khans' have significant influence on the Taliban hierarchy. The ethnicity of tier one commanders in Helmand is predominantly local or out-of-area Afghan Pashtu rather than foreign fighters.

Tier two Taliban are the full-time fighters and facilitators. Most tier two fighters are aligned to a specific tier one commander. Some are motivated by ideology; most are motivated by finance or loyalty to a commander. Although the majority of tier two are local to Helmand, there are some out-of-area fighters and a few foreign fighters.

Tier three Taliban are part-time fighters, facilitators and observers who have varied motivations to fight the International Stabilisation Force, or ISAF, and the Afghan National Security Forces or ANSF. A few are motivated by ideology, but more are motivated by financial incentives and a need for personal status.

A day's work for the Taliban earns a man four times more than he will receive for unskilled labour. Some are motivated by a specific grievance against ISAF or the ANSF. Others are victims of Taliban coercion and intimidation and fight out of fear. Tier three Taliban are always local and are not likely to move away from their local area. In the Inkerman area these fighters were based in Mazak and Mian Rud across the green zone and then came forward to engage ISAF. IED layers were reported to be from out of our area. Some become tier two Taliban if they show an increased commitment, but most tier three fighters' loyalty can be bought by whoever offers the greater chance of long-term success and can provide them with financial stability.

The Taliban franchise uses five lines of operation to fight its campaign. They are: Strike ISAF, Impose Shadow Governance, Win the People, Undermine the Government of Afghanistan and Sustain the Force. Each is described below.

The military main effort of the Taliban was to deny ISAF freedom of movement through IED emplacement, a tactic I had previously thought did not apply, but recent events had proven otherwise. The favoured IED was the Victim Operated IED; however, the Taliban maintained a strong capability in Command Wire IEDs and Radio Controlled IEDs. As well as emplacement on routes, the insurgents would lay IED belts and fields in order to slow and canalise ISAF movement. The Taliban would also use Suicide IEDs in urban areas; this had the dual effect of striking ISAF and undermining Afghan confidence that the government of the Islamic Republic of Afghanistan could deliver security. IEDs were the preferred method of attack due to the economy of human and financial effort, and the fact that they were relatively low risk, easy to emplace and required minimal central control. In Inkerman area of operations IEDs had been used on route 611 to deny resupply, in the local village of Sareagar to disrupt and deny patrols, and around firing points in the green zone for protection. The Taliban might still engage in force-on-force contacts to ambush ISAF or strike a perceived weakness – normally static locations, although this was now less common. Coordinated multi-weapon engagements would be launched only if the Taliban had an excellent knowledge of the ground and been able to prepare weapons dumps and escape routes. They initiated an IED and followed up with rocket-propelled grenades or small arms attacks from pre-prepared positions. This was less common in the Inkerman AO. They also used secondary IEDs on likely ISAF cordon positions. The Taliban continued to use indirect fire, mortars and rockets to fix ISAF in base locations or when they identified a static ISAF patrol that could be engaged. Their accuracy was generally poor, but the threat was still high. The final method for striking ISAF was for the Taliban to attempt a 'spectacular' attack onto ISAF aviation or low-flying aircraft. They favoured the DshKA machine gun which could be brought to bear at short notice, but they also used rocket-propelled grenades or, if available, the 'Man Portable Air Defence system', the SA-7 MANPADs. The success of these attacks was relatively low, but the threat was credible. This was the reason Inkerman helicopter landing site was code red, making resupply by air very difficult.

The concept of 'shadow governance' aimed to illustrate to the local population that the Taliban is the authority in a given area. Vehicle checkpoints and patrolling in district centres and bazaars were a common way of demonstrating to locals that they were the policing force. There was alleged to be an illegal checkpoint two kilometres north of Inkerman. The Taliban would also impose their own justice system and try individuals who were accused of breaking their law. The Taliban was particularly keen on trying individuals who were accused of spying on behalf of security forces or the government. This had the effect of discouraging people from any engagement with us where the Taliban was strong and held power. There had been a number of instances of this in the Inkerman area, and many locals believed a man had been beheaded two years before we arrived and the fear still permeated the community. The Taliban tried to dominate local infrastructure and taxed the provision of services to local nationals. They tried to control electricity and water supplies and then tax people for its use, having the dual effect of providing money for the insurgency and showing that they were the controlling force in an area. Schooling in Taliban-controlled areas was strictly controlled, with girls prevented from attending. Food was also taxed; at the time we thought wheat was taxed particularly highly to discourage people from growing it over poppy.

To achieve the support of the people, the Taliban seek to empower tribes, elders and individuals who show them active support. Similarly, they isolate and intimidate hostile tribes, elders and individuals who do not support them or seek to oppose them. The Taliban can promote themselves to a larger audience by ensuring that they have the support of the clergy and the Taliban message is promoted in mosques. We knew nothing of this in the Inkerman area so it immediately became a Commander's Critical Information Requirement (CCIR) – something I wanted to know as soon as possible. The Taliban will protect civilian livelihoods in industries that suit them. This included the narcotics industry where the Taliban benefited. Taliban propaganda will threaten and intimidate and give reasons for not supporting ISAF, but rarely positive reasons for supporting the Taliban. Methods of delivering this propaganda are radio, word of mouth, leaflets and night letters. The most important feature of the Taliban influence campaign is that they aim to be the first to deliver news to the people with their version of the truth. This was especially relevant during an alleged civilian casualty incident.

To continue their campaign, the Taliban maintain communications with the Quetta Shura in Pakistan. Direction from Quetta is not always followed to the letter, but the overall intent is known by tier one and two commanders in Helmand. Financial support to the insurgency is offered from Quetta, but tier one commanders also support themselves through taxation of locals and involvement in protecting the narcotics industry. The force is armed and supplied through a variety of means. Moreover, the Taliban use Pashtunwali's hospitality ethos, turning to locals when they require a bed or food. Weapons are supplied from many locations, primarily Pakistan, and the Taliban place great emphasis on protecting these lines of communication. Recruiting and training takes place both in Helmand and other parts of Afghanistan, but specialist training is usually conducted in Pakistan. This is particularly relevant for foreign fighters who train in Pakistan prior to moving into Afghanistan.

The Taliban wish to disrupt the democratic process, as had been evident in the then recent presidential elections. During the summer 2009 elections intimidation of locals was successful in the Inkerman area, and no one in the area voted in the election. Officials within the government of Afghanistan were also targets for the Taliban, who attempted assassinations and kidnappings. Physical signs of the government of Afghanistan were also targeted. The government of Afghanistan is frequently derided and portrayed by the Taliban as a puppet state of the USA and un-Islamic. The Afghan Security Forces are targeted, particularly the police, to bribe, subvert and intimidate. The greater the failings of the Afghan National Police, the more successful the counter-insurgency is. Any reconstruction project that is sponsored or supported by the Government is a target for the Taliban. They will either try to destroy the project during construction or wait until it is built and security has been reduced before inflicting damage against the symbol.

The Taliban no longer deliberately becomes involved in protracted engagements against our security forces. They are aware of our superior firepower and aviation assets. The Taliban are aware of response times of our close air support and attack helicopters and will fight to ensure that they can withdraw in cover. Engagements are typically no longer than twenty minutes but have lasted up to three hours. There is a lack of coordination and cooperation between commanders and therefore fighting between different Taliban cells is not uncommon. The brutality and intimidation towards local nationals ensures that the Taliban is often accepted through fear rather than active support. Shadow governance is inconsistent and harsh.

*     *     *     *     *

The Brigadier intended, in accordance with General McChrystal's wishes, to place the people at the centre of our mission. Our understanding of insurgent and community intentions and motivations – 'what is going on' – had to be improved. Battlegroups were to conduct Human Terrain Mapping (HTM) through biometric testing and the employment of the Tactical Conflict Assessment Framework (TCAF). He wanted to build a common intelligence picture as well a common sense of purpose with Afghan partners.

He was also absolutely clear that in judging the wisdom of any course of action, we had to take into account the Afghan, coalition and domestic perspectives, recognising the strategic to tactical compression that accompanied our actions. In other words, one tactical mistake on the ground if captured and broadcast could make international headlines and have a strategic effect.

According to the Brigadier, Sangin was less important than central Helmand, but it remained the key northern town and our hold of the area had to be improved. He exhorted the northern battlegroups to establish their reputations by showing ingenuity with limited resources and that reconciliation could be furthered without full security and, if handled cleverly, could represent a viable alternative to mainstream security operations.

He gave us advice on Improvised Explosive Devices (IEDs). Acknowledged as a potent weapon, he wanted to make sure communities turned against their use, that we attacked the network behind them and defeated the technology in them. Partnership with Afghan forces formed a significant part of his plan to improve security; he wanted partnership at every level. Narcotics were a threat, but most interestingly the HQ believed less because of the revenue stream to the insurgency, than because of the corrosive effect of corruption on the Afghan government and the power that narco-warlords thereby derived.

It was then, and it is now, an uncomfortable truth that drug production was far less under the Taliban. The people who really stand to lose if Afghan poppies are burned are the government officials who take a cut of the illicit trade. Your average farmer knows this and whilst the Taliban tax the poppy crop, they would tax any crop to fund the insurgency in areas they control. The Afghan population know who the villain of this piece is, even if we seem unwilling to say so publicly.

The final thought from the Brigade HQ was that in a campaign where perception mattered as much as reality, it was important to show the progress of the campaign. Measures of effect had tended in the past to present a lot of information and very little understanding; they also tended toward a conspiracy of optimism. We had to demonstrate change through simple and telling metrics to show where progress had been made to a sceptical public (Afghan, British or international). And where the right 'positive trends' were not emerging quickly enough, we could make a persuasive case for a change in approach or an increase in resources.

My job was to understand the Brigadier's intent and the mission he had given to my superior. The précis of the set of orders that I gave on 19 October, an hour after the last of B Company left, is in Appendix 1. I have tried to cure it of 'militareze', but some of it was written in plain English and some in a gobbledegook of three-letter abbreviations and words without vowels. The words in capitals have fairly precise meanings in the context of a military mission, which meant that the orders were clearer to those sitting around than they appear there. As I had not yet received anything other than a warning order that included a mission I was not in a position, in formal terms, to give this as the final order. Those who were there were left under no illusions that this was the foundation from which we would build. To mix my metaphors it was the outline sketch of our current position and the direction of travel. In sum we would conduct platoon-level familiarisation patrols and then, as we had worked out the reality of how to operate and become familiar with the ground and our drills, we would patrol further at greater strength, led through the areas close to the Forward Operating Base by those who were most familiar with that ground. The next stage would be to go back a few times to each place to be familiar to locals, piece together the information and then exploit the intelligence. Much of the detail of exactly how we would undertake all this was in coordinating instructions which are not included here for security reasons.

The discerning reader might well ask why this was not already done. Patrol reports from my predecessors were available, as were the incident reports. But there was no intelligence database for the AO, nothing searchable and no way of comparing or contrasting. After four years in Helmand, as the Brigadier had already highlighted, there was no common intelligence picture. That is a military crime of epic proportions and led directly to people dying in the same compound where others had died not six months before. In Inkerman at least there were a series of incident logs so we could identify compounds where previous units had searched or had an incident. This identified every compound within 400 metres, but there was nothing on the human geography, no contacts other than a single Afghan who dropped in to the base after dark who sold cans of pop and blankets to cold soldiers and dispensed some of the latest gossip as he made a tidy, if risky, profit. B Company 2 Rifles, to their credit, had started a database, but from 13 June to 19 October they had barely been able to fill it in because of the nature of the operations they undertook. So anything we already had was useful for historical purposes, but would have to be confirmed.

I committed at this stage to trying to identify locations for patrol bases. The US had found a measure of success in Iraq by 'living amongst the people'. I had lived as a platoon commander in two platoon houses in Bosnia. I was a fan of the tactic. There are many in the military that are not because it ties men down to guarding a location and limits the opportunity for patrolling. But patrolling is not necessarily manoeuvre, and patrol bases can be 'manoeuvrist' in the military sense of the term – i.e. to out manoeuvre the enemy. Again only time would tell.

# Chapter 7

# Buckle Up

At the beginning of the first week I had my first, and fortunately my last, encounter with the Afghan trots. Not a bad case by any stretch, and certainly not the sprints to which some were subjected. When they annoyingly did not clear up I took twenty-four hours off food and that did the trick. It coincided with a getting a speck of dust behind a contact lens. For twenty-four hours I wondered what the hell was happening to me: sound body and you keep a sound mind. I always felt I wanted to be if not in good shape, then at least in good health, not so much for the physical effort of patrols, but because physical ailments undermine confidence. At that stage I felt confidence was most important when making decisions, and because we didn't really have enough experience or information to warrant it, it was simply a case of going for it.

I had been out with 3 Platoon on an uneventful green zone patrol. I just mooched along at the back, doing the job of peg pick-up man. In training, we had developed a procedure for marking the cleared path by putting down pegs. The last man had to pick them up. When the second man in the patrol had run out, they were passed up the line. Having had so clear a reminder that the cleared path is not always obvious to the last man I was sure that the sacrifice of speed across the ground was worth it for the protection it afforded to all. That said, it was a good reminder to me that if you are carrying 55kg then doing lunges every ten metres becomes tiring and tiresome quite quickly. Other methods for route marking had been used in training, but talc and spray-paint both left ground sign for the enemy to assess tactics, yet what shocked all of us was the number of 'mark and avoid' signs on the ground. I was determined that we should not do this. Going out into Sareagar, it had felt as though we were surrounded by potential IEDs – clearly not the case – or at least not in that number. These areas that had made the Vallons respond needed to be investigated and dealt with. So initial patrols were painstakingly slow, as the Vallon men swept the path ahead and stopped to uproot the various bits of metal they detected. We waited twenty minutes just outside the gates of Inkerman while a Rifleman dug out an old Coke can. In time, the Riflemen became very proficient at knowing what constituted a suspicious signal on the Vallon. They also began to get a better appreciation of 'vulnerable areas' and 'vulnerable points'. Yet it was always a question of their judgement, and incredibly difficult to get right all the time, given the plethora of factors involved. For the time being they exercised extreme caution.

I was happy that they got their drills sorted out. I had given two weeks for this process to happen, with each platoon to conduct a variety of patrols; to the village, to the green zone, vehicle checkpoints and to make sure that all of the Riflemen had guarded the camp from each of the guard posts or 'sangars'. 'Sangar duty', or time on guard, is part of the British Army idiom. The irony is that it is the Afghan word for outpost or checkpoint. The Army might have adopted it 140 years before, not far from where we were now based.

The Company Headquarters personnel, me included, would go with the platoons. Not as an independent section, but to add numbers and to get everyone over the first nerves of going on patrol. 3 Platoon found four IEDs in the first week. All in areas too close to the base for comfort. We sent up the required reports, but at each stage we were told that the 'assets', the counter-IED team or bomb disposal team, were not available to come. So, much against my better judgement, we were told to mark and avoid those locations. I began to see why my predecessors had taken their decisions. You only need to find a couple of these things and then be told to leave them in the ground to begin not to even bother with doing the frankly epically nerve-wracking and dangerous bit of uncovering a device in the first place. To be finding them though was a good start; it gave us confidence in the drills and skills we had learned.

On the morning of 26 October, I was just about to go out with 2 Platoon. Briefed and ready to go, I was called back from the gate to go to the operations room. I was briefed over the radio by the CO that we were about to get a warning order for an operation. The details were pretty sketchy, but it involved the 'lift' of a mid-level Taliban commander. We were going to support this operation. The memory of that day blends into a confusing haze. First we were going to be needed, then we were not; just an exclusion zone in the middle of our area. Well in fact about two kilometres across the green zone from our area and not somewhere that anyone had been since early June, some five months before. Fine. Then news that we might do the cordon and search ourselves. What? By early afternoon we had firmed up that we would be getting some visitors: a combination of Afghan and UK Special Forces (SF). 'Didn't train for this one,' I remember thinking, as two Chinooks'-worth of beefy-looking fellows got off the aircraft.

A couple of my own previous company commanders had done time with Special Forces before coming into the 'green' Army to take command, as had one of my previous COs. I sort of knew what to expect. If you are able to select and train the best, then it makes speed of thought and action routine business. If you have a company of 140 very junior Riflemen, doing things 'on the bounce' is nearly always a recipe for disaster. The leader of the Special Forces group and I cobbled together a plan. We, 'A' Company, would 'path find' across the green zone and guard a forming-up point and the route, while the Special Forces would breeze down the marked route, do their stuff in the compounds, get the bad guys, destroy the weapons and be back before dawn. Simple. Or so it sounds, writing it now. At the time we were just 'kissing' it. Keep It Simple, Stupid (KISS) – one of the best acronyms the army has. It was now about six in the evening.

1 Platoon set off at about 2030. Progress was very slow. The Vallon man at the front was on his fourth patrol. The hardest thing the SF asked of us was not to 'light up'. That is to say, no torches or infra-red lights were to be used, and definitely no smoking; just standard practice, but tempting in the dead of a cold night. Several times the lead section had to box around areas littered with metal. The minutes turned into hours and 1 Platoon was only half-way there after two and a half hours. One of the SF commanders indicated they really needed to be on the objective by midnight. This was beginning to unravel; we just weren't quick enough. Another SF commander steadied the ship – 'I think we'll be OK. Let's see how they get on in the next hour'. 1 Platoon made better progress in the next hour and the burly team set off after them. They got a bit held up towards the end, but at nearly one o'clock in the morning everything was ready. The next two hours were punctuated by little more than monosyllabic updates from the SF liaison officer to the headquarters. 'They're in.' 'They've got Bravos.' 'Found some weapons.'

The upshot was we had five detainees on the way back, including one who seemed too old for the perils of insurgency, and a stash of weapons and ammunition to dispose of. The ATO, Ammunition Technical Officer, or bomb disposal bloke, did not have enough explosive with him to deal with the weapons. They made a decision to destroy the stash in place using the AC130 'Spectre' Gunship with its 105mm gun. It was an impressive show of force. As the sun rose, the last of 2 Platoon, who had been guarding the route, made it back into Inkerman. The Rifleman who Valloned his way to the objective and ensured the success of the operation was cited for his actions that night. Eighteen years old, and 5ft 3in on a tall day, by the time he got in he was collapsing with exhaustion. The SF commander wrote him a letter of which he is as proud as his medal. Rifleman Reece Terry received a Queen's Gallantry Medal in September 2010. As we worked on through the morning sending reports up the various chains, Chinooks came for the prisoners to take them to a proper detention facility and we let Old Man Rivers go.

'Well, if you've got any more like that we'd be glad to help out,' I mentioned to our newfound friends. The SF lads slept and then, as swiftly as they had come, they were gone. The effect of this operation was to give an intravenous injection of confidence to the whole company. From the top to the bottom, none of us had ever thought that on day seven, after only one or two local patrols, we would reach out across the green zone to play our own small but critical part in a

Special Forces operation. I think it was more shocking for those who had been around a bit longer. In the normal course of affairs the exclusion zone goes in and that is that. The young Riflemen just thought this was how things rolled in the 'stan. It took a while to realise that we were not going to spend the rest of the tour on first-name terms or calling each other by nicknames, SF-stylee, or with a Spectre gunship covering our every move.

All this had an effect not only within A Company, but also up the chain of command. The daily brief to the CO with all the other company commanders on the net was pure gold that night. It is always pleasing to be able to report the good stuff. Modesty must prevail, but you know when someone's had a good day. There were enough days when all of us, the company commanders, broadcasting to anyone who had an ear to the battlegroup net, had to face down the grief and emerge from the reaper's shadow to explain why an incident had happened that for all the world one wished had gone differently. But 27 October was not that night. The CO was never given to effusive praise, but he had received reports from all levels of the chain of command thanking him and us for the way we had conducted ourselves. If I hadn't been so tired after thirty-six hours awake I would have done a jig round the Ops room. Meeting triumph and disaster just the same – durch.

The key question was, what would be the enemy response?

We got a response, and it came in the form of a delegation of elders. They came on the first day when we released the old man. We were not ready to talk at that stage so Ed, the company 'Influence officer', asked them to come back the following day. He promised that I would be there and that we would serve tea. Eighty of them came in. Ed started off the meeting, or shura, before I joined them. Having seen the report from the initial meeting I knew that there would be a fair amount of theatre in this gathering. So I dressed to impress in my clean combats and sported a pistol on my belt. The only time I ever wore one was in meetings of this nature, both as a mark of rank and for easier personal protection – not that I ever felt threatened.

I settled down to listen to them protest the innocence of the men we had detained. There was no doubt that they had been sent by insurgents, but they were a notable gathering. In Afghanistan, age, gender and facial hair are all indicators of seniority and gravitas outside the compound wall. Inside the compound there is alleged to be a matriarchy; but outside, in Helmand, mature men with long beards get respect. It was as an impressive bunch of beards as you are likely to find. We talked for about two hours. They are good talkers and the conversation moved at a sedate pace. 'You have the watches but we have the time,' is a popular Afghan jibe. We sat on our haunches until my Western joints creaked and we moved to benches. Green tobacco was taken with care but not by me. Small globules of spit formed a circle of dust balls on the ground around each chewer. Afghans often suffer myopia, alleged to be the result of a lifetime of dehydration. They break into your personal space to look closely from behind a beard and leathery skin tanned by a thousand Afghan suns.

At one point I was told by one of the elders who seemed to command a good deal of respect that we both believed in the same God. 'There is only one God,' he assured me. We had been going for an hour and a half at that point and I felt we might have only just warmed up if the theology continued. So I felt inclined to agree and left it at that. We arranged to meet again in three days to see if their issue had progressed. It all appeared to be a caricature and a slightly idyllic one, but it was not.

I had been delayed getting to the shura because of another ongoing incident. The shura had been postponed for an hour in the first place because two children, both aged nine, had been brought to the Forward Operating Base having stepped on an IED. These were the innocent victims in the battle of wills being hammered out in the meeting. I will not describe the full extent of their injuries, but horrific barely does the scene justice. Our doctor, medics and medically-trained Riflemen worked for thirty-five minutes to save them. They were alive when we put them on the Chinook helicopter to fly to the hospital in Camp Bastion with relatives. They died of their injuries there. It is hard not to believe it was a small mercy. Their uncles returned later in a taxi with the two small coffins on the back seat, and they were buried the following day. And we were left with the moral dilemma of having found, marked clearly and avoided that device, only for two children to detonate it.

The fate of those children caused a good deal of anguish. Collette, Jodie and the team had taken them from the arms of their parents at the gate while a team of Riflemen held drips and dressings as they tried in vain to save them. It was our first brush with post-traumatic stress and the trauma-management process. The platoon that had found the devices was particularly aggrieved. Then there were those who had thought they might be able to help and had gone to the gate only to watch the horror unfold. Once you have the image in your head, it is difficult to shake; even harder if you feel helpless in doing anything about it, harder still if you are not expecting it. It is a great irony that we had trained rigidly to cope, both mentally and physically, with the injuries of battle amongst our own. We accepted that possibility as part of what we were going to do. Children are a different matter – especially for those who have children. As we discussed the events afterwards in the team, Pat Hyde set out a plan that would limit the exposure to such things to those who were needed for treatment and evacuation.

The first week ended with a visit from the Brigadier. As he left, the enemy fired a couple of rocket-propelled grenades at the helicopters for good measure. He had come as part of his first round of visits to all the Company locations. He was obviously pleased that the Company had managed an early success, but he was worried about the effect that IEDs were having. He suggested that route selection might avoid the issue. I was quick to point out, probably too quick, that route selection had its place, but that Inkerman had been occupied for over two years. There were not enough helicopters to lift us *over* the IEDs so we were walking through them. My assessment was that given the size of our force and the enemy's method of operating, we had no way of telling the depth of the minefield that surrounded us, but the warning signs were already there. We had found as many IEDs in our first week as our predecessors had found in their first three months. What was more, not having the assets to deal with them had resulted in the deaths of two children and this undermined the confidence of the very people he wanted us to protect, the locals.

We also discussed the future of Forward Operating Base Inkerman. My view was that Inkerman was out on a limb and we spent far too much time protecting resupply for it to be worth sustaining the base unless there were serious plans to try to dominate the whole of the Upper Sangin Valley, in which case it would be a very good place from which to launch. There were too many unknowns in all of this. What he did know was that Inkerman was getting an upgrade in terms of living accommodation and facilities and that it was very late or even too late in the day to turn all of that off. Knowing what I know now, I would not have been giving him options.

Nevertheless, it was going to stay and we were going to have to work round the difficulties. I made the case for mine-protected vehicles to come to Inkerman. Being on foot is important in the last two metres of a patrol; having properly protected vehicles or helicopters to get you there means you keep your feet until you need to use them. In October 2009 A Company had access to neither. We covered this very briefly. He brought with him an American general who would be part of the coming American surge into Helmand. As the US general left he pulled a large 'stogie' cigar from his pocket. 'That's for the little guy, the one who led the patrol.'

\* \* \* \* \*

The second week of the tour was dominated by two company operations. Flushed with success from working with the Special Forces group, with the platoons now well into the swing, it was time to get the A Company Group acting as one. I wanted to flex our muscles a little, give the insurgent something else to think about. We had opened up a decent dialogue with the elders with our second and third shuras with them, although they came in rather fewer numbers. We discovered they were from three villages, Jusalay, Mazak and Mian Ruud, the villages in the middle of the green zone. Ross Kemp went to Jusalay with 1 Royal Anglian in 2007. So we began to piece together who was who in each of the villages and a rough hierarchy.

The platoon patrols were getting into small arms fire-fights, or 'contacts', as the army calls them, each time they went out. 1 Platoon had a near miss with a command-wire IED on 28 October. 2 Platoon got caught in the open with the Fire Support Group and needed smoke and high explosive from the mortars to extract themselves. The mortar line learned a valuable lesson about getting the first round on target. It was all a little bit close for comfort; in fact it was far too close for comfort – the smoke had landed ten metres from the platoon, but luckily the high-explosive rounds had gone out to the correct distance. The after-action review was a fractious affair. To their credit the 3 Rifles mortar section spent the next two days practising for all they were worth. It paid off. The epitome of 'it's alright to make a mistake, but only make it once'. The reason for the fractiousness was not only generated by how close they had come to being shot by the enemy and then smoked by our own mortars, but also principally due to the time it had taken to get the mortars into action to suppress the enemy and give the platoon on the ground space to manoeuvre. We went over what had happened three or four times, minute by minute, second by second. It was a difficult situation because those on the ground felt that they had been caught in an ambush and needed the indirect fire immediately to facilitate their extraction. Charlie had not had time to bring his machine-guns to bear to try to win the fire fight before they were all taking cover behind a small mound of earth and wishing they could lie flat as Dover sole. In the end I had authorised the mortars to fire based on judgement rather than fact. The fire had been delayed by a minute or so as a result, but the real delay, as we discovered in the review, had come in clearing the airspace. It was not a happy situation. This represented the start of a month of discussions with the Fire Support Team on how we could speed the process up and the nature of their role. Now was the time, for sure, to get out on the ground as a Company to see what we could do to overmatch the enemy without having recourse to artillery and mortars.

The plan was to patrol up to the site of a former patrol base about two kilometres northeast of Inkerman. It had been occupied during the summer of 2008 as Patrol Base Emerald, but abandoned after the electricity-generating turbine had been taken to the hydroelectric dam at Kajaki by a different route. 2 Para had put it in as part of the deception plan for the move, then, when Y Company 45 Commando wanted to free up more men for patrolling, it was taken out. Since then it had become an enemy scouting point; B Company 2 Rifles had dropped a couple of 500-pound bombs on it at one stage in their tour and much of what had been an impressive compound was now composed mostly of rubble. In the last week a 2 Platoon patrol had been fired upon sporadically from the vicinity of the compound. We planned to go up there, do a search, and then go on to the village of Jokhoran to do some 'Human Terrain Mapping' – HTM as it inevitably became known – our first attempt to build a database of information on our local population. Due to the variety of approaches of previous battlegroups there was no standard information that we asked. This was the Brigade's attempt to rectify this. I generally put human terrain mapping as a task on any patrol, just to reinforce the point that we were there to talk to people not to drive them away. Coupled with a Tactical Combat Assessment Framework (TCAF) aiming to establish what needed doing and where, it gave all of the patrols a start point for conversations. The Company was lucky to have two 'influence' officers whose sole job was this type of engagement; they accompanied every patrol. Jessie was a young platoon commander, yet to take over a platoon, and Ed was a policeman who was a Territorial Army reserve engineer officer. Ed brought his policing skills, which proved just as handy as his demolition officer qualification. Jessie was also there as R and R cover for the other platoon commanders, but the extra manpower and especially the brainpower at the start of the tour was very useful.

Very early in the morning of 2 November, after a full day of battle preparation on All Saints Day, A Company set off for PB Emerald. Having set off at 0500, we made it into our cordon positions by 0800, two kilometres in a little under three hours. If that seems a long time, remember that not only were we all carrying at least 55kg of equipment, but we were also now all going at the pace required to properly sweep the ground ahead of the lead man with the Vallon. There were also the occasions when the pace slowed to that dictated by the irrigated poppy field or the ditch knee-high with mud and thigh-high with water. Choosing the least obvious and therefore safest route does not make for a speedy insertion. Importantly, we had not been seen on the way out and the enemy did not really know where we were until about 0830. They got things going shortly thereafter.

2 Platoon were given extra search training before we left the UK and consequently I had tasked them with conducting the search of the compound. 3 Platoon and the FSG provided the cordon troops and the guard. 1 Platoon provided the Quick Reaction Force (QRF) in Inkerman. The Company HQ was based on a compound roof 200 metres west of Emerald on the edge of the green zone. The CSM and the resupply party were an equivalent distance to the east, on the desert side, with the Fire Support Group vehicles with him in over watch.

2 Platoon started the search supported by engineers, also based in Inkerman, from the close support troop. Pretty quickly after that the forward cordon positions were attacked with small arms fire. The insurgents began to probe. Every time they did, the search team had to stop. It was painstaking. Eventually the search team approached the building. They came under fire again, but as they moved back into cover Corporal 'Chico' Bryant reported that he had seen some very suspicious material in the compound. I do not recollect why we didn't call for the bomb disposal team at that stage. Communications with Battlegroup HQ were difficult; we had to work back through the ops room in Inkerman. Perhaps they wanted a higher level of confirmation than a hurried glance. Anyway, I decided to go ahead with the explosive entry at a random point to

reduce the risk of booby trap. It was certainly part of the original plan to go in this way. The hole was exploded in the wall of the compound by Corporal Aidy Dixon and his team. The search team moved to see if they could get in. Chico Bryant confirmed the explosion had created a good entry point and they were moving in…

BOOM.

It was about 11 o'clock in the morning and the heat was beginning to build. But the shock wave from the blast seemed peculiarly strong by comparison to the one I had felt two weeks earlier. The mushroom cloud of dust was almost perfect against the clear blue sky.

Then silence.

Pause. Breathe. Trying to keep my voice as neutral as impossible. 'Hello Hades Four Two Echo this is Hades Four Zero Alpha. Send Sit Rep, over.'

Pause for five of the longest seconds. And again:

'Hello Hades Four Two Echo this is Hades Four Zero Alpha. Send Sit Rep, over.'

Nothing. Charlie chimed in, more concerned, checking it wasn't simply my signal not getting to him. 'Hades Four Two Echo this is Hades Four Two Alpha. Radio check, over'.

Pause. Then, breaking the silence, Chico in slightly irritated tones: 'Hades Four Zero Alpha and Four Two Alpha this is Four Two Echo; just getting my fucking ten-liner together.'

Swearing on the net is usually met with a reprimand but I could have forgiven Chico anything at that particular moment just for being alive. He reported that the device had been outside the main door of the compound. Most of the team had been shielded from the blast because they were already in through the hole ten metres from the door and inside the compound as well. Chico and the other Rifleman guarding the entrance had sat down seconds before the device went off about ten metres from their position. A very near miss.

Corporal Dixon was able to confirm beyond all doubt that there was a lot of paraphernalia for making IEDs in the compound: palm oil containers, wire, kite string, batteries… it was time to go firm and get the bomb disposal team in. They showed up by helicopter at about 1530. Time was beginning to get tight; we had aimed to finish this phase by midday. The high-risk search of the compound was going to take at least two hours and we had about three hours of daylight left. The cordon was still being attacked at regular intervals. We got support from an Apache attack helicopter and an A-10 Warthog ground-attack aircraft rumbled in, farting across the sky. The Apache pilot fired fifty rounds as a 'warning shot' just beyond a tree line to the northwest. I had thought we were getting a warning burst of three to five rounds; instead we got fifty. 'Get him under control', I implored Lance Serjeant 'Dinger' Bellman, the Joint

Tactical Air Controller in my Fire Support Team. Dinger just looked at me with a 'you know what these pilots are like' kind of look.

With the pukka Royal Engineer search team now in full swing things were getting back on track. No human terrain mapping in Jokhoran, but a good day nonetheless. One of the pilots then called in to Dinger and said that he had about ten minutes before he was going. Eh? He would have to avoid the sandstorm. The what? On the top of the roof we looked north and from the desert on the other side of the green zone the sandstorm was coming. 'You've got about twenty minutes before it arrives', radioed the pilot.

My first thought was 'Holy shit'. If they could replicate sandstorms in Norfolk I might have a clue what this was going to be like. Get on the radio. How long is this thing going to last? Get the disposal team out of the compound and into a protected position. Get everyone in tight so the perimeter can't be breached. How long is this thing going to last? CSM needs to get round whoever he can to resupply. Everyone report when firm. With locations. Patrol minimise, no movement. MIRT won't be able to come in. How long is this thing going to bloody last?

I was hammering down the radio at Ben in the Ops room to try and get someone onto the 'Met' section in Camp Bastion. Then, on his final pass, the pilot called in to Dinger on the Air Net. 'I've flown over it. It'll last about an hour.'

Thank fuck for that.

Then day turned to brown. It was my first and last sandstorm. Nothing like the three days to a week versions of Iraq legend, but enough to see us through to darkness. While the dust penetrated every crack Al, my FST commander, came up with an illumination plan to support the remainder of the search, which involved firing a lot of mortar shells. The Artillery boys were desperate to get in on the act, but mortar light is far better. It is all about the trajectory of the round; the artillery sends long and the mortars send high, and so the area gets lit for longer with a mortar round. The search finally finished at 2300. While it went on I gave orders for our withdrawal. From sunset onwards the enemy withdrew and we were not attacked after dark. This became our regular experience. Only once did they lay an ambush for us at night. And even then it didn't trigger. The fact that it didn't provoked a stream of invective from 'Haksar', a local Taliban commander, but that is another tale.

We snaked back across the desert in bright moonlight, arriving back at Inkerman at 0100. I was shattered. It had been a good day, but I quickly realised that the single point of failure in A Company was going to be me. A previous commander at Inkerman had told me that he had planned and conducted three such patrols in six days. It had taken him a long time to recover. I began to see why. The constant quest of the commander is for a tempo of operations that out-manoeuvres the enemy. Go faster than he can react. Unbalance him. Attack weakness. Do not get into a battle of attrition. These were fine words, but putting them into action was going to be hard work. The last act of the day was definitely bad news on two fronts. Staff Serjeant Olaf 'Oz' Schmid had been killed by an IED in Sangin. We had not been told while we were out on the ground, but he was the first guy that we had worked with who had been killed. The second came from the Ammunition Technical Officer who had collected the evidence at the end of the search of the compound. He brought a plastic bag to me.

'Well, we removed enough stuff for about fifteen IEDs.'

'Great.'

'But we also found these.' He showed me black carbon graphite rods plucked from ubiquitous motorbike batteries. 'You'll need to tell your blokes they'll be looking for low metal content IEDs'.

Shit.

# Chapter 8

# Reality Bites

The closest village to Inkerman was Sareagar. No more than a hamlet in 2007, it had grown up to about seventy compounds as the locals left their homes in the green zone to avoid the fighting. At almost every level Afghan society has been disrupted by the insurgency. A great many of those who could left altogether. In 2009 there were 56,000 Afghans living in the UK. At a local level those who wished to avoid the fighting moved away to other towns or at the very least to the villages on the far side of the green zone, Mazak or Mian Ruud. These villages were only five or six kilometres away, but far enough from Inkerman not to be too troubled. Only those who could not afford to move had stayed. Sareagar village had a pharmacy, of a type that sold a few potions, none of which had any real medical benefit; a garage (a shed where someone tried to fix motorbikes) and a couple of mosques. All in all it was a fairly random collection of families from different tribes with little loyalty to each other and no social structure, few of whom had lived in Sareagar before 2006.

It was, however, all we had, so we had to protect it. In the aftermath of the events at the Emerald patrol base and the sheer number of IEDs we had encountered I confessed to Pat Hyde and Ben Shuttleworth, and they were quick to agree, that I thought that so far we had just been very *very* lucky. It was a strange conversation, because they had clearly been thinking the same thing, but none of us wanted to put a commentator's jinx on our run. We had experienced at least five IED explosions that members of the company had been freakishly fortunate to walk away from. I felt like we needed to take some of the risk of moving out from Inkerman again and again in the same way. In addition, given the fire-fights we were having, it wasn't doing much for the safety of the locals, so I devised a plan to conjoin two operations.

Operation Hornet was a Helmand-wide plan that aimed to reduce the effect of IEDs. We were a perfect candidate for the extra support this required, given that we had found so many in our first two weeks. Coupled with this I also wanted to try to generate a persistent surveillance presence in the village so that we could understand the pattern of life better. It would be as risky as any other operation to get observation posts in, but after that it should take out some of the risk for a few days by being static in amongst the population. The original idea was to have a total of five observation points. Four would be in the village and there would be an 'Anchor' Point on high ground outside the built-up area. The high hills two kilometres to the south of Inkerman were the obvious 'key terrain', to use the military jargon, for this operation. One of the hills had been used to protect the incoming logistics patrol so we would need to be careful in the approach. With the ground observed we could then clear the routes on the eastern side of the village and continue to watch over them to try and prevent reseeding of IEDs.

My hope was that if we could get the locals using the routes again then the bomb layers would not only be restricting our use of the tracks, but it would also be a very obvious show of what we were trying to do for the locals. Too often the villagers had been caught in the middle of the crossfire. Not literally, because many of them ran for cover at the first sign of trouble. But Sareagar was living proof that they had been forced to move house, and how many had had their crops destroyed, or were forced to work overnight to avoid the fighting? I was determined that we should conduct operations that put us genuinely on the side of the locals without disrupting their lives too badly. There was going to have to be some disruption. The only time forces had occupied locals' houses was for the protection of logistics patrols. Going into an Afghan home, even just to sit on their roof, is culturally very sensitive. If an Englishman's house is his castle, then an Afghan's home is his honour, or more correctly it protects his honour, which is personified by his wife. Forced entries were now prohibited by President Karzai, so we would have to proceed with due deference, but firmly enough to demonstrate that we were on their side. Nothing ventured…

Two bomb disposal crews came up for the clearance. One was led by Staff Sergeant Karl 'Badger' Ley, and the other by WO2 Dave Markland, who was subsequently killed by an IED strike in another area in February. Dave Markland's search team were Ghurkhas and truly exceptional. I am not qualified to say if one search team is better than another; they are all highly trained and some of the bravest of the brave. The Badger was awarded the George Medal for actions during Herrick 11. He and his team got through a terrifying amount of work. We worked with most of the technical officers and search teams who were in Helmand for Operation Herrick 11 and they all had their idiosyncrasies. The Ghurkhas seemed to rely less on the Vallon and more on what they could see in front of them. If they stopped to assess an area they always stepped on the spot after they had made their decision. On the first day they found one device and cleared the remaining area where the two local kids had been so grievously injured. As part of the follow-up we discovered that the Taliban would fine the family who lived closest to the IEDs for allowing the children to set the devices off. It would be unlikely that they could afford to pay. The Taliban used to extract the payment in other ways, usually forcing another son to spend a period fighting for them. We had heard this in many briefings and now it was going on within view of our front gate. So much for protecting the population. We observed their house day in, day out, but not once had we seen suspicious activity. The IEDs had been put in behind the house, out of our view, but they must have got there. It was extremely frustrating that the family did not feel they could come and tell us. Yet on that point, as I have mentioned already, there was only one Afghan who came to the Forward Operating Base with any regularity. Just one.

2 Platoon were first into the Observation Posts (OP). 1 Platoon provided the protection for the bomb disposal teams and the FSG made their way painstakingly to the top of one of the hills to provide the anchor observation point. 2 Platoon had some interesting negotiations that day. As the lay of the land became clearer they requested that they man three rather than four posts. They explained what we were trying to do to three rather confused Afghan heads of households and offered a good rent for the loan of their roof. We agreed the patrols would get down from the roofs outside the compound twice a day for an hour to allow the women time to move about the compound. This was a risk in terms of surveillance, but one I was more than prepared to take given the implications of 'dishonouring' the home. The negotiations done, they began to settle into, or rather onto, their new abodes. As for the FSG, when they reached the top of the hill to be the anchor point WO2 'Freddie' Fryer reported that they had reached the position. Inside the operations room, with 1 Platoon beginning to move back in with the bomb disposal team, I felt that we had achieved a reasonable start.

From my recollection, and because I was directly involved in relatively few, I nearly always heard an IED explosion before I felt it, and then saw the cloud of dust. The explosion on top of the hill that evening pulsed through the ops room over a mile away. With one exception I am not going to go into the minute-by-minute details of how people died. The families of those who were killed from A Company and those attached to the Company who died in our area have all endured the detail of a coroner's court to hear as precisely as possible those events. My individual, and very partial recollection of precisely what happened will not help you or them. In this case Rifleman Philip Allen, who had been attached to us from 2 Rifles, was killed by that explosion. He was one of four young men that we were due to send back to 2 Rifles in early December with some operational experience under their belts, and we had been the happy recipients of the extra manpower. But on the evening of 7 November, despite the very best efforts of Lance Corporal Hall, another of our medics, and the rest of the Fire Support Group, he died of his wounds.

He was very obviously dead on arrival at the evacuation point that had been selected. Freddie radioed in. Then we did something that we would never do again. I changed the helicopter evacuation into an 'angel' flight. The dead can be evacuated in a number of ways; risking the most important helicopter asset in Helmand flying to a 'hot' landing zone when the casualty is already dead is not the way. If you want a really harrowing account of what this means in practice and in detail then Toby Harnden's account in *Dead Men Risen*, of Lieutenant Colonel Rupert Thorneloe's death and subsequent transport, is a better bet. For us that meant the transport of Philip Allen's body back to Inkerman, where it could be evacuated from a protected helicopter landing site.

I had a choice between bringing Philip Allen to the base straight away or facing a greater danger tomorrow. I radioed Freddie. Never one to either mask his feelings very well, or to disobey an order, he agreed to protect the bomb disposal team, enabling them to fetch the missing equipment, which included a weapon, and exploit the scene. Exploitation really means that the Ammunition Technical Officer and the intelligence officer in the bomb disposal team can gather information from the site to see what kind of IED it was. The bomb-makers generally have a signature construction and this can be pieced together, which leads, ultimately, to a better chance of prosecution. The 'Badger', who was still on the ground, felt he would prefer to do the 'exploitation' of the scene that evening, given that it was a marked cleared route to the site of the explosion, rather than clear to the top again the following day when there was a greater risk of booby trap. It was sound logic, but set against this was our desire to return Rifleman Allen to Inkerman as quickly as possible. The choice was not out of any military manual I had ever read.

It was about 2100 when the FSG made it back into camp. The CSM had prepared a place for Rifleman Allen. Freddie came into the briefing area.

'Fuck… Fuckin' hell… That was… I'm … Fuckin' hell, boss, give me fifteen minutes to get mi shit together, 'na wot I mean.' Fifteen minutes later he was back.

'Sorry about that. I was just. I never ever ever fuckin' want to do that again.'

The FSG arrived in dribs and drabs for the after-action review. The reaction poured out of some and was bottled up tight in others, but none was immune. All were touched and most traumatised by what they had seen. The FSG had most of the more experienced riflemen and commanders. Even the most sanguine were struggling to reconcile what they had just been through. Just around midnight they carried Philip Allen's body to the waiting helicopter. Prayers. Last Post. And back to the FSG accommodation to talk into the small hours. On the same flight that Rifleman Allen went out, the Special Investigation Branch of the Royal Military Police came in.

Most of the information about the process of investigating the deaths of those killed came from Iain during the recce and the handover. The advice from Operational Training Advisory Group, those who facilitate and support operational training in the UK, and the chain of command, can be summarised in one line: 'You ought to think about what you are going to say and do in the aftermath of an incident'. Very helpful – durch. I had done plenty of thinking, but in hindsight the lack of technical training on post-incident reports and Special Investigation Branch procedures seems like a glaring error. I admit to being more than slightly nervous about the SIB appearing at this stage. The last thing I wanted was inept handling at a difficult time, but I should not have worried. The two coppers were as well trained and adept as I was inexperienced. Luckily we had seen the post-incident report being done at close hand as a result of the IED strike during our handover. Ben and I worked into the small hours. 1 Platoon had not done the final resupply of the 2 Platoon positions because they had helped escort the search team to the hill, and as a result Pat Hyde was going to take them first thing in the morning. We adjusted the plan. FSG would provide an extra patrol as a Quick Reaction Force if we needed to extract the observation posts. They would then provide a 'lurk' overnight in one of the areas that had now been cleared and observed, if we felt that the enemy was going to attack the posts. That would depend on what kind of reaction we got during the following day. I got to bed about four in the morning and Ben still had a few more hours to push.

I do not remember hearing or feeling the IED that struck the resupply patrol. All I did know was that by 8.30 that morning we had put Rifleman Sam Bassett on an MIRT. Alive, but very badly wounded. Corporal 'Fish' Fisher had gone with him, after getting shrapnel from the blast in his neck. Rifleman Ross Robinson, the other Vallon man, had been blasted into the air. But as Pat Hyde had got to them he had got up and started to clear the area so that the patrol could evacuate the two casualties. A few hours later, as the tingling in Robbo's legs got worse, the doc strapped him to a spinal board, diagnosing a serious back injury. He was flown out later that day. Sam Bassett died of his wounds in Camp Bastion; Ross Robinson was awarded a Queen's Gallantry Medal for his actions that day. He spent the rest of the tour in the UK recovering from his injuries, both physical and mental. Another Rifleman had to be evacuated later because the explosion had deafened him. After all my imploring to wear ear protection, by now most of the Company had ceased to wear it. They could not tell where the incoming bullets were coming from and shouted rather than radioed instructions became impossible to hear. Faced with what felt like the greater danger of a loss of situational awareness they stopped wearing them. Some persisted, but by the end only one of 140 had worn them all the way through, and it was not me.

I got the call telling me that Sam Bassett had died in the middle of the day. 1 Platoon was still out with the bomb disposal team clearing the routes around the observation posts. To tell or not to tell the troops on the ground, that was the question. I knew I was going to have to break the news at some point, but they needed their concentration on full beam while they were on the ground. As Mike came in through the gate at the end of the day I was there to meet him. 'Not good news, I'm afraid...' I let him have half an hour with the platoon before we did the after-action review. As soon as I had finished with Mike I went back to the operations room and informed the rest of the company who were in the base and told those in the OPs over the radio. In the aftermath of the news earlier in the afternoon I had been subjected to a long chat from the CO. He quite rightly wanted reassurance that we were going to continue with the mission we had set ourselves. I never for a moment doubted we would. But, and it was a big but, I wanted to make some adjustment to the clearance objectives in order to give the Vallon men a chance to learn from the Royal Engineer searchers in the bomb disposal teams. He was vehemently opposed to any adjustment. I was too tired for negotiations. I told him that we had got some very strong advice from the technical officer that given the threat that this would be time well spent. The posts would stay and the Vallon men would hopefully get a much-needed boost. Still he opposed any change. To make matters worse I got the strong feeling, never overtly articulated but clear as daylight in the body language and tone of most in Inkerman, that doubts about the merits of this operation were very close to the surface. What were they achieving? And whatever they were achieving couldn't be worth this price on the butcher's bill just twenty-four hours in.

\* \* \* \* \*

Three days later, at 0630 on Remembrance Day, I was woken by what became known as the 'Taliban alarm clock' – the noise of an IED somewhere in the vicinity being detonated by a bomb-layer, local, livestock or patrol. One sits up pretty quickly, throwing on the nearest clothing and scampering in a rather dishevelled heap into the operations room, only to find a completely relaxed serjeant leaning back safe in the knowledge that at least it wasn't one of us that got it. We always hoped it was an 'own goal' by the bomb-layer, but on this occasion it was impossible to tell.

I have had plenty of time since to reflect on the act of remembrance conducted that day. The preceding days had been bloody and the shock of grief and its subsequent suppression weighed on us all. My thoughts at the time did not do justice to the event. I had decided to bring in those manning the Observation Posts so they could make use of the Royal Engineer team and their training, against the wishes of the CO. By now the view had been expressed to me several times that sitting in observation posts was not proper soldiering. I was having to use a good deal of personal capital, especially with those not from the Company. The Fire Support Team and the Gunners required lengthy explanations of why this was a better way of doing counter-insurgency. When a soldier cannot understand why, some just need telling what to do. Just telling someone what they must do expends a commander's personal credibility at an alarming rate because soldiers will generally obey orders, but unwilling compliance is often worse than not doing something at all. For the Gunners and the Fire Support Team they could see there was no chance that they would be used while we were in these positions, at least not for anything other than sangar duty. That meant they were bored. They wanted us to be out in the green zone battling, so they could do their job. I had precious little sympathy. A feature of the conflict in Afghanistan is that soldiers of every type want to do their job 'for real'. If you are an expert in sniping, you want to snipe, the mortar section and the gun troop want to fire smoke and high explosive rounds to 'smash' the enemy, a natural if thoroughly counterproductive desire. It led to a certain amount of chat that I was happy to talk through. I spent a whole evening in the social area the FST had made for themselves going over and over different aspects of the argument. But however hard I tried they just found it difficult to accept that every shell we fired made it less likely that we would win the hearts and minds of the population. It seems an argument that has yet to be fully understood. The bulk of military training for Afghanistan still reflects technical competence rather than everyone's part in mission success.

So as the OPs were packing up we gathered around the memorial in the middle of the camp, with the names of the fallen in front of us on brass plaques under a cross. The memorial stands at the highest point in the camp. I had debated the risks of being gathered together in clear line of sight at such an obvious time and place – a lucky mortar or RPG might have some serious repercussions. I quickly decided that it was more important to do the service than reduce the unquantifiable risk. We gathered. The company Sergeant Major, Pat Hyde, brought them to attention, marched over to me and we exchanged salutes.

'Sir. A Company are present and ready for the Service of Remembrance. May I have your leave to stand the Company at ease?'

'Please do, Serjeant Major.'

Because the Rifles use 'light' drill and the bulk of the attachments to the Company use what we call 'heavy' drill, but is in fact the drill that is practised across most of the Army, the Battery Sergeant Major, Gordie Caufield of the Chestnut Troop 1st Regiment Royal Horse Artillery, called out the drill movements for the attached units. Light drill has two or three movements for every command given whereas in more normal drill every move has a command. It meant that every time we formed up in this way it was done with a curious syncopated echo.

All the usual parts of the service were there. The names from the roll of honour, prayers, eulogies, exhortation, Last Post, Reveille and a hymn. We were lucky to have with us one of the best buglers in the Battalion, Lance Corporal 'Chip' Newbury, or 'Noobs' as he was known to some. He had been called upon too many times in Iraq in 2007 and declared that he never wanted to play the Last Post again on arrival in Afghanistan. We had other buglers with us, but he played that day. The guys packing up the OPs stopped as they heard it. A pitch-perfect lament. My only contribution was a few words on why it was all so important. That day it was so self-evidently important that I could have said nothing at all.

As I say, my thoughts at the time did little justice to the way we felt. Those of us who are a little older have mostly been exposed to grief. We have lived through the death of grandparents or others close to us. But for the majority of the Company, who were mostly under twenty-one, this was their first such exposure. So the reassurance and guidance through the torrent of emotion that comes with sorrow and survival was a significant task for the leadership team in the Company. It just didn't feel as though there were enough words or the right words to capture it, to help them understand and explain. So my only real contribution was a near solo effort on 'Oh God our help in ages past'. I set off with enough gusto to keep me going to the end. After the end of the service, as the assembled company fell out, the doctor passed by muttering something about 'he must have been a wonderful choirboy at some point'. Such was my enthusiasm, I had not realised that the rest of the Company were listening rather than singing. Riflemen tend not to sing sober, unlike some other regiments that used to do their best impression of the Worzels at every conceivable opportunity. So I walked back to the ops room feeling slightly sheepish, but at least I had made them smile.

By early afternoon the last platoon was in and everybody was split up getting the extra training from the search teams and preparing for the following day's patrols. As they paid the money to those locals who had put up with us for five days the sections got radically different responses. One family took the money and we left on good terms. Another took the money and said that he never wanted to see us in his house again. And the owner of the last compound refused to take the money. He said that it was wonderful what we were trying to do. He said it was the first time that troops had tried to 'share his life'. I was unreasonably pleased that at least we had won over one member of the population. If he took that message to the mosque it would mean more than a hundred patrols.

Having done some work on marketing as part of a previous job in the Army I often used to talk about message – medium – audience. I felt that local support was vital in turning the awareness of what we were doing into advocacy of what we were trying to do, and then, the hardest leap of all, to actually support us. This was the first positive indicator from any local, other than the ephemeral gratitude of those we had given money to for consent-winning activities or development projects. Needless to say I made a lot of it in the briefing that night. There was a grudging acceptance. Pat Hyde wondered what he might have been hiding!

We took a hundred good lessons from the extra training done on the afternoon of 11 November and one bad one. The bad one was that we came to believe that the only way we could see the ground sign that might give us a better idea of the location of the IEDs was during the light of day. If we wanted to be out at night then it would have to be in an OP or in a position that had been cleared in daylight. It was very strong advice. Dave Markland had seen enough in the previous five days for it to be something I would have to accept until we were more experienced. It didn't bode well for 'owning the night' in the way that the Brigade Commander wanted us to. The CO too, was deeply sceptical. I was between a rock and a hard place. Two deaths in twenty-four hours certainly sharpens the focus, and for now force protection was a higher priority than night ownership. I took the view that everybody had heard the advice; going against it at this stage would have undermined credibility and confidence. We had built up a stock of goodwill about night activity. The OPs had increased our night patrol hours markedly, so we had some time before the analysts realised we were not patrolling at night. In short, consent and evade. 'Consent and evade' was one of the late Professor Richard Holmes' diseases of military leadership. For interest the others are: lack of moral courage; failure to realise opposition can be loyal; need to know and you don't need to know; don't bother me with the facts; quest for the 100 per cent solution; associate the quality of advice with status of advisor; I'm too busy to win; I can do your job too; big man, long shadow (no one is irreplaceable). Sixteen years of military service and I suggest that most of these weeds are still composted in the Army of today.

The next day it was to back to routine patrolling. 2 Platoon went off to see a mosque being built in Sadul Kariz, which meant a full day patrol to the village in the desert where the most well-off of our neighbours lived. Others were going to work the vehicle checkpoint with the Tiger Team. The Tiger Team were Afghan Army but recruited from Helmand. They had already proved themselves invaluable in dealing with locals. What was more, if the Ghurkhas were good at spotting something unusual on the ground, these boys were mustard. Iain, my predecessor, had worked very hard to get a regular Tiger Team into Inkerman and we were the happy recipients of his success. The regular Afghan Army Platoon had left Inkerman ten months before we arrived. There was an incident where the ANA commander allegedly stole money from a local compound. The allegation and subsequent search of his belongings was enough of an insult to see the ANA Platoon pack up and leave. It was a considerable boon to have Afghan military back on operations from Inkerman.

The day passed quietly until Lance Corporal 'Simo' Simpson trod on a pressure-pad IED on the way back with 2 Platoon. Simo was the seventh or eighth man in the patrol. He lost one leg at the knee. Corporal Ricky Furgusson gave the first aid. He had been early on the scene with Sam Bassett as well. It was beginning to become a habit. Furgie had walked over the device that Simo triggered. A Vallon man had been over it, and the route was marked with pegs. Another IED was found by Corporal 'Woodie' Haywood as they cleared the helicopter landing site (HLS). Luckily Simo lived to tell the tale and has made as good a recovery as it is possible to make. In the minds of those on the patrol there could only be one reason for missing the device – low metal content. Everyone was shocked that it struck so far back in the patrol. Luck. There was a definite sense that the luck that had seen us through the first couple of weeks was turning fast. More hurtful to most was that it seemed the enemy could do what they liked to us without getting anything back. The incident map was beginning to fill up around Inkerman. By now we knew we had IEDs all around Inkerman from 250 metres onwards. In what depth? Who knew? We had not found it, but we had to try to get past them.

My task that day was to plan the next company operation: it was time to go into the green zone. The harvest was almost complete and the green zone was now fast becoming a brown zone except for the banks of the irrigation ditches which formed the tree lines. Beyond the third tree line directly north of Inkerman lies the end of the village of Jusallay. We were going to attempt a bit of Human Terrain Mapping in Jusallay. I think my summary to the CO written on the night of 13 November captures the intent:

> While the week has seen our first casualties in quick succession the Company remains undaunted. Getting into the GZ will give us an opportunity to understand how things have progressed over the summer and to gauge the insurgent appetite for a direct confrontation.

\* \* \* \* \*

When I was training to be an infantry officer one of the directing staff on the platoon commanders' course talked about the section commanders being the 'Dogs of War'. These men, who have probably been in the Army for five or six years and often nearer ten, and hold the rank of corporal, are the guys that have to show the greatest physical and moral courage in conflict. They are right at the front, the point of the tip of the spear of the chain of command, leading their section of eight men, and in Afghanistan usually twelve or more, taking the instructions that are given to them and making sure that it actually happens. If they don't do it then it is unlikely anyone else will.

The Army works on a system of understanding what the commander two ranks above you actually wants to achieve. In my case it meant trying to understand the Commanding Officer's instructions in the context of the Brigade Commander's 'intent'. For the section commanders this meant that they had to understand and carry out the instructions of their respective platoon commanders in the context of my overall intent. In this way we try to ensure that we are all working towards the same end result. The intent on 14 November did not need much explaining. This was going out with everything we could muster. It may have had a counter-insurgency fig leaf in the form of human terrain mapping, but I certainly expected nothing less than an advance to contact. The formations, grouping, routes and tactics were all straight out of the war fighting tactical *aide memoire*. For a variety of reasons I had a group of fairly inexperienced but very talented section commanders. There were two who had been on previous operational tours as section commanders, but most were newly promoted. This was going to be their day.

Having become so ground sign aware I made one of the few decisions of the tour that I really regretted afterwards. We left at dawn. If you are leave from a single point with 140 men it takes time to get into the correct formation. Almost forty-five minutes in this case. And by the time the last man was out of the gate, the ICOM transmissions had begun.

ICOM is a collective noun for the insurgents' chatter on their radios. They use open frequency radios that anyone can listen to. Indeed the local population had them to find out what was happening: all the radios in the market in Sangin picked up ICOM frequencies. As a consequence it was a source of information, rumour, propaganda and disinformation. We had scanners that could only receive. Local insurgent commanders used local codes to hop around frequencies for more private conversations and instructions. Most of the informal chit-chat was on a rebroadcast frequency. We tried to do a study of this badinage, but in the end the translators got so fed up with detailing the daily round of greetings and enquiries of general health and well-being that we gave it up. At this point in the tour our most potent weapon was still away getting shrapnel removed from his back. Adam, one of the interpreters, had become so adept at tracking the various local commanders around the different frequencies that he could often get to the private conversations before they started. On the cool morning as the sun rose threatening thirty degrees of midday sun, the enemy scouts began to broadcast that we were coming.

The enemy had a pretty fixed routine. By the end of the tour we realised that it was pretty much immutably fixed. Get up before dawn, pray, send scouts out about forty minutes to an hour later. If we were out, they would get the fighters ready. This would take another hour or so. Their first attack would generally come between eight-thirty and nine o'clock. Same detail at the end of the day, and come last light they would disappear. Insurgency was, by and large, a nine-to-five job in the Upper Sangin Valley. Counter-insurgency is rather more time-consuming. As the last platoon left the Forward Operating Base we knew that we had been seen. We were not yet experienced enough to know that we had another hour before the fighters would be ready. The information was broadcast around the Company, and the pace slowed still further as the platoons tried to take sensible tactical precautions, using better cover on less exposed routes. We were still all moving simultaneously when the first attacks came. 3 Platoon on the north-east flank took some rather ineffective fire. 2 Platoon reached the third tree line with 1 Platoon. Company HQ was tucked in a tactical bound behind 2 Platoon. A tactical bound is very much ground dependent. It is close enough to be able to get up to the platoon without too much difficulty but far enough away not to be involved in the immediate fire-fight. The FSG were providing the rear guard. Given the limited number of routes back to the base I did not want IEDs laid for our return, so a cleared route was picketed by sections of the FSG.

There are a number of abandoned villages on military training areas around the UK; Imber on Salisbury plain, Tynham on Lulworth Ranges in Dorset, as well as a number of fabricated villages for training purposes; Cellini village in Brecon, Copehill Down in Wiltshire. To someone in the military they all have the same atmosphere. You walk in there on exercise and you know the enemy is there and it is all about to kick off. The absence of anyone else gives it the atmosphere of a gunslingers confrontation in an early western movie, all dust spirals and tumbleweed. As we moved through the first and second treelines north of Inkerman the tilled fields had been abandoned. The holed and derelict compounds gave the further impression of a no man's land. It was from one of these compounds that Company HQ was attacked. The first thing I knew about it was the close crack of gunfire. It was simultaneous with the ground around us throwing up puffs of dust like a puddle throws up splash from hailstones.

Martin Kinggett, our Vallon man, borrowed from 3 Platoon, was the first to react. He returned a heavy rate of fire. As I threw myself to the ground I fired my rifle for the first time in fourteen years in anger. Two shots. The HQ erupted around me. At this point I began to feel more in danger from them than I did from the insurgent. I bellowed at them to cease firing. 'Watch and shoot! Watch and shoot!'. In the most clichéd of ways the training had done exactly what it was supposed to and kicked in like a Red Bull on a long drive. The rule for Afghanistan is aimed shots only, but in my case the years of training for a conventional reaction to enemy fire took over. As it had done with everyone else. Get some fire down, get in cover and then get on with locating the enemy, winning the fire-fight, etc, etc. The gunman made his escape. I don't think anyone hit him. But I will be forever thankful that Martin Kinggett was as quick to react. A second burst from the insurgent would undoubtedly have been more accurate and could well have finished the operation for the day with half of the company tactical HQ injured or worse.

Elsewhere on the battlefield things were beginning to happen pretty thick and fast. 2 Platoon had got to the third treeline and begun to cross; Chico Bryant with Danny Pearson and a Vallon man, and Rifleman Ben Nash. Up until now we had just had harassing fire: this was the real deal. Two hundred metres or so ahead the lead poured in and the ricochet whistled around us. Rifleman Nash was shot through the thighs; Danny Pearson got a ricochet above the knee. What followed was one of the best five minutes of section commanding I have ever had the fortune to witness. With the bullets landing about him Corporal Chico Bryant treated Rifleman Nash. Ben Nash had a catastrophic bleed from his femoral artery. Unless that bleeding gets stopped and stopped very fast it's game over. It only gets stopped by the application of a tourniquet. We had all made ourselves as proficient as possible in their application. You can do it quite quickly in camp but the real tests are when there is the irritating but compelling distraction of lead coming in at high velocity or you have to do it with one hand. Furthermore, Chico's section was divided over a drainage ditch. He proceeded to treat and then evacuate the casualties under fire, over an obstacle, all the time controlling the covering fire thus imposing a semblance of control on a chaotic situation. Commanding and controlling a group of twelve in the most demanding situation requires a huge amount of self-control and clearheaded thinking. Below is part of a citation I wrote for Corporal Bryant after we got back.

> On 14th November A Company conducted a patrol to interdict enemy capability in an area 1km from Forward Operating Base INKERMAN. Bryant's section was the lead section. Crossing an irrigation ditch the section was subjected to withering small arms fire from multiple firing points. During the initial engagement Rifleman Nash was hit, smashing his femur and opening his femoral artery. With his section split across the ditch Bryant directed his other fire team to suppress the insurgent firing points. He moved with his VALLON man and one other to Nash. Under fire, in the open, he gave lifesaving first aid. The other man realised he too had been wounded by ricochet. Bryant then organised the evacuation of the casualty back across the irrigation ditch. Waist deep in water and still under sporadic fire his section moved Nash to the casualty exchange point. Bryant continued to organise his section to carry the casualties and suppress the enemy. In the opinion of the medical team in the Role 3 Hospital it was only the speed and quality of the immediate treatment that saved Nash's life. For a further four hours and through numerous other small arms engagements Bryant's section remained at the forefront of the Company patrol. For his actions under fire, leadership in the face of the enemy and the maintenance of the highest professional standards in the finest tradition of the service Bryant is especially deserving of official recognition.

Corporal Bryant received a mention in dispatches at the end of the tour for this and many other acts of absolute sang-froid. A later passage will deal with the iniquity of the military honours and awards system. Suffice to say for now that Chico Bryant will appear a few more times and a mention in dispatches does no justice, in my opinion, to his courage. And it would be quite remiss of me not to mention the RAF pilot who came into a white hot landing zone to pick up Ben Nash. Luckily it was the compound wall that took the RPG explosion, otherwise we might have had a real disaster on our hands.

We pressed on. I went up to the treeline to have a face-to-face with the platoon commanders. It was one of the few moments I went to 'look into the whites of their eyes'. With 3 Platoon under pretty much constant harassing fire, but doing a good job of protecting the flank, 2 Platoon had a ditch to move up and 1 Platoon would have to cross some open ground. 2 Platoon to move first! By this stage we had an Apache attack helicopter in support. Al, my FST commander, came up with a fire plan to support the move. Warning rounds with artillery into an open field and then smoke and high explosive from mortars on call. Dandy. Apache off to the other flank looking for enemy movement in depth. 2 Platoon moved carefully forward. Given the length of time we had been now been on the ground there was a reasonable likelihood of some kind of nasty surprise. It was now 1200. Not a soul in the fields: just us and the enemy. The Apache identified insurgents and asked for permission to engage with hellfire. Hell yes.

The insurgents had been identified in the line of compounds beyond where 1 and 2 Platoon had now taken up positions. The Apache reckoned he killed a number of insurgents in the strike. It was now in the heat of the day. We had been going since six and been up since four. Stick or twist. Stick. The choice: pull in 3 Platoon to protect a route back and press on to the next irrigation line, or bring up the FSG and progress in a bubble. The thing that decided it, as in most operations, is logistics. In this case that meant batteries for electronic counter-measures and radios. With one on and two off you have about twelve hours of operating time; we had been out for seven hours. Previously we had been able to extend this by being static and switching the sets off. You can't take that risk on the move.

As we began to withdraw through the 'open gate', held by the FSG who had had a very dull day, the ICOM sparked up again. One insurgent gave some of the game away. 'Thank God they are going; they almost got to the mosque.' As I looked at the map it appeared there were three possible mosques that could have been serving a nefarious purpose and a bit of me is sorry now that we did not carry on to find out. It was clear we had given them a shock. We had been lucky, but all save the FSG had been in the action enough of the day to know that whilst it made them feel like soldiers, it didn't get us very far with winning over the population. The farmers were coming back into the fields as we made our way back. It was amazing how quickly they knew it was starting and finishing. I am dismayed every time I see in media reports or documentaries that a local is identified as an enemy because they are carrying a walkie-talkie radio or scanner. You need a direction finder and a translator to achieve the positive identification required by law to kill him as an insurgent: anything else is tantamount to murder. The locals were nervous and industrious as we passed, trying to do a day's work in the few hours before they would be required at the mosque.

As we got back in it was clear that the mission had been accomplished, at least in terms of company morale. Every section chattered with the exploits of the day, the mortars, the artillery, the hellfire strike. As dusk fell we were treated to a Taliban riposte. An RPG exploded on the walls of Inkerman. Our locating equipment indicated that it had been fired at the very limit of range. Clearly someone felt they needed to do something to show both us and the locals that they were still out there. It was a contemptuously poor attempt in comparison to previous attacks on Inkerman and everyone knew it. Yet I was left with the impression we had been the bull charging at the matador's cape. We felt better for the charge, but the enemy held all the cards between nine and five. They had the light, knew the ground, and were indistinguishable from the local population within a second of discarding a firearm. All commanders are told to exploit weakness and neutralise strength; it is a *sine qua non* of military doctrine. The 14 November would be the last time we tried to take on the enemy strength in this way.

Rifleman Nash recovered from his wounds, reached full fitness and is still serving with 4 Rifles. Danny Pearson, who was wounded by the ricochet, returned to Inkerman three weeks later, after an ill-deserved break in Camp Bastion. It was also the last time the A Company Group would patrol at full strength. I had orders that a platoon would move in less than a week to partner an Afghan Army Platoon on the outskirts of Sangin. They would be located at Patrol Base Blenheim, four kilometres, or in other words a helicopter ride, from Inkerman. The question was, which platoon should go?

# Chapter 9

# Afghans

The elders of Mian Ruud, one village beyond where we had got to on 14 November, were not happy. By now they thought we were just tagging them along and they were fed up with coming across the green zone for no apparent end, but it did not stop the Taliban making one final play to get their man back. It had become clear since the operation at the end of October that we, or more properly our Special friends with our help, had captured Najibullah, the area commander of the Taliban. But we had also detained three sons who should have been involved in the harvest, who were still in custody. By the time we had our seventh meeting it was just a family group that came to plead the innocence of the captured men. What was most surprising to me was that they brought the men's mother with them.

It was the only time in six months that I spoke to an Afghan woman. Given the cultural sensitivities I found it astonishing that she should come to the camp in this way. She did not wear a burkha like the rest of the female population. She came with her head covered but no more. Trained as we are to look for the presence of the abnormal, or the absence of the normal, I had to be concerned when something like that happened.

As Afghan legend would have it, the battle of Maiwand created an unlikely hero in the shape of an Afghan woman called Malalai, who, on seeing the Afghan forces falter, used her veil as a standard and encouraged the men by shouting out: 'Young love, if you do not fall in the battle of Maiwand; by God someone is saving you as a token of shame'.

She also spoke the following landay (Pashto poetry):

With a drop of my sweetheart's blood,
Shed in defence of the Motherland,
Will I put a beauty spot on my forehead,
Such as would put to shame the rose in the garden

The Afghans were spurred on by the shame of letting the infidel see an Afghan woman unveiled and the rest is history.

So 129 years later, if this woman's presence was meant to inspire or shame local fighters it was a strange way of going about it. For unveiled as she was she certainly did not have Malalai's alleged beauty. She had, in the words of a droll Rifleman describing a Bosniac crone, 'Regimental teeth; one black, one green, one AWOL'. She brought her uncle, her husband (Old Man Rivers) and another man who claimed to be another son. The meeting was intense, more so than with the larger groups. She simply would not believe that we had taken her sons because they were involved in the insurgency and she certainly had no faith they would be given justice in the Afghan system. She had a strong point. There is much anecdotal evidence that it is the size of your wallet rather than the strength of the evidence that secures freedom or punishment in Afghanistan. This is of course true to some extent in all countries, including our own, although the Afghan system is rather more direct, cutting out 'm'well-remunerated learn'd friend'.

She blazed for about an hour. We took tea. She wept. She persuaded and cajoled; it was a very good performance from an experienced negotiator. It remains my only evidence of the fact that inside the home it is Afghan women who are all-powerful. Outside the compound they were quite literally faceless. I often bridled at the unbounded patriarchy. It was during this time that President Karzai's government passed a law that entitled Afghan husbands to conjugal rights. It was the only time during the six months on the ground when I really questioned what we were fighting for. Was the government of the Islamic Republic of Afghanistan really the lesser of two evils? The rest of the time it was very obvious. Innocent people were being subjected to a brutal form of coercion, and at least in our area I was going to have a good go at stopping it.

The arrival of the woman in our camp must, if I read the culture right, have brought some shame to her and her family. Would it inspire or appal the locals? It was not only us who were in danger of treading on cultural sensitivities. I hope that the gossip in the mosque extended to, 'You know they made the boys' mother go to the fort in shame', rather than 'she unveiled herself so her shame is our shame'. Or perhaps to prevent cooperation with the enemy was the threat of shame on their household. But it seemed a risky move, even for them. Still, in this instance it did not prevent some interesting information from coming out.

Adam the interpreter had just got back to Inkerman. Having had six long, fairly interesting but seemingly unproductive meetings exchanging views we had a bit of a breakthrough. One of the things we could offer that was not available in the villages was medical treatment. There had been an edict from a fool to the military doctors that they should not routinely treat locals. Something about making them reliant on us rather than local healthcare. There was no local healthcare; medical treatment was a sure way to induce a level of sympathy that was not possible when armed to the teeth on patrol. Anyway, after a few discussions on the ethics and tactics of all of this with Collette, she agreed that at the very least we would examine and potentially diagnose, but pills would not be handed out. The uncle had a bad back. Adam went with him while I sipped tea and chatted poppy farming with Mr, Mrs and Master Rivers.

It turned out that before the war (I don't know which one, there are too many to choose in Afghanistan's recent history), the old uncle had been in the NDS, the Afghan intelligence service, described to me as a cross between Special Branch and MI5. They seemed a bit more local than that, but nonetheless, during his treatment – and I hasten to add, given other events in the Army's recent past of which we can be truly ashamed, that is in no way a euphemism – Adam found out that we had our man, Najibullah. It was the first local confirmation. Not only that, but he described how the Taliban were forcing themselves on the local population. The three sons had fought for the Taliban but he made a good case for their innocence. He asked a telling question. 'Why do you stay here? We need a base in the village then the population would support you.'

Adam told me this on his return with the man. As the meeting broke up Adam went to each of the men who were there in turn, offering his best wishes. As they left I wondered how close the relationship was between interpreter and locals. Adam was clearly trusted by them as an honest broker. He was trusted by me; he had almost been killed enough times to be beyond reproach. Others were not so sure. I had a 'trust everyone – trust no one' philosophy. I set out with the attitude to try and trust people, especially locals, until they proved they could not be trusted. Behind closed doors and in the planning process I tried to ensure that at no point were we completely reliant on one piece of information before deciding a course of action. You might think that either too risky or too risk averse! But in November 2009, in what was an alarmingly effective tactic, five British soldiers had been shot by an Afghan policeman in central Helmand. You cannot help it, for a second you are grateful that there is not an armed Afghan in the camp. I say for a second, because whilst things seem to have gone from bad to worse in the type of incidents that have bred deeper mistrust between the local armed forces and NATO troops, I cannot reiterate too strongly that the key relationship in fighting an insurgency is with local security forces, both civil and military. We had worked hard to get the Tiger Team back and there just happened not to be one with us the day the news came through. But the requirement to appear to trust what might very well be extremely untrustworthy is a difficult trick to pull.

Several journalists have written about how distrust has grown, but that in their experience the Afghan is entirely trustworthy. But that is not in the rules of the Afghan game. 'If you want to understand the Afghan then look no further than Buzkashi'. Those are not my words; in fact they are the words of one Winston Churchill, but they are still relevant. The national Afghan game is called Buzkashi. The translation of the name is 'goat pulling'. It involves two teams of fifteen setting off from a single point on horseback. They race towards a dead goat placed in a circle. The goat is grabbed and they gallop towards a second marker. The teams must get the goat round the marker and back into the circle. The game is violent. The peculiarly Afghan element of this game is that once a team has the upper hand the goat will often be stolen by players within that team in order to get the final glory. The game is played in the barren desert with distances of over a mile between the markers and the circle.

I asked our interpreters whether Buzkashi was played in our area. The answer was yes, but that was before the fighting. The cultural point is, rather obviously, that faced with a common enemy the Afghans unite, but quickly argue amongst themselves when the external catalyst is gone. Perhaps our answer to this is cricket, where the game may be played over five days, a good tea is very important, and the most likely result is a draw, leaving aside the niceties of a winning draw or a losing draw. But cricket is also played in Afghanistan courtesy of our imperialist past. We had several six-a-side games in the base. Our interpreters, generally from Kabul, were archetypically good slow bowlers or wristy batsmen with a good eye. The playing surface definitely left a little to be desired, which made the occasional LBW hotly contested.

The common ground was found in football, for which we had enough room for a small five-a-side pitch. After work, if there was still enough light, I often found a group of Tiger Team Afghan troops mixed with Riflemen, interpreters, and our locally-employed civilians enjoying a kick-about that more often than not turned into an international friendly. Sport was doing its bit to turn colleagues into friends. Furthermore I was always invited to dine with the Tiger Team and the interpreters sometime during their weeks with us. I have no doubt I was invited out of respect and politeness, and Collette and Jodie out of respect, politeness and fascination. I ate with every team we had up to Inkerman and never once felt anything other than a soldierly comradeship. Given how dangerous they knew the area to be I was surprised when, having flown out after two weeks, half the same team flew back a day later with a new mentor. He said they wanted to come back, which I think said more about their desire for medical care than our patrols, but either way I took it as a strong vote of confidence.

Things were beginning to come into focus at the end of the first month. The Battlegroup had given its first set of orders setting out the direction of progress. Three of the five companies had suffered fatalities as well as a number of wounded. The IED threat, especially round Inkerman, was much higher than we had previously thought. Early success had given us momentum and we had been handed a golden opportunity to engage with a population that had been little understood. We had shown the enemy that we could stand toe-to-toe and slug it out if required. What concerned me most of all was our requirement to walk out of the base on every occasion. We now had a picture of an almost perfect circle of IED incidents around Inkerman. This matched identically the areas we could not see from our various observation posts inside the camp.

On taking over the base we had been shown where our predecessors had mounted the 'Revivor' camera. It was on top of one of the guard posts. It is more usually deployed under-slung on a helium balloon. There had been a number of teething problems. Once up it had become a target for every amateur marksman in the area; in other words the whole male population. The balloon can be easily patched, but the helium had to be brought in by helicopter. And the helicopters were bringing mortar and artillery ammunition so Iain had made the decision to place it on the highest point of the camp. Now that we were not firing as much ammo it was time to experiment with the balloon again.

It is a curious aspect of life in the infantry that we have a group of individuals trained in radio communications. The CIS Platoon, as they have become (Communications and Information Systems), are an idiosyncratic bunch. They attract some of the best and worst of all battalions and 4 Rifles was no different. In our case Corporal 'Archie' Archer was ably assisted by lance corporals 'Sonny' Patterson and 'Compass' Northeast, as well as a couple of Riflemen and Signallers from the Royal Signals. These guys started in Helmand on easy street doing eight hours of radio stag a day: earlies, lates or nights. By the end of the tour they were doing a lot more. They became the Company 'experts' in almost anything with a battery and a circuit board. Rifleman 'Dicky' Sheldon and Archie were our 'trained' Revivor operators. Trained in the loosest sense of the term.

Things with the balloon went like a mouse (sic) on fire. First it got shot at very regularly. But we got quite good at patching it up. Next we received a delegation from Sareagar concerned that we could see the women in the compounds. We argued strongly that we were not looking at the women in the compounds and that we were only interested in the IED layers in the alleyways. Whilst of course we could see the people in the compounds, I was prepared to ride this one out. The same rate of attrition as we had in the first month to IEDs would make life very difficult; we needed everything we could get in the fight. And then, a week or so after the Revivor went up, it showed its greatest failing. In a sudden strong wind pretty common in late autumn it snapped its tether and blew off towards the central highlands of Afghanistan.

There was much banter as a result. 'Spot the balloon' competitions appeared all over camp and Archie never really lived it down. Unfortunately we had missed a directive about a second tether due to the fact that our balloon was not flying, as a number had already failed across Helmand. I made it my highest priority to get another. In the fight against the IED persistent surveillance was going to be vital. Having got another one we then experimented with locations around camp, but the need to get it down quickly in freak winds to prevent another loss meant that it stayed beside the ops room.

I was also desperate at this point for more radios and the use of more helicopters. An OC doesn't make many requests direct to his CO to get involved in the administrative side of operations. It is by and large handled by the CQMS or the 2IC. If you need to escalate it still further to add the weight of the chain of command it is a sign of desperation, however gentlemanly the language. I know that our desperate need for more of these items extended all the way to the top of the Battlegroup. But at least we had a balloon; others did not.

The ability to see further and to focus into the alleyways had an instantaneous effect on command and control of the Company. All of a sudden from the ops room I was able to see exactly where all the patrols were. I could see the quality or otherwise of patrol spacing, of whether a Rifleman had adopted a fire position or was turtled on his back. Platoon commanders came in and planned patrol routes taking their sections over the ground. For the purpose of command and control this was an amazing tool. I could feel the Tolkien-like pull of the zoom lens. Every workplace has a boss who wants to control minute detail, the leadership disease: 'I can do your job too', but if you are doing someone else's job, who is doing yours? I have often noted that being a details man, which I am certainly not, is a great strength but a greater weakness. After many years of wondering who first came up with this idea I recently discovered, quite by chance, that this is a Rochefoucauld maxim. That one's greatest strength is also one's greatest weakness. It remains true that getting the right balance between knowing enough detail while having a sense of the entire scope of the operation was a constant battle, just as making time for an individual issue in detail can be an equally important part of getting the whole dynamic right. The equilibrium between distance and intimacy needs to be found. Whatever the temptation to identify the minor imperfection, a great benefit of such equipment is the same feeling of security that one gets from having the Apache, a drone or jet in the sky above, the sense that someone has your back.

The balloon a hundred feet up also allowed us to study and understand the pattern of life. Focusing on what the population are doing gives you a chance to do something about it. We got very excited one evening when we thought we saw an IED being emplaced. Luckily Adam was on hand to say that the hotspot was in fact the generator for a well that had been turned on to get water for washing before evening prayers. Until that point at least half of the ops room had convinced themselves this was an insurgent bomb-layer in the act. With Adam back we suddenly had an great increase in understanding and an ability to turn information into intelligence, not only because he had patrolled the ground with countless units, but also because he knew each of the local Taliban commanders by voice on their radios. The 'eye in the sky' was doing its stuff and the platoons knew the ground. My report at the end of that week summarised it thus;

> The Coy continues to make progress in the AO. Our understanding has increased ten-fold from handover. We have been less kinetic than our predecessors. We will try to be more proactive with the application of

firepower. I would imagine that this approach will take some time to come to fruition but there are early signs that the battle for the consent of the local population is eminently winnable.

So who should go to Blenheim? Sounds like a nice day out in the English countryside, but the reality was that Patrol Base Blenheim was 'hard pressed'. 'Hard pressed' is a military euphemism for 'pretty much constantly under attack'. Even from four clicks away we could feel the intensity of the daily fire-fights as the insurgents tried to neutralise the effect of this relatively small outpost in the most northern built-up area of Sangin.

I sat down first with Pat Hyde and then with Ben to talk about who should go. The FSG was quickly discounted as they were already weakened by having to provide short-term replacements for 1 Platoon. 1 Platoon had trained for the patrol base scenario, but I felt they were still recovering their mojo from what had been a tough period. That left 2 and 3. It was a close call. In the end I opted for 2 Platoon, seniority and experience being the decisive factor. I am certain that either of the other platoons would have done the job, but circumstance had mitigated against two of them and of the other two 2 Platoon nudged it.

So in the middle of November 2 Platoon packed up and went to Blenheim. The first month for them was little short of epic. If the first month of the tour was a series of highs and lows it was at least punctuated by 'equipment care days' and 'battle prep days', with which I could regulate the energy expended. However, 20 November represented the start of the time when the activity was almost constant. There became no such thing as a 'normal' day in the newly-expanded Inkerman area of operations. The Afghans in Blenheim had already got a small team of UK mentors from the Yorkshire Regiment in their camp. The 2 Platoon move was part of a renewed effort to help the Afghan National Army take on the insurgency with more vigour. 2 Platoon had one central task, to build up the capability of the Afghan National Army, the ANA. Charlie and I talked about it before he left. The first part of the mission was to demonstrate that one could patrol from Blenheim. The activity from the base had been limited to manning a vehicle checkpoint on the road and daily trips into town to pick up food supplies. 2 Platoon mounted three or four patrols a day in their first week. Nearly every one was attacked. It was a transformative experience for them all. You can really tell the quality of a unit simply by listening to them on the radio. Sloppy, elongated speech turns into sharp concise messages delivered with urgency, never panic, and most of all, people are concentrating enough on the radio as well as their horizon not to have to repeat messages. I have heard it said that a good net is one that is mainly silent. I absolutely agree. The temptation for commanders to fill the air with overly-detailed messages that need to be checked and checked again is damaging. 2 Platoon were beginning to get it.

All the planning and conduct of patrols was done jointly. The Platoon worked extremely hard in the first forty-eight hours to give their new home enough protection – they were all up for the whole period. On the third day they were there the insurgents outdid themselves. The Afghan Army Platoon had received some information in the vehicle checkpoint on the road that the insurgents were going to try to strap an IED to a donkey and send it towards the camp. Donkeys do not have the reputation of being the most compliant animal, so Charlie and Neil, the Yorks mentor, treated it all with some scepticism.

Then, in the afternoon, the gate guard realised there was something suspicious going on. A group had just let go of a donkey a short way from camp and hurried off. He tried to divert the animal with flares and other warnings. Obstinacy not being the best quality in that situation, the beast of burden eventually had to be stopped by a rifle shot. It was immediately taken away by locals. We had just had a new satellite telephone system put in to Inkerman so I was able to speak privately to the Battlegroup Headquarters for the first time on the tour. As this situation developed their attitude was something along the lines of 'What the hell are you doing shooting donkeys?' Their all-too-obvious message was that the donkey was someone's livelihood and shooting it was going to do nothing for winning the hearts and minds of the local population.

So when a second donkey carrying a huge bundle of hay was slapped on the arse and sent up the hill towards the gate, it was with some dismay that I heard on the radio that it too had been shot. This time it was closer to the gate and 2 Platoon had got into a cordon around the dead donkey. Down in Blenheim Charlie and Neil managed to persuade the ANA that this was something they could do, the dead donkey being so close to the camp. The team went out and established there was something very suspicious under the bundle of hay carried by the donkey. We called for the bomb disposal team, whom we discovered could not be with us until the following morning. The ANA were staring down the barrel of a night on guard of a dead donkey. It was too much for one enterprising ANA warrior, who set fire to the hay with a flare. A minute or so later, in the middle of the 'What the hell are you doing?' conversation, the explosion was audible in Inkerman.

By the time we had shot the second donkey there was an even greater sense from HQ that the Platoon had gone rogue and was behaving like the ANA, firing at the first sign of danger. Neil was livid with the ANA but I was more sanguine, knowing that the Rifleman on the gate had in fact taken swift appropriate action that had saved them from an unusual attack. Luckily no one was hurt and that, I reasoned, was the best outcome. But it is impossible to report a donkey IED up the chain of command without either a wry smile at the ridiculousness of it or a feeling that the world is slightly off its axis.

The donkey IED further exposed the fact that there was always a little frisson between 3 Rifles and A Company 4 Rifles. Despite a successful amalgamation of four regiments, 3 Rifles was heavily laden with those who had been in the Light Infantry. 4 Rifles had been a Green Jacket Battalion. To the untrained eye you might think that we had quite a lot in common. And indeed we did, like siblings in the same family: from the outside you look the same, but on the inside there is a fierce struggle for identity and attention. The Green Jacket to the Light Infantryman is a scruffy arrogant individual who is as likely to stab you as pat your back. There were quite a lot of equally harsh views in the other direction. They were generally shared in good nature but occasionally taken too far. In an effort to dilute some of this auld rivalry the Commanding Officers of all the Rifles Battalions had been jumbled up, not taking account of their previous cap badges, with some very mixed results. In the case of CO 3 Rifles he had been a Green Jacket, so quite liked the kind of banter he got whenever he managed to make the journey up route 611. In this case they only calmed down after the second donkey exploded and we started to get credit rather than criticism.

Still. Given that I had to get a helicopter to the base in central Sangin and then a lift to Blenheim it was a week or so before Pat Hyde and I paid our first visit. I had a lunch date with the ANA commander, but prior to that went on patrol with 2 Platoon and a group of the ANA. We supported an operation conducted by B Company 3 Rifles, who had responsibility for central Sangin, acting as flank protection. We went at dawn. The calls to prayer echoed across the town. It still sends shivers up my spine, too closely associated with the proximity of the fight as supposed to religious observance. The mosques in urban Sangin were more tightly grouped and with better sound systems, each Mullah doing his best to out-call his neighbour. What was incredible to me was how different the human and physical geography was between Blenheim and Inkerman. Around Blenheim hardly a compound was destroyed. There were large numbers of farmers in the fields. The whole place had a more normal feel. That said, B Company were attacked on the patrol, but 2 Platoon were never under fire. It was the first patrol that 2 Platoon had conducted without being attacked. As Pat Hyde remarked when we got back in late morning, 'Don't know what all the fuss is about myself'. Corporals Bryant, Haywood and Furgusson grinned rueful smiles. They knew exactly what the fuss was about and two of them would be evacuated in a MIRT helicopter at different times later in the tour as a result.

The ANA commander had not come with us on patrol. He often went into Sangin, but rarely on patrol with his men. The British mentoring team were beginning to get quite frustrated by his inactivity. The small group from the Yorkshire Regiment headed up by Neil had been with this group of the ANA for a couple of months. The previous ANA Company Commander had left early in their tour and with him any sense of purpose had disappeared. He was due to return in the last month of our tour after being trained in the UK. It gave hope for the future, but meant that progress was hard.

The good news was that we had just completed our first proper patrol together, and it was further than the Afghans had been for some time. So there was plenty to be positive about. I was presented a delicious combination of meat, rice, cucumber and tomato, with fruit and nuts and a cup of 'chai'. We were provided spoons, but the Afghan way is to take the rice and meat in a pinch of flat bread. It was very well cooked and a welcome change from rations. Our conversation ranged widely. Mohammed had been based in Sangin for three years. He had worked with a number of British units and his current mentor was his sixth. The Afghan Army at that point was probably the most trusted Afghan institution; the least corrupt. The soldiers in the patrol base came from all over Afghanistan, making them less subject to local cultural pressures. They are well paid but they are still subject to the usual pressures of soldiering. As time went on getting new recruits to go to Sangin became impossible. Rumour spread fast that as soon as they knew where they were going they went AWOL. This was a man who had not seen his family in a year although he was shortly to go on leave. It became apparent during our conversation that he had lost many friends in the fighting. He and his men had occupied the hinterland between insurgent and the government, but were unenthused and demoralised.

To get to and from the base we travelled from the centre of Sangin by road. From my perspective Sangin District Centre (SDC) was a revelation; a bustling bazaar, coffee shops, bread stalls, a shop full of bird cages. We occupied a Forward Operating Base away from the areas of burgeoning development. This was the appearance of normal life, lived in relative freedom. It gave me a renewed sense of our collective purpose in Afghanistan. Over chai the commander offered a very Afghan solution to the problem of insurgents. The tribal and ethnic divisions in Afghanistan, and three years in Sangin, certainly hadn't promoted a culture of tolerance, rather the reverse. And despite a common religion the ethnic gene seemed dominant. He would have taken a far more robust approach given the chance; he seemed genuinely confused as to why we did not use our technology to obliterate them all, locals and insurgents alike. The meal ended with an agreement that we had a lot to learn from each other in the coming weeks and months but that we were both sure our partnership would be successful.

After a couple of months I got Charlie to write a short piece covering his experience of the ANA to send back to the UK. It has been reproduced several times in various military journals and gives his perspective as the man very much on the front line. It can be read in full at Appendix 2.

\* \* \* \* \*

At the other end of our part of route 611, 1 and 3 Platoons, with help of the Fire Support Group, were making the best of being stuck with HQ. I found myself being overtaken by Mike, Tom, Jessie and Ed in understanding the ground and especially understanding the locals. They were beginning to meet people for the fourth, fifth and sixth times – beginning to gain familiarity, if not respect. We were due to bring another resupply through the desert during the time that 2 Platoon were occupying Blenheim. We had to secure the resupply route through the desert for a couple of days, which precluded Company patrols and generally slowed the tempo of activity. In some respects this was a good thing, giving me time to pause for thought. But Mike, in command of 1 Platoon, was straining at the leash.

He had really begun to understand some of the dynamics in Sareagar and had some credible theories that would need to be tested. So we did three operations into Sareagar and the resupply. The first of these was a recce to possible new patrol base sites. These operations were all largely conceived by Mike, who had the best knowledge, but supported by the Company with company resources. By company resources I mean that the platoons were inflated in size with various assets attached; search dogs, sappers from the Royal Engineers, Royal Military Police men and women, all designed to help the situation on the ground but not integral to a Platoon. The other critical way in which the Company HQ could help was with the control of helicopters, jet aircraft and drones, both armed and unarmed. These last three were controlled and allocated by the Brigade HQ and some by the Divisional and Theatre HQs.

The thing I remember being most troubled by, forty-eight hours before we commenced these operations, was where I should put myself. Going into Sareagar with my tactical HQ was one option; staying in Inkerman in the Ops room was the other. There is a strong sense in the current British army that if you aren't at the front, then you aren't in command, which is backed up with a desire to get commanders to 'smell' the battle. Like most fairly sensible edicts from above, it had been taken to extreme by commanders lower down who wished to prove beyond doubt that they had 'got it'. The logical end to it was that commanders found themselves actually at the very front of patrols doing someone else's job, reaching the ultimate paradox of not being in command by proving that they were in command. I am not advocating armchair command: you do need to be in the right place to have the most influence on the battle. But from Company Commander up that is rarely going toe-to-toe with the enemy. And by going toe-to-toe I mean putting yourself deliberately in the way of his most deadly threat. If you're doing your job, you'll be close enough as it is. There seems to me a subtle but very important difference between not ordering a task done that you would not be prepared to do yourself, and not ordering someone to do it because you *haven't* done it yourself.

In Afghanistan, 'going on the Vallon' seemed to have become a rite of passage. I was always uncomfortable with this. Commanders are high-value targets for the enemy because they are the brains of the operation. Take them out and however good the recovery, 2 Para at Goose Green, the Welsh Guards in Helmand and the Battlegroup would always have been better off with its original commander than without him. They have become heroes and I would not dispute that in some way they are; that posthumous silver lining is rather less significant than the inclemency the cloud brings. So the only time I went on a Vallon was in training. I knew how to do it if I had to, but I also knew that if I was the one on the Vallon we were in real trouble and that it would have to be the crucial intervention in the battle.

Leadership is an extension of personality and I have a half-baked theory that there are two types of officer. There are of course many more, but in military leadership there is an interesting fault line between those who really want to be leaders and those who really want to be soldiers who through happenstance are in a leadership role. I think of myself as the former rather than the latter. My professionalism as a soldier was to a standard. I don't pretend I had the smartest uniform or the most organised kit; I was not the fittest, the bravest or the best shot. I could do all of that to a very professional standard, but it is not what motivated me to want to be in the army. I wanted to be in the army to command.

'It's a question of leadership' is a phrase often trotted out when things haven't gone the way a senior commander would wish them; a euphemism for 'You need to put more effort in here'. It induced an internal eyeball-rolling every time I heard it during sixteen years in the army. The true leadership moment is when you have to persuade people to do things that they would not otherwise do. I enjoy the task of persuading people to do things they would not undertake in normal circumstances. There is, in that persuasion, a requirement for a certain amount of personal example, but it only goes so far. It doesn't help if the example is a bad one! It is certainly not only about personal example; rank, experience, and character all play their part in leadership. I would put special emphasis on knowing what motivates your people. And this is astonishingly easy to say but devilishly difficult to achieve. No subordinate wants to expose a weakness to a superior, but it is precisely by having the intimate knowledge of those strengths and weaknesses in character and skills that one can exercise the best leadership. Get the right man or group of men for the job and then know when they might just need extra support or when one can concentrate on something else; that is a balance that needs constant adjustment. My personal leadership maxim is a misquote from Karl Marx: 'From each according to his ability; to each according to his need'. I try to treat everyone equally by treating them all differently. To stick to one method of operating just because that is how one has trained leaves no place for experience and evolution.

At the Company level and below team spirit, respect, collective ownership and personal accountability are powerful catalysts to persuasion. This is achieved in a structural way through training and living together in garrisons and messes. And then, and far more importantly, by shared experience on the ground. A lot had already happened in a few short weeks and for the most part it had cemented our mutual trust rather than undermined it.

Undoubtedly there are times, especially when things go wrong, that one feels lonely in command, or sometimes quite the reverse when trusted subordinates take opposing views. My personal cure for those times when the question of leadership was posed, if ever things got more than a little difficult, and there had been a few of those days, was to look no further than the Riflemen. Common sense, a bit of humour and to be trusted by them to make the right decision despite the associated risks always inspired me to do my best, to do better and get the best out of them. If one is going to exercise 'leadership' it has to be coupled with *mutual* trust and a common understanding of approach. It would be an interesting qualitative assessment to ask how mutual the trust is between commanders and commanded in the Army before and after a tour. Likewise, on the common understanding of the approach, hindsight suggests that this is one area where the Army has come unstuck in Afghanistan, as there has been no consistent agreement on the goal, the approach or the resources needed to undertake those tasks. And that was as true at Battlegroup level as further up. Two months previously my predecessor had exactly the same task to undertake with a third of the manpower; same goal, different approach, different resources. But I digress.

So, for these patrols into Sareagar, were the platoons ready to enact what I said without me being right there? Having done things a certain way up to that point the situation had now changed and we had to change with it. At this stage in proceedings the question of leadership was more practical than philosophical. These operations extended out 500 metres from the Forward Operating Base. Going with a section from one of the platoons would be an option, but in the compounds I might easily find myself unable to see or speak to platoon commanders due to high compound walls and the vagaries of VHF radio waves. In the end I opted for Inkerman, to my discomfort more than Mike's.

The first operation went well. In fact it was the first of this size where we were not attacked. I had decided the risk of IED under the view of the Sangers meant the troops on the ground could do the first 400 metres in the dark along the 611. Getting the appropriate tactics to balance between the threat of IEDs and small arms fire was a delicate one. Dave Markland's sound advice to only move in daylight had opened a weak flank that had been exposed on all of our subsequent patrols; we could not move fast enough under fire to find the enemy, fix him in place, and strike to defeat him. On the hoof in daylight he was nearly always one step ahead. We went early, very early, and were able to get all the information we wanted on the potential sites for a new patrol base on the other side of Sareagar and get back before the enemy were formed up. The platoons came back through the village using the protection of the compounds to make it as difficult as possible for him to attack us. We were all done by 10am and it all felt very strange. No shots fired. It had been close, but by the time they were ready they were too close to the heavy machine-guns in Inkerman.

The resupply operation brought good news and bad news. In clearing the route we uncovered a large mortar shell filled with home-made explosive. It was a bit obvious. What was not so obvious, but was uncovered by some excellent work by the 3 Platoon Vallon men, were the three low-metal IEDs placed in close proximity to the more obvious device. The game of cat and mouse between the IED layer and the Vallon men was really underway.

The resupply brought fresh food for us, fresh helium and a new balloon. The fresh rations from the last resupply had run out after two weeks, so we had been on ten-man ration packs for the previous fortnight. It was nothing like as long as was to be the case in the second half of the tour, but the arrival of the 'fresh' was welcome. For all soldiers in Afghanistan, the basics of living assume much greater importance. Food, drink, sleep, cigarettes for some, press-ups for others, or a visit to the deep trench latrine, are all important rituals in the day.

Food is by far the most important element of this. There is an army joke that the chef's course is the hardest in the Services because no chef seems to have passed it. Whilst variety and taste have improved immeasurably in recent years the staples are still there: bacon grill, sausages, tinned tomatoes, powdered egg and beans for breakfast, generally after porridge. Noodles and soup for lunch with a couple of rice or pasta choices for supper. Military efficiency being what it is, the food is chosen for its nutritional value and ease of preparation. In Inkerman we were particularly lucky that the chefs did an outstanding job; given the limited ingredients of the ration pack the four chefs from the Royal Logistic Corps let their imaginations run wild. Processed cheese cheesecake, tinned fruit crumble, pizza, spam balls in sweet and sour sauce, chicken jerky and fresh bread were all added to the daily fare. We all ate together on bench tables in the cook house. Cardboard plates and plastic cutlery prevent the spread of illness but give a feeling that you might be as disposable as they are. Whilst there is much that is functional about the food, the best days were certainly reserved for when fresh rations come in. Steaks to order were a particular highlight, as well as fresh fruit in place of the processed fruit bar. Being well fed is probably the single most important aspect of a soldier's morale. We definitely marched on our stomachs.

The recce and resupply operations were quickly followed up by two more, Bultair 1 and 2. We started to name the operations in Pashtun after animals; *Bultair* means bulldog, a masterstroke of originality – durch. Mike had identified locations in Sareagar that were suspicious for the kind of activity we had glimpsed around them from the ground and the air. He had a list of compounds he wanted to search, but of course we were not in the business of forced entry.

At least *we* weren't, but the Tiger team were not covered by the Karzai edict. They always went in having been 'invited', but I don't think the local population were under any illusions as to their purpose. The operations had some success in turning up items that could be used for IED-making, including a 105mm shell, but nothing conclusive enough to detain on. It was all very suspicious to us at the time, but a later operation stopped a vehicle with over fifty shells that were being taken to Sangin market to be sold as scrap. Given the number that had been fired over the summer it should not have been a surprise. The Royal Artillery were doing their bit for the local economy!

I only regretted the decision to command from Inkerman once during these operations, when I found myself having a public conversation with one of the platoon commanders that might have been done better face-to-face. They probably do not even remember it, because by the time we had finished the tour there was no way I could be in nine places at once, so all of those kind of conversations were conducted over the radio. In between these company operations we launched the Fire Support Group into the desert overnight. They had a very good patrol getting totally different feedback from locals away from the principal area of fighting. Unfortunately we tried it for a second time and trying to get through the IED belt took so long confirming potential devices that I made the decision to bring them back in. This was not good news. Getting vehicles into the desert to interdict the back routes into Sangin by setting up vehicle checkpoints was what I had sold to the FSG, who were of limited use in the villages and the green zone. Their ability to manoeuvre in vehicles and the range of their weapon systems were almost utterly negated in such close country. But if they couldn't get beyond 500 metres it was going to be a long tour. Freddie was not a happy man. He made a reasonable point that he was negotiating a minefield in unprotected vehicles with four men out front waving metal detectors at explosives that did not have a great deal of metal in and in some cases none at all. 'F'ckin' fucked-up – kna wot I mean?' I did and it was.

\* \* \* \* \*

We had gathered some useful titbits of information from platoon patrols so I put together a Company operation to go to Jokhoran, the village we had intended to visit a month earlier but never got to as a result of being held up in PB Emerald. Using the same tactics as the success in Sareagar, we would release the FSG early on day one, giving them all day this time to get to the open desert. Then the following morning we would try to get to the mosque in Jokhoran at first light to see whether the information we had gleaned from locals that it housed a group of insurgents was true.

The Fire Support Group set off into the desert to the south-east of Inkerman on 7 December. Watching Freddie and his men make scrupulous snail-paced progress was a nervous time. We had opted for using a route up the 611 to the north-east before breaking right into the desert in the hope than we would avoid the most obvious unobserved ground around Inkerman. Every hour or so we would get an update. It was five or six hours before they had broken into what we considered 'safe' territory.

The idea was to get them into the desert and make a night move so they would lose the insurgent scouts. They could then appear as flank protection and diversion if we were held up in Jokhoran, able to escape back into the desert if required without having to conduct a fighting withdrawal to Inkerman.

1 and 3 Platoons, this time with the company tactical headquarters attached to 3 Platoon, used the 611 the following morning. The road had been carefully watched the previous day after the FSG had passed along and as far as we could tell traffic had been normal. I was confident that even in the dark we would be able to get a kilometre up the road almost to PB Emerald before breaking left into the green zone. Using the cover of darkness speed would be our deception, so no fancy tactical formations just one long 'Afghan Snake'. Snake is about right. Momentum is all important for moves at night. As soon as the human traffic halts the concertina effect of a bad day on the M25 is created. Not only that, but the physical effort of multiple lunges onto one knee with six stone of weight on your back is exertion one would rather not expend.

Before we set out to Jokhoran I was witness to a small, but in my own mind very significant, act of courage. There was a Rifleman who, in early November, had been shot on a patrol. 3 Platoon had finished their task and were just coming home when Rifleman Armstrong Pollock took a bullet through his leg. He was casevac'd in the usual way, but such is the quality of care that the hospital in Bastion gave he was able not only to have the wound cleaned, but also to make a recovery in Bastion. Remarkably the bullet had not damaged, to any significant degree, the muscles, nerves or tendons in his leg and so he stayed in Bastion. A little over three weeks later he was just about to do his first patrol since being shot. I was astounded. He had been required to do the usual physical tests before returning to front line duty. There is of course a difference between the usual physical tests and patrolling into enemy territory at four o'clock in the morning, but here he was. I watched him in the briefing area raise and lower himself from one knee to the other.

'Alright Rifleman Pollock?'

'Yes Sir…just testing.'

If ever I need an example of physical courage or mental strength I often think of that 'just testing' moment.

So into the early hours we set off, trying to find the best way round the IEDs and the eyes that would wake up to find us unusually close. We got to the outskirts of Jokhoran at first light. I had selected a building 100 metres to the west of the main village as the location for my Company HQ. From there the

A Company 4 Rifles in FOB Inkerman.

Me and Emily on the
promenade in Southwold.

Ed Dutton on the
range. Influence this.

Hardest job in the Army: one pip wonder.

Jodie instructs Rfn Davies treating Corporal Furgusson, a scene played out for real nine months later.

Charlie and Furgie at Lydd Ranges.

Spacious accommodation on the Brigade Exercise, July 2009.

Chinook on the HLS outside
Inkerman protected by the
Fire Support Group.

Taking over from Iain
on 19 October in front
of the briefing board.

The officers' mess. Mike, Tom, Charlie, me, Ben, Ed and Jessie.

Jona, Jimmy, H, Pat Hyde,
Dave Rider and Freddie
Fryer.

Tim Lush.

Freddie Fryer and a
new friend.

Corporal Hayley
Wright on the front
line.

Coming back in to
Inkerman from patrol,
November 2009.

High walls and heavy loads = slow going.

Showers in PB Blenheim.

In the desert.

Hearts and minds.

Over-watch outside Jokhoran.

Adam and me having a little chat with a farmer on the way back from Jokhoran.

Shura time.

The Chestnut Troop
waiting and hoping.

The Tiger Team
question a local.

The Revivor balloon.

Corporal Galespie,
chef extraodinaire.

The washing machines.

Over-watch waiting to get into PB Bariolai.

The makeshift defence on day one in PB Bariolai.

Find.

Mastiff passing a picnic.

Pat Hyde.

Mastiff strike.

Mohammed Sharif, Governor of Sangin District, March 2010.

Chico Bryant with the ANA patrol commander.

Corporal Fox getting to know people around Ezeray.

Rob Fellows in a shura after prayers.

ANA in the lead from PB Blenheim.

The medics.

LCpl Michael Pritchard.

'Pritchard's post' below the Russian trenches.

Mark Charlton, Reece Terry, Pete Aldridge and two others, 25 October 2009.

Sam Bassett.

Martin Kinggett.

Tom Keogh.

Carlo.

Ross Robinson.

Afghan sunset.

two platoons would push into the village, with the Tiger Team being the ones who would make entry to the mosque and deal with any locals. All had gone to plan thus far. It was about six am when dawn broke and we paused to change night sights for day sights. I had given the platoons ninety minutes to find out what we could and then we were going to head for home. I had no desire to spend all day in a fire-fight.

I have described previously the ravages that the campaign had left on areas of the green zone. Compounds destroyed, a village full of refugees, and a minefield with a small ISAF enclave in the middle of it… but nothing prepared me for Jokhoran. Having seen it from 500 metres away during our first company patrol to Emerald I had assumed that all was quiet because of the activity around the search. The compounds had looked intact from the south. As we approached from the east it became apparent that Jokhoran was a ghost village. The compounds had high walls but each roof had a hole bored into the top of it. After thirty minutes of looking into compounds the platoons were reporting that no one was there. It was 3 Platoon and specifically Corporal 'Cat' Felix who poked his head over the compound next to the mosque and identified the first signs of human habitation. Like all the A Company section commanders he was to have one or two exceptionally close calls, but not today. The Tiger Team moved in.

The Afghans spoke for about thirty minutes before I began to think about the withdrawal. It was seven am and all was still quiet on the insurgent radio, ICOM. Someone suggested we stay until eight just to see what happened. It didn't take me long to decide against it. Adam pointed half a kilometre to our north. 'That's where the marines were down to their last magazine each.' he remarked.

'Fine. Let's go.'

As the platoons came back I did a hot debrief with the platoon commanders. It was all very strange. The mosque had a load of blankets in but the Mullah had not aroused any suspicion in the Tiger Team during their conversation. The Mullah said he was trying to start up the village again. There was one other family living next door; he hoped there would be more soon. He expected that the reduced fighting would allow things to get back to normal. 'Normal' – now there is a thought.

The platoons reported the extent of the devastation in Jokhoran. Whatever had happened there was little short of appalling. I was appalled. We, and by we I mean it in the broadest possible sense as ISAF, had destroyed that village. To what military purpose I know not. Perhaps there were positively identified insurgents in every property? Perhaps we didn't feel the need to compensate the families who lived there so that they could continue living there. These were large compounds of relative prosperity, now deserted. We had moved from roof to roof in our quest to find people, and the thought of the potential IED threat lurking in the alleys was unsettling. To me, whenever I wanted to give an example as to why we were not trusted in this area, 200 years of history is one thing, and Jokhoran represented a large part of its latest manifestation.

It was seven-thirty when we left. Right on time at eight the ICOM sparked up. I only ever witnessed one escalation in threat worse than that morning on the way back from Jokhoran. All the local Taliban commanders came on to the airwaves, vying to be the first to attack us, inadvertently telling us exactly who was operating in that area, but that really wasn't the most pressing concern. The compounds on the south side of the 611 and the few that were occupied on the north side spewed out livestock, women and children.

Adam, just ahead of me, was like a cat on hot tin roof.

'Over there in the trees and over there in the compounds', he said, pointing out individuals moving counter to the torrent of humanity and animals. Time for the FSG. The FSG had begun to approach an area known as the power station. It was 800 metres further on from Emerald. They had identified a group of men but had not seen anything to identify them as insurgents. The Royal Marines had killed a large group of insurgents in precisely that area the previous year. And being creatures of habit I hoped they would form up there again. With the rest of the Company so exposed it would be useful if we could be first to the punch. The FSG bounced back into the desert and then forward in a concerted thrust towards route 611.

The 611 sounds like a major route and in Afghan terms it was. After all, there were places where you could have two lanes. It was a graded route, once upon a time; traffic, weather and neglect had carved ruts and potholes to make cars bob and weave wildly down the trail. It marked the division between the desert and the green zone, following the Helmand valley from the Afghan ring road in central Helmand north through Geresk and Sangin and then on to the damn at Kajakai. Local freedom of movement was bound up in control of this road. We now knew of two Taliban tolls operating with impunity beyond the reach of our patrols, marked by no more than a bottle in the road and a few men sitting outside a compound taking their dues.

The FSG provided just enough distraction; the platoons, with Company HQ in between, moved just fast enough to be inside the range of the machine-guns in Inkerman; and the women, children and livestock, despite their best efforts, moved just slowly enough to allow us safe passage. The commanders changed their tone from the argy bargy of the first contact to goading us to turn round. 'They are like thieves in the night', 'Look at them run like dogs from their angry master!', 'We own the day'.

To this day as a Company Commander the Jokhoran operation is the one that I am most proud of. We accomplished the mission without a shot being fired. The risk was balanced with the reward and the resources available. Well, almost. I would of course have turned round and gone toe-to-toe if it could have proved decisive. My issues with our Fire Support Group had not really got much better. They were increasingly desperate to live their Afghan dream of fire missions smashing the hell out of the enemy. I was equally determined that we weren't going to smash the hell out of anything unless it was the absolute last option to save ourselves or others. On this occasion, as a planned operation we had booked helicopters, drones and jets to help well in advance. Various fire plans had been discussed and we had targets for every conceivable option to help us manoeuvre against the enemy or help us extract if we got into difficulty. But as we strode out of the gate early in the morning, all of those assets that had been previously allocated to us were taken elsewhere by the Brigade and Divisional HQs. So whilst we were as well positioned on the ground as we could be, the crucial element of observation in depth, flank protection and a fixing force had been stripped from us. To stand and fight in such inglorious isolation on ground of the enemy's choosing would have been to invite a General Custer moment.

Military commanders need these resources to be able to manoeuvre. Tactical manoeuvre is based on an incredibly simple triumvirate of activities: being able to find, fix and strike. If your principal resources to find and fix are taken, all that is left is to strike or, in Afghanistan, pound randomly, with increasing desperation, at a more mobile enemy that you can't see. And then you end up destroying the village in order to save it. We simply did not have the integral capacity nor the assets from elsewhere to out-manoeuvre the enemy on the ground. The deepest irony is that there was always a reserve of attack helicopters held to help us get out of contact. My view was, and still is, that 'held in reserve' is too late. By the time you have had the fire-fight you have by and large lost the population, unless of course you have managed to ambush a group of insurgents and killed only them and done it quickly.

We strolled back into Inkerman being watched on all sides by sullen men. Adam beckoned one over and we quizzed him. Nothing doing. We were all back on the stroke of 0900. For the people who lived around Jokhoran I like to think that their attitude was shifted by events that day. Not that it had an immediate effect, but three months later one of the families from those compounds came to us with a plea. It ran something along the lines of 'We know you don't want to destroy our compounds but when the insurgent comes we move to the desert side. We can rebuild our compound.' Within a week a hellfire missile had destroyed a compound wall along with a very persistent and deadly insurgent who had been using it for cover. The insurgents never used their compound again during our tour.

The internal PR campaign that this type of patrol represented success, and that exchanging lead and other heavy metal represented failure, was a hard sell. Everyone had seen the rush of humanity, felt the imminence of action: 'How grateful,' I argued, 'do you think those women and children are that the firing did not start? How annoyed were the Taliban? Did we get the information we were after? We all get to fight another day.'

At about this time I wrote a piece for the radio as an amalgam of the assault on our senses and emotions that we had experienced in our first two months since arrival in Afghanistan.

Sounds, sights and smells of Afghanistan. The comfort of the sleeping bag in the chill of the morning air. The invigorating shock of the occasional cold shower. Clean combats dried in the dusty air. Hot coffee, bacon slice, beans and porridge. The acrid ammonia of the desert rose and the rich odour of the deep trench latrine. 80 pounds of armour, ammunition, kit and clobber. The crackle of radio communications, clipped and terse. High walls, narrow alleys, open fields, dusty roads and clothes; heat shimmer, rain on hot stones, mist in the green zone. The Somme like suction of the irrigated poppy field. Waist-deep ditch water, bobbing with excrement. Sweat and steam on protective specs. Careful steps. The adrenaline injection of imminent action. The crack and thump of lead through the air, the fizz of a rocket-propelled grenade. The hornet drone of the helicopter spitting fire. The high octane, low pass of the jet. Sweat, mud, blood, fear, bravery. Calm after the storm. Eerie calm. Tobacco spat, bines puffed, the smoke of dung fires. Bravado, banter, humour, laughter. Grief like a stone. The IED explosion, the slam of a metal container door too similar to distinguish. Nervous relaxation. Sunset on jagged peaks, bright stars, crisp nights, moon shadow. Noodles, meat and boiled tinned carrots, chocolate sponge. The tapping of the keyboard reporting to commanders. Late nights and gentle snoring of men at rest.

The FSG picked their way back through the minefield and I got a set of orders for the defining operation of the tour. Operation Ghartse Gahadme 4 or GG4 for short. Opening up route 611 to Sangin.

# Chapter 10

# The Road into Hel(mand)

In the headquarters above us the cogs were now whirring fast. GG4, as the operation became known, was simple in concept – open the road for uninhibited ISAF and local use – but difficult in practice. It was ground that we didn't know, or not in the kind of detail to compete with our enemy. Halfway between Inkerman and Blenheim, just on the desert side of the road, lies a series of old Russian trenches. I don't think the irony of being about to emplace two patrol bases either side of the Russian trenches was lost on anybody. Nor that we knew the local Taliban were playing 'at home'.

The CO's intent was to place three patrol bases about one kilometre apart between 2 Platoon in Blenheim and A Company in Inkerman. In order to achieve this I would need an extra platoon and so the Battlegroup took a platoon from C Company in Kajakai and gave it to A Company. 7 Platoon, commanded by Lieutenant Rob Fellows with Serjeant 'Billy' Bain as his 2IC, arrived. We got a bomb disposal team in at the same time. 1 and 3 Platoon would go to Sangin and make their way up a newly-cleared 611 under command of D Company 3 Rifles. They would be dropped off in Viking vehicles to compounds that had been identified either by recce or from a map, where they would stay and permanently picket the route. Once established they would then come back under my command.

Our part in all of this was to use 7 Platoon and the FSG to put in another patrol base at the far end of Sareagar on the 611. We would do this after we had taken in a large resupply of the stores required to fortify the compounds. We would also get more ammunition, helium and other essentials to be able to sustain the patrol bases without resupply for thirty days. That included thirty days' worth of bottled water at six litres a day for each of the thirty-five men. If it was simple in concept the logistics were epic – 15,000 bottles of water was just the start. The combat logistics patrol bringing this stuff in from the south through the desert could only leave back down the 611. We did not have the troops to keep both routes open. So failure to open the route out, down the 611, was not an option.

Before all this got underway we needed to celebrate Christmas. It was the last time that the majority of the A Company group was going to be together. The previous resupply had brought our Christmas food six weeks early, so after a quick chat with the Company Sergeant Major and Ben, we decided that now was as good a time as any.

There is a tradition in the British Army that at Christmas the officers, warrant officers and serjeants serve Christmas dinner to everybody else. It is a chance to recognise that for the majority of time it is the Riflemen who do most of the thankless tasks. In the base, because I had so many different 'cap badges' under command the team served not only to Riflemen, but to signallers, policemen, gunners, chefs, engineers, mechanics, medics, dog handlers and a trooper. A meal of three courses and two sittings: soup, a selection of fresh meat and fresh veg, with Christmas pudding. Christmas cake to finish. Shrunken stomachs ached with the pleasure. There was a lot of good-natured chat that went on, with the boot well and truly on the other foot; not quite as bad as a boozy cookhouse in Bulford but a good attempt to recreate the same atmosphere. Collette made an 'entrance' as a Christmas pixie with Ed dressed as a very alternative Santa. The black bin bag dress, what there was of it, induced whoops and cheers as well as multiple photo calls.

And once the world outside was forgotten the banter started. There was no talk of future ops or loved ones, just a few moments out of the game. Then the applause for the chefs and they stumbled into a cold night, a cigarette for some but a return to the sentry post for others. The Company would celebrate a memorable Christmas ten days later amongst friends, but away from loved ones. A few, a lucky few, had Christmas on R and R – married men with young children – and then for New Year single men became the priority. Those of us in forward operating bases were all thinking of those who had no choice but to spend Christmas apart.

As well as Christmas there was the delayed celebration of Bonfire Night by the bomb disposal team that nearly delayed the whole operation. With the number of extra troops in Inkerman the accommodation was bulging at the seams. On operations personal space is at a premium, so shifting up even further for extra units is bad news. New units nearly always bring new infections, and living close to one another means that coughs, colds and worse can spread very fast. In some sense we were lucky in Inkerman because all the time we were there a group of engineers had been revamping our accommodation. But it was not yet ready and the new units had to go into a transit shelter. These had been declared unsafe because of their design, with one hesco (a giant basket of earth) container on top of another. Safety demands had increased, after this design collapsed at another base, to two containers below to support the one above. But even the transit was better, and safer, than outside in mid-December.

The weather during the Afghan winter of 2009–10 was not at all bad by local standards. It got down to minus five degrees Centigrade at night and was up in the twenties during the day. It is not the absolute cold that makes life so difficult, but the extent of the variation in twenty-four hours. One is constantly either donning or doffing fleeces or jackets. In my case I was rarely without my down-feather puffa jacket when around camp. Previous units had built wooden stoves in all the transit accommodation blocks. They too were now regarded as too dangerous to use and had signs on to that effect, but just having them there was temptation enough for our visitors. The fire that started in the transit accommodation grew from a flicker to a monster in a flash. Within a few minutes the bomb disposal team ammunition started to cook off. 'Bones', the Engineer troop commander who was first on the scene, had to beat a hasty retreat under fire as the ammo pinged around the inside of the building.

It is testament to the strength of a condemned block of hesco and the isolation of that transit block that the fire did not spread further. However, for a while we were treated to what sounded like the most vicious fire-fight. Grenades, bar mines, weapons, bomb disposal kit: all either exploded or melted. A great plume of black smoke rose over Inkerman. 7 Platoon were due to set up a patrol base in three days and 60 per cent of their kit was gone. Luckily they were doing a kit inspection at the time, so all of the stuff they wore on patrol and their weapons were saved. Lists were put together and materiel readied to be loaded onto the resupply. Back in Bastion the Quartermaster's department worked round the clock. There would have to be some sharp work in a couple of days in Inkerman when it arrived. For too many hours for comfort D-Day hung in the balance. I got a statement from one of the search team sappers saying there was no sign on the fire. It was reminiscent of the Baldrick defence of the Flanders pigeon murderer. 'Captain Blackadder definitely did not shoot this delicious plump-breasted pigeon.' In this case 'There was no sign on the fire saying, "DANGER – Do not use this fire"'.

Unlike the rest of the chain of command all the way to the Brigadier, whom I was told wanted charges brought, I was minded to forgive the search team. They had found and diffused four IEDs that day on the resupply route. Despite the loss of kit no one had been hurt. We cobbled together enough spare kit for 7 Platoon to be ready and the specialist kit for the search team was flown up from Bastion. We were still good to go. I could have charged the sapper and stripped him of a month's wages but it would have done neither him nor me nor the team any good at all. He had his punishment and more from his fellows; it would not surprise me if he wasn't still called 'Goldie', or some other fire-starting nickname. There was no malice, just a desire to keep warm. The military justice system allows an officer in command of a company to be effectively the prosecutor, judge and jury. And only Sapper Safety Matches would be able to speak in his own defence, if he did not take the option for a court martial. Not for the first time I felt that good order and military discipline was best administered through his sense of shame, albeit with considerable shame enhancement in the form of well-chosen words from pretty much everyone round camp. Taking it a more formal route would compromise my sense that the chain of command had at least as much to answer for as the sorry Sapper Sparks.

More interestingly, the incident brought out the Taliban spies. A week previously a young boy had brought in his blind grandfather for a medical examination. The kid had been very interested in the camp, but we put it down to childlike curiosity. The day after the fire he was back with his grandfather for a further examination. This time the questions were rather too direct; clearly a list of things to ask about the fire. He was turned out. Another innocent caught up in a situation way beyond his control.

The resupply made it through the desert. Slowly but surely the road up from Sangin was cleared and opened, but not without a considerable fight. From 14 to 20 December there were some forty IED finds or strikes in our area of operations. Corporal Goodson, who had been with us a matter of weeks as a replacement for Corporal Fisher, was shot and wounded in the shoulder and evacuated. Rifleman Neil from the FSG was also shot and wounded. 1 Platoon was having a battle and a half. Their new home was located on the site of a former patrol base, PB Downes. It was a double irony that we had opted again to retake ground once held in sight of the Russian trenches. They were being attacked hourly through the day. The search team working with them clearing routes out of the new base found eight devices in an alleyway and cleared them under fire. The requirement to fill sandbags for fortifications in order to make sure the new bases were well enough protected meant little sleep for anyone involved.

The total number of forces in the company area pushed up to nearly 500: two rifle companies, an armoured squadron, a combat logistics patrol of over ninety and a troop of Americans, code name 'Thor'. The Americans do a good line in call-sign names, even if the irony is lost on them. After all, what could be more ironic, in an Alanis Morrisette kind of a way, than being stuck in a river valley in Helmand with the call-sign 'Hades'. We paid the boatman on the Styx rather more often than we crossed the Helmand. 'Hades' was the call-sign that all of the Sangin Battlegroup used. And as the fourth Company of the Battlegroup we were Hades 4-0, four zero rather than forty, with each of the platoons being 4-1, 4-2, 4-3, 4-4 and so on.

The 'Thor' call-sign designated a type of bomb-disposal unit. The Americans have a rather different attitude to bomb-disposal to our own and they were aptly named. Our method had its genesis in Northern Ireland, where if the bomb could be diffused and analysed it would help with forensic evidence and give some kind of intelligence. The US army is much happier to detonate the devices and be done with it as a means of clearing the area. So there are a small group of people who drive heavily-protected vehicles with a multitude of ways to explode devices protruding from them. They then simply drive them over uncleared routes. Nutters.

More euphemistically, they were an 'eclectic' bunch. The officer, or 'L.T.', was a relative new boy, but his platoon sergeant was in the finest tradition of US forces. Utterly committed to the mission, he reassured me that if there was anything that needed clearing then he and his team were the men for the job. For three days they helped us out non-stop. He was seven weeks away from completing a tour of duty that had lasted ten months and taken him from Iraq directly to Afghanistan. His fourth child had been born during his time away. In three days they blew up over twenty improvised explosive devices.

The attitude of that US sergeant encapsulates everything you need to know about the US army attitude to the wars in Afghanistan and Iraq. Whilst they are, by almost any definition, counter-insurgency campaigns (or in the case of Iraq transformed fairly rapidly into counter-insurgency) the Americans managed to generate the kind of political will that is more usually consistent with a war of national survival. It is only in the last couple of years that this has waned. The British army has been intoxicated by this attitude. I was clearly in the grip of it in late 2009. Hindsight will have hopefully taught our leadership and theirs the truth of the Clauswitzian maxim: 'No one starts a war – or rather, no one in his sense ought to do so – without first being clear in his mind what he intends to achieve by the war and how he intends to conduct it.'

On the afternoon of 18 December I took 1 and 3 Platoon back under command and on 20 December I travelled for the first time down the road to visit 2 Platoon in Blenheim. It had been a tough fight for six days. And it continued to be so. The insurgents attacked the three new patrol bases every day, sometimes simultaneously, with rocket-propelled grenades and machine-gun fire. Inkerman was mortared three times, which I mainly remember for a furious discussion with Battlegroup HQ over whether we could fire back with mortars and artillery with a counter-battery mission. Denied. I was apoplectic, not only because for once it met all the right criteria for protecting our own troops from the threat, but also because the enemy rounds were not actually landing in Inkerman but in the local village. If we were going to protect the local population and, most importantly, make them *feel* protected, we needed to fire back. On the third occasion we did. I had long been an advocate of what was misguidedly titled 'courageous restraint'. But like anything that is taken too far to make a point, it undermines its own validity. Luckily I was now able to go to Sangin and talk it through face-to-face rather than over the phone.

The battle rhythm for the company changed markedly in this period: twenty engagements a day was not unusual. Each platoon was also trying to put out a patrol a day so there was an exponential rise in radio traffic to and from the Company Headquarters, but still no extra radios despite repeated requests. On the upside was the arrival of three Mastiff vehicles, proper protection for troops going up and down the road.

Immediately there was the problem of who should command and man these new vehicles. The short-term solution was to give them to the CSMs group. Commanded by Hayley Wright, the clerk, and Pat Hyde, with drivers taken from the platoons and gunners from HQ, this merry band, who travelled under the Company Sergeant Major's call-sign, Hades 4-9, became synonymous with our fight to keep the 611 open. They escorted the resupply truck and the bomb-disposal teams, took people on R and R, evacuated casualties and brought in the replacements. Needless to say the short-term solution turned into a medium and then a long-term one. By the end of the tour Hades 4-9 and Pat himself had done more time on patrol than any other call-sign in the Battlegroup and been blown up no fewer than fourteen times by IEDs. Whilst injuries were suffered to knees, backs and pretty much everywhere else, no one lost a limb. In doing so Company Serjeant Major Pat Hyde garnered a considerable reputation in the Battlegroup, and more widely, which I was not so worried about, but to the Company he became the embodiment of a will to continue in extreme adversity. It also meant that he got to keep an eye on professional standards throughout the Company and keep his finger on the Company pulse as he picked up and dropped off. Even if I began to wonder what it would do to morale if he really got hurt.

\* \* \* \* \*

The worst two hours in seven months in Helmand were undoubtedly between 1930 and 2130 on 20 December 2009. Somehow we, and again I mean we in a broad way, contrived to allow a sniper attached to A Company to take a shot at and kill Lance Corporal Michael Pritchard, one of the two members of the Royal Military Police attached to the Company.

Much of this story has been covered in a very well-documented coroner's inquest. And because of that publicity and the fact that I sat through five days of evidence that we gave in open court, I am going to make a sole exception to my earlier rule of not discussing my view of why people died. The coroner concluded that Michael had been accidentally shot whilst on active service. But the accident was wholly preventable. The coroner asserted that poor communications, poor briefing and the broader situation all contributed. What follows by way of my view relies principally on the evidence of that inquest, but also on my experience leading up to the incident. For of course it was I and the rest of the chain of command that generated the broader situation in which we had a disastrous two hours.

There are a myriad of bits of data that seem more or less important three years and some months on from the incident. And what was very important to us immediately before the incident now seems much less so, given the fact of Pritch's death. There is much to be learned from such an experience. Making sure those lessons are really learned and acted upon would be a very thin silver lining to what remains a very large cloud.

I took over the area of operations from D Company 3 Rifles on the afternoon of 18 December. There was only one problem. The area between 1 and 3 Platoon in their newly-constructed patrol bases had a huge blind spot. Several IEDs had been found in this area when the road had been cleared on 15 and 16 December. It had been protected by the Viking vehicles until the morning of 19 December. They had been retasked in a hurry and I was left insisting that we re-clear the road before putting a standing patrol in place to observe the blind spot between the bases.

Somehow the orders for a standing patrol morphed into it being an observation post during the inquest, which was indeed what it became but it was not then. Observation post intimates an air of permanence, whereas when I gave orders it was needs must to send a patrol to cover the blind spot to buy time to get the necessary equipment for a more permanent manned checkpoint. The road was re-cleared on the morning of 20 December, during which time a legacy IED was found and disposed of in the very area that I wanted the standing patrol located.

Tom and Corporal 'Decks' Decker moved up the road and tried to establish the best position from which to observe the blind spot – what is known as 'dead ground' in military parlance – between the two new patrol bases. Once this had been done and the Afghan occupant of the compound had been duly compensated for his trouble a couple more things happened. The inter-platoon boundary changed to reflect the new layout on the ground between 1 and 3 Platoon and the standing patrol got communications with the remote sangar of the patrol base in Bariolai. We had reopened the road, something we had to do again and again over the next three months. At this stage I was happy that all seemed to be going well.

But all was not well. For whatever reason the location of the standing patrol in the compound did not get passed on from one Rifleman to another in the sangar in Bariolai. Nor did the information about where the boundary line was now located between the platoons. In the aftermath of the incident neither we nor the Military Police investigation established who was in the sangar when 'comms' were established. In hindsight it pains me beyond words when I consider how many fledgling sangar briefs I heard during training, how many range cards we practised making, how many times I had checked the sangars in Inkerman. But somehow the chain of communication broke and this information was not passed on. We will now never know why or how that happened.

Three hours later, as dusk fell and the night sights were being used for the first time that day, the Riflemen in Patrol Base 2, later named Bariolai, in a sangar that was seventy-five metres away from the base in order to be able to observe the road, observed heat sources that looked like they were in the road. IED layers? Given previous experience and the current intelligence picture, it was a distinct possibility.

They reported it up and continued to observe. During this time illumination was put up. Still there was no positive identification but they, the supposed enemy, were not going away.

Communications were difficult. Aren't they always, and especially so if you need more radios, but in this case the work-around was to relay the messages via another sangar that had line of sight to the ops room. This put another man in the loop. Somehow during the transfer of the information from the sangar to the ops room via two other men, the two groups had put the 'people' observed in the 'road' 300 metres apart. Those in the platoon operations room believed them to be on the boundary 400 metres away and those in the sangar knew they were 700 metres away at the site of the inter-platoon boundary prior to its move. At one stage a Rifleman came from the remote sangar to fetch more illumination rockets. This was another opportunity to confirm face-to-face what everyone was talking about that was missed, although the importance of that omission could not have been known at the time. After all, both groups were equally sure the other knew exactly what was going on. The appearance of a lance corporal in the remote sangar who asked for and received permission to fire warning shots did not clarify the situation. The reaction of the 'insurgents' to the warning shots only served to confirm in the minds of those in the remote sangar that the IED layers must be determined to finish their work. This confusion even perpetuated through a conversation initiated by the standing patrol saying rounds had gone over their heads. Those in the remote sangar did not hear the transmission and the Bariolai ops room and everyone else assumed it was ricochet going overhead and not incoming fire. There are two sayings in the army about assumptions: 'Assumption is the mother of all fuck ups' and 'to assume makes an ass of u and me' – both were as true on that day as they ever had been.

The team in the ops room in Bariolai reacted to the transmission and to the threat in a good way. They sent down a section commander and a sniper to the remote sangar. More experience, better observation skills and a more accurate weapon system. Also, in the case of the section commander, certain knowledge of the location of the standing patrol and the line of the new inter-platoon boundary. If this was an opportunity to right the confusion it ultimately only served to fuel it.

The section commander observed the same thing as the Riflemen. So did the sniper. At this stage the moon set. When the moon sets in Afghanistan the stars do not produce enough ambient light to see with image-intensifying telescopic sights. Pitch black does not do justice to the blackness of this black. The image-intensifiers were next to useless unless IR illum was fired. By now the section commander and the sniper, with their thermal scopes, had a 'positive ID of IED layers on the road.' They even confirmed with the ops room that none of the standing patrol were on the road. They were all in the compound. In my mind this was the crucial moment.

Everybody who heard this from Ben in Inkerman to Tom in PB 1, later named Shuga, was now satisfied that those in the remote sangar were not looking at the standing patrol. And even if there was some confusion in PB 1 about where the incident was, the standing patrol was in the compound on the roof and the IED layers were 'on the road'. As the sniper began to fire warning shots the standing patrol reported shots coming very close. Because of the various confirmations that had gone on before, the standing patrol now assumed they were under enemy fire. This was not unreasonable given that the patrol base 400 metres down the road from where they had come had been attacked all day. They were fearful of lighting themselves up in case they could be seen by the enemy. To those in remote sangar it looked even more like IED layers sneaking around.

At this point the sniper, honestly believing he had positively identified insurgents laying an IED, aimed and shot directly at the IED layers. This was between 2040 and 2050. He assessed that he had hit one and he and the section commander both observed a 'casevac'. The coroner tended to the view that there were never any insurgents in the area. If that is so, and it is the most credible view, then it is a cruel twist that the activity in the standing patrol at that time gave the impression of someone bending over another's body, moving it away and then coming back with another man. In hindsight it fits almost exactly with the requests by the ops room at Inkerman of the standing patrol to see if they could observe anything in the road 300 metres to their east, which was the point that all the operations rooms thought the IED layers were at. The Inkerman ops room knew, as did we all, that there was a threat warning out of an IED planned to be emplaced against the wall of a patrol base. Was this it? It turned out to be against PB Almas the other side of Sangin, which exploded a day later.

The section commander and the sniper in the remote sangar continued to observe. They then observed what we now know was a changeover of observers in the standing patrol at 2100, which they interpreted as a renewed attempt to lay the IED after a lull. The Bariolai ops room, having not had any info for fifteen minutes, saw this as a new incident and wanted to re-escalate. i.e. not take lethal shot but provide warning and flares to establish what was really going on. Earlier they had tried to get the large megaphone, known as the 'sound commander', to warn the locals that they were going to be fired upon and now Mike intended to use it. He radioed the sangar. Too late. The sniper had taken aim and shot at another 'IED layer'.

In the standing patrol Corporal Decker had become increasingly concerned that those in the remote sangar might not know exactly where they were. Despite having achieved communications with the remote sangar earlier in the day he could not raise them on the radio nor they him. So from 2100 he began to lay out markers round the compound. Infra-red markers, not visible in the thermal band. I would imagine he looked for all the world like he was crawling into the road and back.

The fatal shot passed through the back of Corporal Decker's body armour, and such is the velocity of a sniper bullet that it continued into Lance Corporal Pritchard and he was dead in a matter of seconds.

The next thing that came over the radio was 'man down'. For those in the remote sangar at PB Bariolai their assumptions and their certainty began to unravel very fast. So too for those in the ops rooms in Bariolai and Inkerman.

For my part during the whole incident I was with Charlie in Blenheim planning to work my way up the new bases now the road was open. Earlier in the day I had given the orders to Tom and Mike when the inter-platoon boundary had been revised and I heard these being reiterated by Ben at the evening briefing. From there I had little knowledge of the developing catastrophe, other than that potential IED layers were being observed, just like most nights, until after the fatal shot was fired. That is not to say I did not make a contribution to the chaos. It just was not on the night in question. The piece for which I was most at fault was the communication situation. I knew we were operating with the bare minimum of radios on 30 October. By mid-December I was certain we were operating below that threshold and that communications in the event of an IED strike were our greatest risk. Whilst I shouted loud I clearly did not shout loud enough. According to the coroner poor communications were one of three elements that caused Pritch's death and I knew it before it happened and so did the rest of the chain of command.

The rest of the chain of command have never acknowledged their part in all this, either for the lack of radios or because of the system of equipping soldiers on operations through the UOR process. The thermal sights used by the sniper and section commander that night were only available in Afghanistan, so the sniper had done no thermal recognition training. The specifications of the sight, in the form of the granularity of the picture at certain ranges, mean that it is technically impossible to positively identify solely with the use of the sight. You cannot see what a man is wearing at that range, so a 'positive' identification had been achieved using his knowledge of the history of the area, the current intelligence picture *and* what he thought could see through his scope. The sight being a UOR meant he had taken it from its packet in Sangin. He had never fired his sniper rifle with it on until that night. He had never experienced the extra weight on the front that would change his point of aim; this is the most likely explanation for the shots which he missed, even though he thought he had hit and seen a casualty evacuated. Furthermore, a feature of thermal sights is that they give fewer visual clues as to depth. In other words, you lose a sense of perspective. To the layman it all looks a bit flat, and things that are different distances away can look similar. In this instance, when viewed from the elevated position of the remote sangar, the standing patrol on the roof of the compound looked as though they were on the road. There are many burdening hypotheticals in all this but one of the most crucial is: if we had been given an opportunity to train with the equipment we were using that night, might Pritch be alive today?

I went back up the 611 that night stopping at each of the patrol bases. 3 Platoon were shocked and angry; Pritch had been a brother in arms. In hindsight they were also shocked that they had made the assumption that they were being fired upon by the enemy until they could do too little too late to prevent the blue on blue. There were certainly things that they could have done, and that they didn't do them was based on an assumption that they were more vulnerable to enemy fire than to fratricide. And no blame should lie with them for that, but blame is different from self-recrimination.

If the emotion in Shuga was grief and anger, then in Bariolai it was already self-recrimination to go with their shock and disbelief. We collected the sniper and his buddy, arriving in Inkerman in the early hours of the morning.

Whilst at Blenheim I had spent ten minutes having the 'condor' moment, but it didn't make me very relaxed. This is not about having a cigar, it is about generating the time and space to think before acting. This was going to get very big, very quickly. Fratricide is mercifully uncommon. When it happens everyone has a view all the way back to the messes in Bulford and the first impulse is to avoid a share of responsibility whilst focusing on others. Before this process started I wanted to set the Company on a path which would guide them through the slings and arrows of this outrageous ill-informed denunciation. I kept it short. We had to be honest, brutally honest, with ourselves and with those who would investigate what happened. Honest for three reasons. Honest because we had to live with ourselves and if we hid anything it would, in time, undermine us. We had to be honest for Pritch. If his death was to mean anything at all it was that the correct lessons should be learned. If we were anything other than entirely forthcoming the wrong lessons would be learned and it would make it more likely it would happen again. Then, most importantly, we had to be honest for his family. For however much the event flew in the face of all of our sense of professionalism, however awkward the emotion, it was but a fraction of what we had imposed on his friends and family. More than anything else we owed it to them.

And so it was. The Royal Military Police came and decided someone was to blame. For the most part the SIB did a very good job in investigating deaths in the Company in Afghanistan. In this case it was disastrous. Somehow, despite good evidence to the contrary, they identified Mike as potentially criminally culpable. All the way through the investigation I never stopped believing, as a result of our initial incident investigation and report, that it was anything other than a series of honest if avoidable mistakes. In the inquest I was advised not to take responsibility for this, although I have always believed that that's what commanders are there for, to take responsibility for the honest actions of their subordinates. This is not about taking the whole blame – they should take their share of the blame, but commanders must take responsibility for the whole and act accordingly.

Eventually, over a year after we got back, the Defence Prosecuting Authority threw it out. The chain of command, on advice from the lawyers, and without all the evidence, and in my opinion much to their discredit, then took administrative action against Mike. They found that on the balance of probabilities there had been 'inefficiency'. At the inquest it became crystal clear that if there had been inefficiency it had not been Mike's. There were at least three people who might be considered less 'efficient', including myself. At the inquest I watched Riflemen, lance corporals, section commanders and officers all shoulder their share of the responsibility, and in one case testimony of such moral courage that it was equal to anything I saw in Afghanistan.

The lack of moral courage in the investigation was highlighted by the nature of the coroner's narrative verdict that was the clearest version yet of what happened and why. But unfortunately he only had the statements taken at the time to go on. If the Special Investigations Branch had been a little more broad-minded and significantly more diligent perhaps they would have discovered the missing range card, the Rifleman who *had* been briefed by his section commander, and included the assessment from me a month later that accused Army HQ of criminal negligence for not giving us enough radios in light of that and other incidents. That would have saved a lot of heartache for us all, but most especially for Pritch's family, who endured a torturously long wait for the truth.

None of that will change the fact that Pritch was a great bloke. He did not deserve to die in such circumstances and I am truly sorry that he died at our hands. He had become a fellow Rifleman. I hope the lessons are really learned; the coroner seemed to think they had been. They might have been 'learned', but the funding for the equipment that would solve the issue and give a true situational awareness picture has been taken out of the programme in the cuts in the MoD. I have rarely been more ashamed than when the Assistant Director of the Combat Capability Directorate reassured the court on oath that it was all in hand, when it clearly is not. The equipment is commercially available and all our allies have it. We don't.

Furthermore, there should be someone who is prepared to take 'command' responsibility for his death. After all, we take enough of the plaudits for others' performance if it goes well. It seems that we have got to a very bad place where the fear of the law overrides the command imperative. It was the same in Afghanistan. Not acting due to fear of failure is far worse than acting in the expectation of success.

I am responsible, just as I know others who played even a small part also feel as though they were in a position to have made a crucial intervention. I have looked up the chain of command for anyone who might be big enough to accept this. I don't anymore. The generals, civil servants and politicians seem to have no desire to accept the consequences of their actions or inaction. It is left for future soldiers and their families, men like Pritch, to live with the consequences.

\*   \*   \*   \*   \*

By the time we got to Christmas I was tired. Ten days of relentless activity had taken their toll. Everyone was given a small boost by the arrival by helicopter of some Christmas mail. Due to various administrative constraints the Christmas mail very nearly did not arrive on time. Then, to obvious relief, vast quantities showed up on Christmas Eve. The level of support that we received from families, friends, anonymous donors and well-wishers great and small was outstanding. I opened a 'to a soldier' card from a primary school and a dollar fell out. The message inside simply read 'get yerself a cup of tea'.

Tea is about the only thing that comes for free but it was deeply touching. I had been the lucky recipient of many parcels from family and friends. The oddest gifts catch you off guard. One parcel came with a bag of autumn leaves and lavender. Freddie Fryer inhaled deeply, declaring 'That is England, it's bloody England – kna' wot I mean'. Even so there are some gifts that don't quite make it. Either my sister could not bear to part with the Christmas truffles, or they got snaffled somewhere along the line. And Merv's plum preserve would have to wait until R and R. I was inundated with puzzles to fill what people must have thought were my copious hours of free time, as well as a fine selection of cake, confectionery, cheese and cured meats. We all had our parcel from the charity UK4U –thanks! It is an incongruous name for a charity that continues the fine tradition of sending a gift box to each soldier serving on operations at Christmas. The arrival of mail and parcels engenders depression for those who have been forgotten and ecstasy for those with news from home. Those with the post-mail blues are often to be heard damning all those involved in the transit of mail. They are often the first to laugh when the boot is on the other foot. In an electronic age it is still handwritten words, read on a camp cot, that bring most happiness to a soldier on operations. That, and a full stomach.

Whilst it was true that we did get a load of mail, there was still a full container of mail for A Company 4 Rifles sitting in another Forward Operating Base in the middle of Helmand, having been blown up on the way up with the combat logistic patrol. So despite the saving grace of parcels on Christmas Eve there was a lot of post that did not make it. It wasn't until the end of January that I got a selection of English cheeses, which had ripened to the point where they could have walked from Geresk if only someone had let them out of the container. The various puzzles and puzzle books stayed in a pile for the rest of the tour, gathering dust. I think I must have said something once about the soldier's lot being 90 per cent boredom and 10 per cent fear and they were trying to relieve the boredom. The truth for soldiers is that tedium comes in an uneventful stag in the sangar. Not so for a commander: command is as long as piece of string, you can do it twenty-four hours a day. I don't think I was ever bored once in seven months. Tired, nervous, fervent, frustrated, fearful, angry, elated, exhausted – but never bored. But with the platoons at their lowest point of manpower due to casualties and R and R the average Rifleman was doing eight hours a day of guard duties before he went on patrol for however long that took. On days when a patrol lasted all day, so did the sangar duty. Luckily there was enough going on for them not to be too bored.

We were 'delighted' to welcome General Rodriguez to the base on Christmas Eve. The five-letter abbreviation for his job title was unfathomable but as the third most senior officer in Afghanistan he was basically in charge of the coalition assistance to the Afghan National Army. I relayed our generally positive experiences of working with his US countrymen and the ANA, pleading the case for more Afghan warriors in this part of Helmand. He came with an international entourage including a Belgian Colonel. The level of commitment and enthusiasm of the US army for the mission in Afghanistan is infectious and energising. I did ask why he, based in Kabul, decided to come to us. 'Well, we're always hearing about Forward Operating Base Inkerman.' Hmmm. There's only one thing worse than being talked about…. There was a trip round the base to grip and grin with the troops. Each stop was peppered with stirring words and heartfelt thanks. Uncle Sam felt like a great friend to have and it still came pretty naturally despite the language barrier.

Pat Hyde and I discussed Christmas Day. Were we going to do a run down to all the PBs in the morning? Waking the Riflemen with rum in tea – a drink known as gunfire. The previous day on a resupply run one of the Mastiffs had been hit by an IED. It was increasingly clear that there were a number of devices that had not been found in the initial search of the road. This was not surprising because we had discovered that these devices were not initially 'active', as they still needed a power source attaching. They were, however, now being activated, either as pressure pads or command-wire IEDs. We came to the reluctant decision that the 'gunfire' could wait and we would do a mail run in the evening. There would not be time to do a full-on visit to each patrol base so I opted for flying visits to each and then, not having seen 3 Platoon except under the most unfortunate of circumstances, I went to them for a couple of days. Or at least I planned to stay for two days, but ended up staying for seven as the fight for the 611 hotted up.

The bomb-disposal teams cleared the 611 for the third time, working their way up from Blenheim to Shuga. I was in Shuga with 3 Platoon. On 26 December 3 Platoon discovered that a blind spot from one of their guard posts had been exploited and a large sackful of explosive had been put under the road in one of the culverts. It had taken a while for Chico Bryant to work out what he was looking at, and Pat Hyde was only a couple of seconds behind him as they realised they were standing in the most dangerous place in Helmand. Luckily they were doing the check at night. In daylight they would in all likelihood have been observed and blown to smithereens.

Next morning a check at first light revealed the string that, if pulled, would trigger the device. It ran into a compound 100 metres up and from there who knew. The team moved forward to cut the string thirty metres from the device. I was standing inside the patrol base 100 metres away.

'Cutting in 5, 4, 3… BOOM.'

The string went taught with the bomb hunter's cutters around it and the bomb exploded. WO2 'Butch' Butcher, 2IC of the Fire Support Group, strode across the patrol base. He had not heard the call and was not expecting the explosion. He seemed to jump three foot in the air as it went off. We quickly established that no one had been hurt, but the culvert had been ruined. The ATO grabbed the string and pulled in 350 metres of cord. 'Trying to isolate the end of that would have been a Battlegroup operation', declared the Staff Sergeant later. But the Mastiffs could not get back to Inkerman until the culvert had been sufficiently repaired. This would be the story of our life for the next week.

It was great to be out of Inkerman and living with a platoon for a while. 3 Platoon and especially Corporal Decker's section were feeling the effects of the loss of Lance Corporal Pritchard very keenly. Due to the rotation of guard duty and patrols there was often an opportunity to talk over a brew or the latest meal. Guys had come and gone from R and R and some were looking forward to the best part of four months in Shuga patrol base. 3 Platoon had moved in when the weather had been dire: on the first night they had huddled round fires trying to dry out and keep warm simultaneously. All the activities of the previous ten days had served to exhaust them. They were not yet in a fixed routine. Patrol, guard, build, eat, sleep when possible with little time for anything else.

If I had walked in to that base as an independent observer I would have been concerned. I knew the context and was less concerned, but I talked to Tom about the list of things that needed doing. He anticipated every one. But his principal concern was security. The culverts they were responsible for had been compromised already, because whilst they could see the top of the road they could not see the side of the road, especially where there was a deep culvert. A new post on the top of the building next door would do the trick. We went up to have a look. Three minutes later we were face down on the roof as the local Taliban opened up again.

Tom had a good point. He was genuinely prioritising, not just writing a list of priorities with no resourcing, and that meant compromising other tasks; not comfortable. His other point was that he was manning the observation post now known as 'Pritch's post', leaving him with less manpower to do other stuff. I had some sympathy. The Battlegroup HQ staff watched the patrolling statistics like a hawk. Ours had noticeably dropped off in the last ten days. I felt forced to make a defence of the number of hours that we were now doing in guard duty before any other tasks were complete. More manpower was the key. Except I had just managed to get the Fire Support Group back together in Inkerman to provide some kind of local patrolling presence and now they seemed the most obvious candidates to assist the platoons. Inkerman would have to wait.

The opening of the 611, despite its difficulties for us, had proved very popular with the locals and commensurately unpopular with the Taliban. The focus of the popularity and the discontent had been the closure of the Taliban checkpoint in the Gul Agha Wadi between 1 Platoon and 7 Platoon. It should have been within striking distance of Inkerman, but in four attempts to get there we had always met fierce resistance. 1 Platoon discovered that locals were charged fifty Afghani every time they went to market and more if they were trading there. We had stopped this overnight and everyone, apart from the Taliban, was very happy. The Taliban operated an impressive traffic control system in response. No illegal checkpoint, but if they wanted to attack us on the road they seemed to be able to divert the traffic at will. We never discovered precisely what the signal was. I would imagine that locals listening to insurgent communications or ICOM had a fair bit to do with it.

Every time the Mastiffs did a run up the road the culverts needed to be checked. Whilst I was with 3 Platoon, Corporal 'Cat' Felix went out early to do a check. Luckily he spotted the tell-tale fishing wire running along the culvert. As he made his rapid retreat another mighty explosion tore up the side of the culvert. The device had not been laid inside the drain, so the road remained intact, but it was an incredibly close call on what became known as the Western Culvert. The 'Cat', which is one way to describe a six foot five inch ripped West Indian, returned to Shuga covered in dust saying 'Fuck' 'Fuckin' or 'Fucked' every second word, or more accurately, three in every four words, as he described how close he had come.

Unlike in Inkerman where the power ran day and night, Shuga had a generator that was used as sparingly as possible. This meant that after dusk you were reliant on a head torch. One evening I went back to my temporary cot in a small Afghan compound room shortly thereafter. I left saying 'I'm knackered, wake me if it kicks off.' At the start of the tour I had been up when there were patrols on the ground. Ben and I had pretty soon come to an understanding that only one of us needed to be up. And two months of experience suggested that the Taliban only got it together from eight-thirty am, so better to get sleep when I could. There were enough sleepless nights inflicted by necessity. Even now I harbour some guilt about the requirement for sleep; I had enough to do to be going twenty-four-seven for six months. There are some glib army phrases about a commander's responsibility to get enough sleep. Much of our training helps to cope with sleep deprivation. There are some who like to test themselves until they are hallucinating. In Helmand that is bad juju. Sleep is not just the commander's requirement, it is the responsibility of all soldiers. Highly traumatised soldiers who have not had enough sleep for whatever reason – fear, the night terrors, or guard duty – are a danger to themselves and others. Commanders who make slow decisions brought on by sleep deprivation endanger the lives of others. Sleep is not just a responsibility, it is quite literally a matter of life and death.

My head touched the pillow. At ten am the following morning I stumbled into the platoon ops room. 'Nothing happened?' I asked incredulously, if a little sluggishly; I felt like Rip van Winkle.

'No.'

'Wow. Well, I feel a lot better for that. Nobody thought to rouse me anyway.'

'You said only if kicks off, sir.'

'Indeed I did.' A mildly ashamed smirk crossed my lips.

Riflemen and lance corporals might not say anything initially, at least not to my face. It wouldn't take long for the banter to start, though, so I weighed in first. You give it, and you get it back.

'Came down here for a rest… much busier in Inkerman.'

'Perhaps you'd like brunch now, sir?'

If all this seems a bit rose-tinted it was not. 3 Platoon needed to get Patrol Base Shuga squared away. Ten days of much ops and little admin makes a patrol base a health hazard. By the time I left I hope I had made it as unambiguous as possible that whilst I had a good deal of sympathy, there were some things that needed reprioritising if only to get to the minimum standard required. This was true of all the platoons; it was just that I happened to be with 3 Platoon on that trip. I made my way back up the 611 on 30 December 2009. The area had been relatively quiet for two days and the ingress of stores after two weeks was close to completion. I paid flying visits to Mike and to Rob. I was trying to make the point that this was just the start; they now had to make their new houses homes, or in this case fully operational bases, with all the same management requirements for health, hygiene, washing, cooking, operations rooms and so on as there were in Inkerman, as well as the day job of directing or leading patrols and becoming a figure of ISAF authority for the local community. Despite the exigencies of the fight to establish these bases, the real work had only just started.

# Chapter 11

# Hellfire and Resurrection

A Company did not have a happy new year. A sapper from the Explosive Ordinance Disposal Team, David Watson, stepped on an IED just before sunset on 31 December. He was helping clear an area round Patrol Base Blenheim. When men like David Watson die it may sound like they are working independently from the company to which they are attached. The reality is that they are working hand in hand and it is a matter of luck not judgement that he, rather than a Rifleman from 2 Platoon, died that day.

My stay with 3 Platoon had given me a thorough and useful insight into life in a new PB, but it meant that I had rather lost touch with what was going on elsewhere. Time in Inkerman was required, time to try to work out what was going on, where we were going to make a difference. First there was some of the dull stuff to do. In years gone by as an officer in one of the antecedent regiments to the Rifles I would undoubtedly have had a 'batman', best described as a mélange of valet, bodyguard, conveyer of orders and general personal assistant. The Household Division still have orderlies who help in the preparation of officers' uniform for ceremonial duties and the Ghurkhas appoint a rifleman to assist junior officers, but for the most part the batman has been consigned to history. Quite right too.

What gets the headlines are the bombs and the bullets, the politics and the heroism, but there is quite a lot about operations that is a good deal more mundane. I had to have a washing day. The signal for washing day was that my hanging shelves in my hesco had only one pair of clean socks left. The bulging washing bag got a hot soak with a bit of dhobi dust. Hot water was taken from the most dangerous piece of equipment in the army – the Puffing Billy. This was the metallic dustbin water heater, the lighting of which had induced cartoon explosions and face blackening in training. Then, in an innovation probably not peculiar to our part of Afghanistan, the Royal Engineers' cement mixers provided the mechanical power for a twenty-minute wash. A change of water and a twenty-minute rinse, a quick soak and if you're lucky most of the dirt is out. In the summer, with temperatures of fifty degrees, un-wrung washing took an hour to dry. In January we looked for two fine days together on the forecast to be sure. Morale had been raised a month before when the shell of a new laundry unit arrived, but the plumbing had yet to follow. I am not ashamed to say that the novelty of this particular experience wore off quite quickly during the tour. But like most domestic activity in Helmand it became a social event and the washing repartee was a bit of a break from the bombs and the bullets.

Another very noticeable thing about being back in Inkerman was that the camp was now usually populated by half a dozen or more who were on their way to or from R and R. Just being away from their patrol base put them in a more reflective frame of mind, more so those who were returning than those excited about going home. One particular conversation with a Rifleman in 3 Platoon gave me pause for thought. When I asked whether he had really told anyone at home what he was doing he just shrugged at me. I was concerned already that the trauma-management process might not survive being in the PBs. Getting Freddie to do interviews between forty-eight and seventy-two hours after an incident had been impossible in the first two weeks. We had to rely on the platoon serjeants doing the job they have done since armies began and keeping a close eye on their men. This, coupled with requests for Mr Fryer's help if required and some enforced visits, I hoped would deal with the worst effects of PTSD. I decided that we needed a visit from the Field Mental Health team. It was not that I saw much evidence of PTSD at this time, it was just that the numbers of potentially traumatic incidents were already off the scale. The Field Mental Health team came knowing what were fast becoming eye-popping statistics: we had our 100th IED event on New Year's Day. The Battlegroup had lost seven men in two weeks, we in A Company had lost two, and in the case of Lance Corporal Prichard in circumstances that were of immediate regret. I wanted to be reassured. So it was an 'advisory' visit rather than a clinical requirement.

The army is getting better at identifying and treating psychological issues early. I had always stated that in line with good practice, I wished to keep any battle shock casualties as far forward as possible with people who better understood the individual and the event. I would discover it was much easier said than done. At the start of the tour, after every event in which we were exposed to trauma we were interviewed collectively and individually. Stress and its effects are now well known, but one can mitigate the impact mainly by talking about it. We have a good system, but culturally in the army we struggle to answer the basic question: how do you feel about that? This is not that surprising really, as our feelings changed from day to day. It is quite difficult to explain to those outside the military how the cocktail of emotions is mixed. A drop of fatigue with a slice of excitement; a splash of adrenaline with a measure of boredom – add fear, relief, elation, frustration and pride and stand well back. Quite honestly most soldiers don't want to explore all of those when the mixture may be more potent tomorrow or even while they are still in the unit with which they serve, because in that unit they are like everyone else, but outside that environment we fall into a tiny minority.

Those returning from two weeks' rest and recuperation talked of lacking either the ability or the desire to explain to others. They had enjoyed themselves in a way only soldiers know. I had been constantly impressed with young men confronting the most difficult events and strongest emotions. They clearly preferred dealing with them amongst colleagues rather than friends.

The support is immeasurably better than it used to be. The Mental Health team, from whom we had two visits during our time, were very useful to provide an independent check. I wanted a candid view and any advice they could give. On both occasions the visiting team talked of the spirit in the company, not just among us Riflemen, but across the Company group. I was very glad of the reassurance. We were being melded in adversity – I just wondered how hot it had to get before we melted. The butcher's bill was adding up and it was not only us who were paying a price. The local nationals suddenly found themselves caught up in the violence in the vicinity of the new patrol bases.

Having achieved relative control of the road to Sangin, the fight was now on to keep control. The Taliban was tenacious as well as brutal. 1 Platoon treated a local who had stepped on and partially detonated an IED. He was flown by us to the hospital in Lashkar Gar. During his stay there his family came to the patrol base where he had been treated to see if we had any news. As they departed they were followed. We found out that the insurgent intended to question them and stop them ever talking to us again: the unveiled threat of the bully. We paid for his father to take a taxi to the hospital. Our man came back in due course, down a foot, unfortunately, but extremely grateful for his treatment and speedy evacuation. Mike, who organised the evacuation, became an instant family friend and was invited to supper. Lance Corporal Jodie Hill, who was now based with 1 Platoon, had treated the man, and provoked a certain amount of interest in the local Afghans. She caused confusion and attracted admiration in equal measure, just as she had done with the Tiger Team.

In counter-insurgency the front line is not a line in the dust, it is waged over the human geography. It is politics with an admixture of other means; the battle for trust and support over coercion. In Afghanistan, however, people trust what they can see. This leads to what I felt at the time was becoming our greatest problem, trying to explain the paradox that the presence of a patrol base may bring explosions and fighting, but people feel safer. It is a hard sell to everyone: locals, soldiers, and especially those back home, who are living every day in fear of the uniformed knock at the door.

The combination of me trying to make positive conversation on the phone set against the stream of bad news with regard to casualties is difficult for anyone to bear. Rachel had got the wives together for lunch before Christmas and they had stayed into the evening. The rest of 4 Rifles were enjoying the Christmas festivities with a note of caution. So if things were difficult in Helmand, then in the UK they were no better.

At the start of the New Year Rachel took Henry for his assessment and diagnosis. At that time things did not look good. Mute, locked in a world that he did not understand aged three years and six months, still not potty trained. He could not make sense of us nor we of him. The diagnosis was unequivocal. Autism. Or more properly, an Autistic Spectrum Disorder, but it was too soon to know what his prospects would be. Autism has powerful negative connotations, one fears the worst, and the worst can indeed be pretty bad: a life in full-time care. Louis Theroux has recently done a good job showing what it is like with a child at the far end of the spectrum in his series *Tough Love*. Rachel waited several days to phone me, wondering if the distraction would be worth it and whether it all could wait until I came back for R and R in the middle of February. She decided it couldn't wait.

I remember the phone call not because I was suddenly inconsolable, but because of my lack of reaction. I would like to say that somehow I had already accepted that he might be autistic after all of our conversations in the summer and during the tour, and this was only confirmation. I would of course be lying. A formal diagnosis jolts your expectations, your hopes and dreams. There are not many autistic England cricketers. Or not that I knew of. Ironically by then I had relinquished most of my hopes and dreams for my family and my children. I had but one left. Let me get out of this alive to see them again. My personal battle was not to let this hope completely overtake what I had to do as a job. I balanced the argument that it was never going to be worth getting back if I was left with a lifetime of regret for simply getting through. That is a strong and destructive paradox of emotion. But in this instance it made me almost instantly accepting of something that I know for many is very difficult. I don't underestimate it; I just happened to be in a situation that made it a good deal easier.

For now Henry had autism and Rachel just had to cope. Whilst I tried to be a supportive husband and loving father through the medium of a thirty-minute phone call once a week, it was never going to be anywhere near enough. Yet diagnosis, as many parents of children on the spectrum will tell you, opened the door to a million useful strategies and represented the start of progress for him and us that continues to this day.

Yet the big decision of early January in northern Sangin was how often to use the road. There were two competing schools of thought. Little and often, or only when necessary? We had been doing little and often for three and half weeks, forced on us by the fact it had taken far longer to get the right quantity of stores and ammunition in place than we had expected, coupled with almost daily trips to escort disposal teams to defuse roadside bombs. Now we had things more or less in place I wanted to go for a routine resupply, just enough, just in time. Do the quick runs down and back up to Inkerman, dropping off and picking up like a bus, then an occasional serious effort escorting the resupply truck down with a full drop-off that always took at least thirty minutes at each base, however much Pat Hyde chivvied and chased. It gave the enemy time to set up nasty surprises. Moreover we were fast running out of places from which to over-watch the blind spots on the side of the route. Going back into compounds that we had previously occupied, even if they had an Afghan resident, was a very dangerous sport. We always tried to use variations in route, but given the fixed nature of our locations this would inevitably be increasingly difficult. So the second option was to limit the trips to once every four or five days. I hoped that this would give the platoons the chance to get into some kind of routine. The new checkpoint, 'Pritch's', built with a Hesco wall and a cuplock sangar, was put up in a herculean overnight effort by Sgt Mac and Corporal Baglin with a section from 1 Platoon, who lifted 3,000 filled sandbags up two floors. Each man lifted 350 sandbags. At one a minute that is nearly seven hours of step climbing with a full sandbag. It would be manned by 1, 2 and 3 platoons on rotation to distribute the burden as equally as possible.

Pat Hyde reckoned that by not going on the route as much it might be more difficult to clear when the time came. We were both right. And the choice, yet again, was one of Hobson's making.

After ten days in Inkerman it was definitely time to get back down the road. The CO wanted to get all the company commanders together in the Battlegroup HQ in Sangin. He was also keen to come and see how we were getting on. He was only coming for a day and given our record at getting up and down the road in a day, which was not all that good, I decided to meet him early. After the meeting in Sangin I would then visit all the platoons on the way back up for a proper visit, or at least that was the plan. It was a bit risky because Ben was going on R and R, so Ed would have to hold the fort in Inkerman for a couple of days before I returned.

The cover for R and R breaks had been planned carefully to ensure that we were not left with any critical weakness. In normal instances a platoon commander might have stepped up to be the 2IC, but they were essential to the patrol bases so it would have to be Ed. There were enough old hands around to give him a steer if required, Freddie Fryer more than anyone, who was beginning to get more than a little fed up with his platoon being used as casualty replacements. That situation was never going to get any better.

So as we began to secure the route for the CO to come up the road the Taliban busied themselves trying to take us on. The escalation in violence in the previous weeks had meant that more resources were allocated to us, those owned by the Divisional and Theatre HQs. Foremost amongst these were the Reaper drones. A Reaper is an armed drone the like of which one hears so much about now, but four years ago they were less notorious. Taking off from Kandahar, they were flown from Las Vegas by a pilot in an armchair, beaming pictures to the Joint Tactical Air Controller on the ground, in my case Lance

Sergeant 'Dinger' Bellman, from which we could confirm the positive identification of an insurgent and authorise a strike with a hellfire missile.

The drone and the firing all happens beyond the limit of sound and view so the attack comes as something of a surprise to the insurgent. A section from 3 Platoon were pinned down and as the gunman was operating from a tight alley in a built up area, precision attack was the only way of dealing with him. It may come as a surprise – no one was more shocked than me – that I had not done a single drone attack in training. Not even in theory. In all we did ten Reaper strikes. It is not knife in teeth, cold steel soldiering, but with the technology at our disposal there are plenty of other ways to 'neutralise' the insurgent – a strange euphemism that does not do justice to the act. For Riflemen it is a matter of professional pride to be able to shoot straight. The trick, as I began to discover, with using the drones is to fuse the information available and set up those controlling the weapon to be in the best situation to fire. According to our rules of engagement, the legal framework that allows us to use lethal force against the insurgents, the final judgement was my responsibility with those above me able to intervene if they felt I had got it wrong. This is often a very difficult finding to make based on a profusion of factors. By far the most important aspect is to make sure that we only kill those who are positively identified as insurgents.

Having got to the point where I had spoken to the Battlegoup HQ and agreed that this was the best way of dealing with the problem, Dinger turned to me and said 'I need your initials'.

'You what?'

'I need your initials for the bomb.' As I looked even more quizzically at him, he explained. 'The pilot who is going to release the weapon needs your authority to fire'.

'OK. R.G.S. Romeo Golf Sierra.'

'Roger that, Romeo Golf Sierra.' Dinger then spoke to the pilot. 'Hello Codie 21 this is Widow 26 (Dinger's callsign, no irony there either), my commander Romeo Golf Sierra authorises launch'.

A brief exchange followed telling us that it would take however many seconds for the rocket to get to the target. Those few seconds can seem like 3,000 hovering over the picture still beaming in.

BOOM. The target was some 400 metres from the patrol base.

'Splash.'

'Target identified, target down.'

We then watched a very slick casualty evacuation chain in progress. The Reaper followed the now dead man for twenty clicks, all the way to a village in the upper Sangin valley where he was taken into a building with a red cross on the roof! The van was tracked back to Sangin, where it was stopped by another company and the driver taken to see the NDS for questioning. Genius.

Ten minutes after the strike Ben arrived at PB Shuga. He had been in the back of the CSMs Mastiff on his way to go out via Sangin on his way to R and R.

'I wait three months and then I'm bloody stuck in a vehicle when it happens...'

'I'm sure there will be more. Enjoy your leave.'

Be under no illusion, those moments were personally some of the most adrenaline-fuelled of the tour. The imminence of the threat, fight or flight, produced the strongest of physiological responses. My judgements were often rather easier than some others: pity the Rifleman with the child laying an IED in his sights. Finding the mental space to make the right decision became easier, but the aftermath always left me cold.

Success in the morning meant an easier ride in the afternoon; the insurgents were busy with their grief and the CO was distracted by the latest news. We travelled into Sangin in the early evening. It was good to see the other OCs. Command can be lonely; a lot is made of it. I felt it most keenly as a platoon commander until I realised that the loneliness is largely self-inflicted. There is an army saying, or at least one that is used a lot in the army, that 95 per cent of pressure is self-induced. I usually found that the antidote to that pressure lay in seeking out Riflemen for a chat. Some would be awkward, but to most I seemed far removed from their daily life and I hope that talking to me did as much for them as it did for me. Nonetheless one's peers have a better sense of the type of pressure one faces daily and it is always good to be able to compare notes in relative privacy. In addition we got the usual pep talk about mid-tour standards and some interesting briefs on the wider political situation in Sangin from the Political Officer and the Stabilisation Officer. It was, in short, diabolical; the place was being run by an illiterate gangster who had little or no interest in bringing public services to the people of Sangin. Propping him up for so long probably put us in bad odour with the locals. None of us were to know, but there were changes afoot for him and his cronies. After we finished I went back to 2 Platoon in PB Blenheim.

I had lunch with Mo, the Afghan Platoon Commander, again. Things were going well with the partnering he assured me. He liked 'Captain Charlie'. Charlie and Neil, the platoon commander mentor from the Yorkshire Regiment, had a good cop–bad cop thing going that was working fairly well. The 2 Platoon accommodation was still very basic, but was much improved from when I had visited in December. I had wanted to go out on a joint patrol to see how things had improved over the last month with the ANA. Corporal Ricky 'Furgie' Furgusson was going to give orders just before sunset for a relatively simple patrol to see if we could catch those trying to lay devices in the Western Culvert between 2 and 3 Platoon. This would mean going out at 2200 and coming back in at about 0400.

Just before orders the Afghans pulled out. Charlie and Neil tried to get them back on board to no avail. At this point I decided that if the Afghans weren't going then I might as well get a good night's sleep. I expressed my disappointment to the ANA commander, but nothing would move him. In hindsight it may have been because he was not going out and I was that he pulled the remainder of his troops. Afghans have a strong concept of 'face' and will do almost anything to save face; I can only imagine he did not want to lose face in front of me, but it was frustrating. We decided Furgie would go anyway.

In the early hours of 13 January Furgie stepped on an IED. He was the fourth man to walk over the piece of ground where the IED was placed. Lance Corporal 'Murph' Murphy had to drag him out of the building. Ricky sustained multiple injuries. Both his legs were missing; five of ten digits from his hands were gone or partly gone, as was a good deal of the flesh from his wrists. Where the force of the IED had picked him up and smashed his head against a wall his left eye was a gaping hole; his lips and most of the left side of his face were badly mangled. Sergeant 'H' Henry charged down the road on his quad to pick him up.

The medics took him to the med tent and made sure the tourniquets were in place and he was getting fluids. He was loaded onto an MIRT, still alive, by a thread. Charlie came into the ops room, ashen. Furgie was an extremely popular member of the platoon, the Company and the Battalion. He had been on the boxing team for years and had fought many legendary battles in the ring. Inter Battalion boxing nights are pure testosterone and partisanship, and the 4 Rifles and 2 RGJ gymnasiums had rung to many a chorus of 'Furgie's goin' t'getchya.' He would be a deep loss.

Charlie, having seen Furgie come in, was not hopeful. I went and did the after-action review with the patrol. They were clearly all very shaken. Furgie was their life. I remembered on a previous visit him turning to one of the young Riflemen and saying with his strong Telford twang in the Brummie style: 'Don't put the knife from the butter in the jam. What would your mam say?'

From manners to matters of life and death he was their man, and now they would have to do without him. Lance Corporal Murphy would step up until a replacement came. Murph had transformed on operations. In camp, back in Bulford the previous year, I had concluded he was not fit enough, too idle: I didn't want him in A Company. What a misjudgement. On operations he was diligent, brave and reacted quickly enough to that IED strike to bring Furgie back to Blenheim alive, even if the prospects for his continued survival were appalling. The casualty evacuation chain starts at the point of wounding. In the platinum ten minutes, and the golden hour, everything has to go right, from horrific injury to hospital. Stemming traumatic bleeding under fire or in the dark is hard, getting the casualty organised, protected and transported back to base in a limited time requires monumental physical effort, taking personal risk and working as a team. It is all against a clock; the body clock of the casualty who is fighting to stay alive. They can only do so if the right first aid drills are carried out, the right fluids, drugs and care are given at the right time and in the right location with the correct facilities. There are some wounds of battle you can do nothing about, but the speed and efficiency of the care given on the ground can only help.

I made it back to Inkerman six days later having been to all the bases. Ed was near the end of his tether. It had been a rough few days. He was being called upon to organise things at the Inkerman end without much top cover. He was fairly relieved to see me return and presented me immediately with a long list of things we needed to do urgently. Everyone was still worried about Furgie, who somehow was still alive, and I could do little to console them. Anyone who had seen him knew that brain damage was a very real possibility. Only after a couple of weeks did any 'good' news start coming out – if one could call it good. It seemed the damage round his eye had allowed his brain to swell and as a result there was a small chance it might not have done significant damage. I began to wonder if death might not be more merciful than what potentially lay ahead for Furgie.

In the aftermath of the Furgie incident I finally shouted as loudly as I could about the acute deficiency of radios. I had been going on about it for for weeks and now months, and the lack of radios had almost caused a critical delay in getting Furgie treatment. By luck a Rifleman on a personal radio was able to relay to a guard post that was able to relay to the ops room what was going on. I emailed a friend who was working on the equipment desk in Army HQ in the UK to see if the requests made already had been passed to someone who could do something about it. This was circumventing five layers of the chain of command, but desperate times called for desperate measures. The reply I got back gave me no faith that the system was responding: each thought the other elements were blocking. So I launched an unignorable missive up the chain. I was grateful to be silent copied in to the version that the CO sent on up, which was equally scathing if a little more to the point.

The risk of IEDs on the road was increasing, as were the number of small arms engagements with rifles and grenades. Corporal Chico Bryant had been blown off his feet by an IED with a directional charge. If he had been closer to the wall it would have taken his head off. Patrols were contacted nearly every time they went out. It was a trying time. Every single platoon had either found IEDs, been hit by them, or been taken to them, in most cases all three. In all of the chaos of the explosions and the rip of lead it appeared, somehow, that we were winning the battle for hearts and minds. Locals would come into the patrol bases to request wheat seed. Others came for medical examination and occasionally we would get the location of an IED. Usually it was one that was near their house that they wanted removed.

We, or rather the Battalion HQ stabilisation team, contracted a local builder to try to repair and strengthen the culverts on the 611. We wanted a mesh and iron grid put on them to prevent explosives being put under the road. The contractor charged a large sum, took a cut and then subcontracted to another: this process went on until four local men were contracted close to PB Shuga. It was an outstanding example of the way corruption works in Afghanistan. The men who got into the culvert were being paid only a handful of dollars for their time and effort. They dragged out a pressure-pad IED from the area where they were working. They stepped on another and Tom found himself organising the evacuation of two of the men and thereafter trying to repair the damage with the local community. The same thing happens on a larger scale as the aid budget goes into the Afghan government and only a miniscule proportion ever gets spent in Afghanistan. Our esteemed ambassador at the time, Sherard Cowper-Coles, thought the army unfit for the responsibility of dealing with aid. My view is that it only gets spent on what people really need by those on the ground. Even at Battlegroup level 90 per cent of the funds went in the subcontracting process. The higher you start the worse it gets.

Trying to protect or destroy just one culvert of the seven on our stretch of the 611 cost fifteen lives. Locals, the ANA, the enemy and A Company all lost men there. In one of the early clearances of that area one of the IED operators had found a wire. Unsure about where it would lead and lacking sufficient protection to find out he sent down an electric pulse. Expecting one explosion, we were slightly shocked when three went off. It was a 'daisy chain' device designed to do damage right along a patrol. The attacks were getting more sophisticated. Up at the Gul Agha Wadi 1 Platoon found three pull-cords leading to the Wadi.

In Sareagar 7 Platoon had done a good job since coming down from Kajaki. As it was marginally quieter than the other areas they had begun to forge links with the locals. The base was right on the edge of the 611 and had good views of the road. The attacks against them came in fits and starts. When they happened it was from multiple firing points and used the whole range of weapons the enemy could throw at them. Whilst there had been lots of attacks further down towards Sangin, 7 Platoon had seen fewer daily attacks. When they came they were spectacular. They, and I, were quietly pleased with their efforts. Then, after a month, the enemy worked out that there was a small blind spot in between two of their sangars. We knew it was there, but did not believe anyone would be audacious enough to put something in. Whilst 7 Platoon couldn't see the ten-metre square patch of road, they had a number of ways to mitigate the problem; they counted the people, cars and other traffic through and it was all within earshot.

Now there was a mangled wreck of Mastiff, no injuries on the inside, under their noses. Rob couldn't believe it. How had they dug in such a large device so close? It must have been enormous to do that much damage. It turned out they had used our own tactics against us and 7 Platoon's problem originated between 1979 and 1989 and in our use of VCPs. It wasn't until three days later that we realised what they had done and with what.

The area round 1 Platoon in Bariolai was becoming increasingly dangerous due to the amount of pattern-setting that 1 Platoon were forced into. Their problem was the Gul Agha Wadi; the largest of the Wadis that had to be crossed from Inkerman to Sangin, and the battle to control it was the focus of most of 1 Platoon's operations. There were very few compounds that overlooked the Wadi and by mid-January we had used all of them more than once. Due to the bombs in the road, which meant that the vehicles needed to move the people around were damaged, the backup plan for moving men back to their patrol bases was to go on foot. It was the least preferable option but workable in extremis.

7 Platoon had a couple of people they needed to get to 1 Platoon, so they patrolled into the green zone to link up. 1 Platoon provided a reserve section, and 7 Platoon would pass back through their location at the end of the patrol. Pat Hyde and his crew were working with a bomb-disposal team further down the road. On the way down they had noticed a dodgy piece of ground which they had avoided, but wanted to investigate on return. Meanwhile 7 Platoon came under fire in the green zone from Jusalay. This was not unusual, but this time Rob had enough troops on the ground and, with 1 Platoon in support, 7 Platoon advanced. The ICOM went wild. 'Quick arm the IEDs the infidel is coming.' There was a building we had suspected was being used as a base for insurgents in Jusalay and Rob got to within a hundred metres. The atmospherics were terrible, with people fleeing out of the area. The HQ tried to get air support to no avail. With no ability to look in depth, no readily deployable reserve and the casevac vehicles the wrong side of a suspect area, I called Rob back. He had made the point going forward, but the risk did not seem to match any potential reward.

The people got dropped off with the 1 Platoon section and 7 Platoon got back safely. Mike, who was with the section from 1 Platoon, aimed to cross the Wadi north of the most vulnerable point and swing back in to Patrol Base Bariolai. As they got into the Wadi they came under fire from the south side; they took cover, but as they got up Rifleman Peter Aldridge stepped on an IED.

The Company Sergeant Major had an ATO called Dan in his wagon. He and his search team had been nicknamed Desperate Dan and the God Squad. The team had suffered early losses in the tour and they all bore the physical and mental scars. That's not to say they weren't extremely good at their job. They operated with us many times. They took great risks on our behalf and that day was no exception. On hearing the situation report on the radio net the CSM turned them round and drove them back to just short of the suspect area.

He put it bluntly to them they had a choice about the risk of driving past again or saving a man with both his legs missing. They agreed to go on and offered prayers as they did so. There was no explosion.

By the time Pat Hyde got there the MIRT was on its way and there was nothing more for him to do. Mike had been injured in the blast as well and needed to get on the MIRT. Jodie Hill was treating Pete and as they loaded him onto the helicopter he turned to her and said 'Tell mum I love her.'

Peter Aldridge, or 'Fatback' as he was known to his platoon, died of his wounds in Camp Bastion. I wrote this eulogy that night.

Rifleman Peter Aldridge was a mighty fine Rifleman. He had joined the Army straight from school and trained for a year at the Army Foundation College in Harrogate. He had brains as well as brawn. Fit, strong and brave he gave his life trying to make sure that the path was safe for his section. He had been trained in specialist weapons. He wanted to be a Sniper. Like all those who had been trained and educated at the College he was a future leader. He aspired to be a section commander. He will be sorely missed, and the Army will be much the poorer for the passing of his talent. But it will be his family and friends that will feel his loss most deeply and our thoughts are with them. He had all the qualities of a true Rifleman. He held no fear of rank; admirably direct; an appetite for adventure; a quick tongue; an easy laugh and broad shoulders. I have enjoyed his company on adventure training tearing down a Welsh hillside on a mountain bike and on operations over a brew putting Afghanistan to rights. On operations he carried the fight to the enemy but was mature enough to understand the requirements for restraint. In England he shared his room with his mountain bike and all his extra kit. In Afghanistan he has helped to wrest control of an area from the insurgent. He was always to be found at the front. Trusted by his superiors and his peers in situations where only those with his qualities can be trusted. We trusted him and he would now trust us to live up to his example.

Others were doing the same thing.

Rifleman Craig Hitchins was in Inkerman on return from R and R. He and Pete had shared all the hardships of battle.

Aldridge was known to most of us as 'Fatback'. He was a bloke full of emotion, who had time for anyone. Fatback would spend most of his time on camp either spray-painting his kit or with his girlfriend. One story has always stuck in my mind about him, from when we spent a long cold night on a lurk, with little warm kit and the odd shower of rain. Neither of us could get any sleep until he turned to me and asked me if we could spoon! Very quickly we were spooning and fighting for the comfy ground. When first light broke he woke me up and whispered 'Everyone is looking at us!'. I opened my eyes to find our platoon staring and sniggering. The banter very quickly started. Fatback was a key member of the platoon who will be dearly missed.

The section from 1 Platoon got back to PB Bariolai. Serjeant 'Jona' Jones was on R and R and Mike was in Camp Bastion having been wounded by the shrapnel from the device. The platoon needed leadership and all of the obvious candidates were the wrong side of several devices that we knew about on the 611. As soon as I had the news of Pete's death confirmed from the hospital in Camp Bastion, I got onto the net to talk to 1 Platoon. The man I spoke to was Corporal Mark 'Bobby' Charlton. Bobby, as he was universally known, was my best corporal. Before the tour he had been on the Platoon Serjeants Course in Brecon where he had got a distinction. Only the top 5 per cent of infantry soldiers ever go on that course, and only three or four on each course of over a hundred gets a distinction – the very best of the very best. He had been the section commander behind Rifleman Reece Terry on the first Company operation with the Special Forces.

I tried to be quite matter of fact, making out that what I was about to ask him to do would be as straightforward as I made it sound.

'Right, Corporal Charlton, I need you to do a few things for me.' This was not a time for familiarity.

'Sir.'

'You need to do the after-action review…'

'Done sir.'

'Well done. You need to break the news to the platoon and then you need to get the platoon to write eulogies; those that want to. Get someone to read them out on the net so we can type them up. Then tonight you need to conduct a memorial service and then you'll need to think about your plan for the patrol in support of the bomb-disposal team tomorrow to try and exploit the area where Rifleman Aldridge was killed.'

'Sir. …Is that all?'

'Yes. I'll give you a call in a couple of hours to hear how you are all getting on. You'll get a new platoon commander just as soon as the road is opened; until then you are the Platoon Commander and JD is the Platoon Serjeant.'

A few hours later, as Collette, our doctor, took down the last of the dictated eulogies, she suddenly looked stunned and was clearly on the verge of tears. She left the ops room in a hurry; I waited a second then followed.

'Tell mum I love her' – the words of a dying man reported by the medic who treated him as part of her eulogy to him. They cannot not fail to affect anyone who has a jot of sympathy for the families of the forces. When I saw Bobby a couple of days later, he felt he had been happy with what he had been asked to do when he came off the radio until it had transformed into the hardest thing of his life: a sudden plunge into the reality of the pastoral and tactical world of the platoon commander. The next day, with 1 Platoon covering, Desperate Dan and the God Squad moved into the Wadi. The Taliban were waiting. They withdrew with bullet holes in their Vallons. And in the stack of traffic that waited in a queue backed up all the way past 7 Platoon the anti-tank mines, proper Russian anti-tank mines, military-grade explosive, none of this fertiliser and fuel rubbish, were being laid in the road by Patrol Base Ezeray.

Colour Serjeant Williams, or unflatteringly, if accurately, 'Bog-eyed Will', took over as 1 Platoon commander. He was the FSG 2IC and a very safe pair of hands. With the FSG split to the four winds he was as bored as Freddie. Freddie could have gone, but with Pat Hyde just about to go on R and R I needed Freddie in Inkerman. We desperately needed to find a more sustainable approach to the security of the road.

*Chapter 12*

# Afghans on the March

The attempted clearance of the Wadi and exploitation of the scene of the explosion had caused the traffic to back up in both directions. Most of the IEDs we faced were made of homemade explosive. This is a simple mix that requires a detonator to accelerate the burn and produce the explosion, but in the hierarchy of explosives it is still relatively slow burning compared to military-grade explosive. It sounds different. It booms, like the slamming of a heavy door, whereas the military grenades and mines have a higher, sharper crack. Needless to say the military stuff is smaller, more easily concealed and considerably more destructive. As Pat Hyde drove back to Inkerman from Bariolai an IED exploded underneath the lead vehicle for the second time in four days. This was no longer funny. How were they getting this stuff in?

For once in his life, Pat Hyde was nervous of moving the vehicles. Just as well. Between the two vehicles was a now obvious patch of fresh earth. The bomb-disposal team, still with them, investigated. It was a double-stacked Russian anti-tank mine in a shallow grave, covered by earth. Not patted down, just in the wheel ruts on the road. Obvious to a foot patrol, but just well enough concealed from the commander and the gunner in a Mastiff. Luckily the Mastiff had done its job again, and there were no injuries except a ringing in the ears, the vehicle absorbing the blast. One of the 1 Platoon sections had noticed people getting out of their cars in the queue. It could only have happened with the cover of the other cars in the queue, just as when we stopped the traffic in VCPs outside Patrol Base Ezeray, Rob assumed. Up to now we had always been more worried about the security of the VCP, so had funnelled cars through. Now it became just as important to keep the traffic flowing, but the risks weren't getting any less.

The average lifespan of a Mastiff between wheel-removing explosions on the 611 at this point was nine days. The team from the Corps of Royal Electrical and Mechanical Engineers (REME) in Inkerman had their work cut out trying to fix them up enough to get them back out of the gate. These guys, and the work they did, rapidly became my top administrative priority. Sergeant Hall and his small team, which included Afghan civilian help, worked some very long days to ensure our safety. I have included a weekly assessment report that I sent at the end of January at Appendix 3. It was summarized thus:

A difficult week in terms of casualties with 42 and 41 bearing the brunt. But the prospect of the ANA in SHUGA and BARIOLAI is extremely heartening. The fact that locals around SHUGA actively encouraged the move is more heartening still.

Pat Hyde, the CSM, reluctantly went on R and R. In his place up stepped WO2 Freddie Fryer. Freddie had been champing at the bit in Inkerman. The events of the previous week had put an end to any notion that we would get his Fire Support Group back together anytime soon, but stepping up to CSM for nearly three weeks would be a welcome distraction. As Pat Hyde left Ben came back, bringing with him another Tom, a Rifles captain who would take over as second-in-command and allow Ben to command the Company while I was away for the best part of three weeks on leave. During the couple of weeks leading up to my departure on R and R, a fresh pair of eyes and the extra manpower was very welcome.

The following week was going to be an important one. The ANA had received orders to move to Patrol Base Shuga from Blenheim. It was barely a kilometre between the two bases, so hardly blitzkrieg, but given the context it was a hugely significant step. Two months previously they had barely left camp. Certainly any suggestion that they might patrol east was dismissed out of hand. Now we had to get them safely into Shuga. For that they would have to cross the western culvert, so before they went anywhere near it we would have to make sure it was clear.

Desperate Dan and his search team were by now a permanent fixture in Sangin and near enough continually in Inkerman. Dan was a captain at the time. ATO's come in all shapes and sizes and Dan was the tallest, thinnest man ever to make the long walk. If physically they are different they share a common virtue: bravery. Karl Ley, aka 'The Badger', might have got the George Medal for his work on Herrick 11, which was phenomenal for its quantity as much as anything else, but three other ATO's were killed in Afghanistan over the winter of 2009–10. Dan was on the more methodical side of a very methodical group of individuals. We had a long discussion about how we would try to clear the culvert, but in any option getting some protection in for the search team would be the first job.

2 and 3 Platoon were tasked with this protection. As 3 Platoon were clearing a compound for their use as an overwatch position, Rifleman Armstrong Pollock stepped on an IED. The explosion tore off two legs and an arm. This was the same Rifleman Pollock who had been shot in the leg and returned to Inkerman three weeks later; now he had no legs at all. The IED launched Rifleman Sergeant some thirty metres, into the next compound, deafening him but otherwise he had scarcely a scratch on him. 3 Platoon did a magnificent job in the casualty evacuation. Having come into the compound over ladders they put

plan C or even plan D into action, blasting out of the compound with a Light Anti-Structure Munition (LASM). Despite the severity of his injuries Rifleman Pollock was medically stable within four hours. At a time when IED victims were routinely getting tens and even hundreds of units of blood to keep them alive he had just nine. The tourniquets had gone on so quickly he had pretty much only lost the blood that was in his legs and arm at the time they were blown off. He is still recovering from his wounds and is still in the Army.

After this Dan and I had a frank exchange about the relative risk of trying to put in a cordon to protect him and the search team and their risk in the search. The whole area had been soaked for days with surveillance drones and we had not seen anything. We could give him close protection but not a cordon. He relented reluctantly. The team had a mechanical device that could investigate the area that would reduce the risk. And then if that didn't work they would use the team. The mechanical device failed almost immediately so the search team went into the Wadi.

Freddie escorted Dan and the team down to the culvert in the Mastiffs. All went well; the search team had completed nearly all of the first part of their task when they found a device. All was quiet on the insurgent radios. The eyes in the sky could see nothing untoward, so Dan went forward to deal with it. The search team huddled in the Wadi. Dan got on his knees to start cutting. There was then an almighty explosion. Freddie was on the net straight away.

'Four Zero Alpha, Four Nine you'll've heard that. The dust is all over the place I'll go forward when it's down but it was right in the middle of them.'

'Four Nine, Four Zero Alpha, roger out.'

Freddie said afterwards it was like seeing ghosts emerge. Covered in dust, every man in the team, and finally Dan, walked out of the Wadi.

'Four Zero Alpha, Four Nine, you're not going to believe this, 'cos I don't an' I can see 'em. They're all alright.'

It was very welcome news and a massive relief. The device had been very large and very close to Dan and his team. After such a close call they came back to Inkerman to regain some compos mentis. Dan had a good point that he was quick to make. 'That's why you have a cordon, to stop that happening.'

I had a point too. 'If we did that we would have cordons for cordons for cordons.'

The discussion wasn't getting us very far and it didn't resolve the fact that we still needed to check the culvert before the ANA came over it.

The next stop was one of calculated risk. If the locals wanted the road open, perhaps all the enemy were trying to do was target the checks. Answer: don't do the check and just drive over the culvert. It was risky, but with few options left the following morning Freddie covered his ears, opened his mouth and drove over the culvert. No bang.

'Four Zero Alpha, Four Nine, well that wasn't very exciting – kna' wot I mean?'

I did but I thought we'd had quite enough excitement getting over that culvert. The way was now clear for the ANA troops to go to Shuga. The Kandack commander Colonel Wadood, named 'Wat-a-dood' by Pat Hyde early on and by the rest of the Company shortly thereafter, wanted to talk to his warriors soon after their arrival. That meant an influx of ANA from central Sangin to guard the route. Charlie briefed them in Blenheim that under no circumstances should they go into the wadi by the western culvert. The route was clear but the culvert was not. Two hours later an ANA warrior stepped on an IED in the western culvert. His comrades watched him bleed to death, too frightened to go in to rescue him. The ANA were paralysed on one of the most dangerous spots in Afghanistan. Too fearful to go and fetch the body, but required to stay to guard the route.

Corporal Chico Bryant turned up. He and his Vallon man, Rifleman Needham, calmly moved into the wadi and collected the dead warrior and then proceeded to Patrol Base Shuga. The ANA followed. Chico became an instant hero to the ANA. He earned a tour's worth of trust in the space of thirty minutes. Colonel Wat-a-dood Wadood welcomed the warriors to PB Shuga later that day.

We then proceeded to visit all of the other bases, showing him where the ANA might be housed in each patrol base and meeting with his general approval. His visit to Inkerman on that day was an interesting moment. He and his Serjeant Major spotted the Russian Kamaz truck that had been left when the ANA platoon had left Inkerman a year earlier. He pointed to it as I tried to joke that we would drive it back in exchange for some warriors for Inkerman. It was a joke that fell utterly flat as he shook his head and spoke the only word of English I ever heard him use, 'Inkerman – bad'. Chico had got us some trust back, but the shame inflicted on the ANA previously in Inkerman had not been expunged even by his courageous recovery of a dead man.

\*  \*  \*  \*  \*

In the first two weeks of February a Rifleman in 7 Platoon observed a child laying an IED in the road, shot at him and missed. My feeling was that he had done so deliberately. In essence it was a warning shot. But warning shots had been banned by ISAF HQ, much to my indignation. The problem was that too many soldiers across Afghanistan were firing 'warning' shots and hitting. Across Afghanistan innocents were being killed. Lots of them. And you can't win a counter-insurgency if you are killing the very people you are supposed to be protecting.

There was only one occasion when warning shots were allowed and that was if there was time when life was threatened and it was the only option in that situation. All soldiers carry a piece of paper on operations outlining the rule that deals with the universal and immutable right to self-defence. If you are being driven at by a car in a checkpoint you can kill the driver to save your life if you cannot get out of the way. If there is time you can fire a round to try to stop the car. Afghan drivers, who must compete with the Bosnians, the Kosovars and the Italians as the world's most erratic drivers, did not seem to notice a checkpoint until they had lead coming at high velocity just in front of them.

For the remainder of the time, for individuals who were arousing suspicion, but not yet positively identified as conducting a hostile act or acting with hostile intent, we had a number of escalation measures. We could shout at them to move away. We had flares. Sometimes we carried a loud-hailer. The population and the enemy were all very used to this and they worked only at relatively close range. The only way to really get someone to move was to pop a bullet five metres from him and he moved pretty sharpish. But to do that you needed the professional skill to make sure five metres is five metres.

We had some reliable information that the enemy thought we were bad shots. It only went to prove in my own mind that most of those we identified as suspicious were indeed Taliban, just that we could not be totally sure at the time. The thing about hostile intent and a hostile act is that just because you *can* shoot someone doesn't mean you *should* and a warning shot was by far and away the best method we had of achieving the effect required. There is of course the alternative of not taking the shot at all and waiting until the suspicious activity is identified as a hostile act and then shooting the man. Unfortunately by that time he is one of a number and then you are in a fire-fight, the local population are terrified and the proportionate response of a section trapped in a fire-fight can be use of heavy machine-guns and from there the escalation can continue until you are raining down 10,000 mortars in six months. Pointless.

Just as pointless is the repetitive slaughter of tier three Taliban foot soldiers who occupy the same positions time and time again. There are many stories from Afghanistan of this kind of turkey shoot masquerading as professional soldiering. The supply of tier three insurgent manpower is limitless. They are the local population, the ones whose hearts and minds we are trying to win, the ones we are trying to protect: kill them and the way of the Pashtun requires revenge. Even with tier two Taliban there were over three million refugees to Pakistan in the Russian war. Educated and politicised in madrassas and now returned to kick out the next bunch. The killing game must really only have one function; to protect the local population. It can have a secondary effect: the enemy must be disrupted and there are times, such as when Bariolai was attacked at the beginning of March, when the platoon in defence is fighting for its life. I wrote an essay during one of my stays in Inkerman and submitted it with the other 'Young' Officers' essays that the CO thought would be useful! It is available at Appendix 4. Please forgive the Peter and Jane style. After fifteen years of Army education I have come to the conclusion that the Army is the only place where simplicity of style is valued over content. Complexity or even explanation of the most simple paradox is thought dangerous rather than useful.

As an aside, but by way of example, during my time in the Army I have written the same essay on Clausewitz three times; at Sandhurst, and on two staff courses. The first time I took some of what I had learned in Political Philosophy during my time at Warwick and got a C, the next time I rewrote it using my History A Level as a guide and got a B. As a newly-promoted major I wrote the same essay a third time using sentences of no more than two lines and words of only two syllables. That time I got an A-. But I digress.

This particular essay went under the title: 'Rules of Engagement: an analysis of current application and effect in Afghanistan.' I tried to look at both the theory and practice of rules of engagement, examining the effect of our rules of engagement from three perspectives: the local national or Afghan perspective; an insurgent perspective; and the effect on friendly (ISAF) forces. My conclusion was that the cry goes up that soldiers are too afraid to fire in the face of potential prosecution, but I thought there was strong evidence to suggest that they are not afraid enough. We are not at war. We fight in Afghanistan at the invitation of the government of Afghanistan. If we are to enforce the rule of law we must abide by the rule of law. The lack of investigations and prosecutions with regard to the adherence to the law of armed conflict, especially in regard to proportionality and discrimination, is not necessarily evidence of a conflict well fought; it might well hint at a lack of judgement and of moral courage on the part of soldiers and commanders alike. The essay is available at Appendix 4.

\* \* \* \* \*

The first two weeks of February were, in army slang, a bit of an epic. At the back end of the move of the ANA I decided that we could no longer afford to do the vulnerable point checks in the Gul Agha Wadi and the western culvert. The cost and further threat to life and limb had become too great. They needed a permanent guard. So we set up two more observation posts. The 611 south of Inkerman now had bases and checkpoints every 500 metres. The one on the Gul Agha Wadi became known as Pete's Post and the Western Checkpoint was at the western culvert. Occupying these caused some local dismay. They too came under regular attack, especially Pete's, which did seem to relieve some of the pressure on the patrol bases, at least in the short term. When attacking the posts the enemy often used the same firing points. We were doing to them what they had done to us: forcing them into patterns that we could exploit. Although, for those on the receiving end, there was a sense that we were being tied down to guarding fixed points. Hobson's choice – again.

This solution further exacerbated the problem of generating a patrolling force from each of the bases. Any potential solution relied on getting Tiger Team troops into 1 Platoon and the ANA with 2 and 3 Platoon. During February local troops were on hand most of the time. The spike in violence brought a renewed focus on us from the chain of command. We needed to get the patrol bases in a better state; build better sangars and have better observation equipment in them. The reinforcement of the culverts would be the next way to improve security on the road. Planning began for Operation Ghartse Ghadme 5, an operation that would take place at the end of February, after Moshtarak and immediately on my return from R and R. Until then we just had to hang on in there.

We could not move until then because to our south, in central Helmand, the largest operation of 11 Brigade's time in Afghanistan was about to get under way in the form of Operation Moshtarak, or 'Togetherness'. Moshtarak was an open secret. It had been planned that way. The imminent threat of overwhelming force in central Helmand was jointly planned with the ANA and had political backing at the highest level. Unsurprisingly, aside from a few strongholds there was relatively little resistance when it took place.

Even the most basic intelligence work might have deduced that unless the Taliban were going to dig in then they might go and attack where the bulk of the forces weren't, and that place might be the Sangin Valley. There was good evidence that fighters came north just at the point when the resources to defeat them were moving south. My engineer troop, Bones, Staff Mac and the lads, went off to build new bases. Bases that would have fortified 'cuplock' sangars, water pumps, telephones and generators – in fact everything we wanted and had not got, in the harsh reality of being down the Brigadier's list of priorities.

There were three obvious changes to the insurgent tactics: fewer IEDS, more small arms attacks for longer and against all the bases in a day. The sheer volume of incidents in this time frame was beginning to make us all jittery. Especially with sections of ten sitting in the checkpoints, I certainly was nearly at the end of my tether. I remember the only time I lost my temper with those in the operations room and particularly with Ben was at about this time. I have always believed that it is better for commanders to exude a calm authority rather than ranting and raving, even if that is what is going on inside. My favourite saying from my early education as a Green Jacket officer is 'Everything matters but nothing matters frightfully.' As a company commander, if one continually yanks on the tiller or bawls people out progress inevitably slows down. If every step requires an instruction and confirmation to and from the top to move, or stop, with feedback on progress, people get more worried about the reporting than they do about the progress. The higher you get the worse the effect.

On the day in question we were discussing a simple administrative move that involved Pat Hyde's group and a couple of the platoons. The role of the Company HQ in this instance is a simple coordination role: an assessment of the risks and deciding what happens where and when. I had weighed the risk of a particular platoon moving first as too great, because it would have left another going through a very dangerous area after nine am, even though it might have been easier for the remainder. Having done their estimate the platoon commanders came back to Ben and asked if they could change the running order. Ben agreed and then came to find me to confirm. I was clearly having a bad day and for once I saw red. There were hot words in the ops room. I remember saying something along the lines of 'It's my plan and don't fuck with it.' The truth of it was that Ben had done everything right except checking *after* agreeing rather than before. And to give him his due he had tried to do that as well; I was doing something else no one else could do for me not immediately in the vicinity of the ops room. The public savaging in any circumstance has to be used sparingly as a management tool. I found the message is rarely heard by the individual getting the rebuke and the rest of the audience take away a whole variety of messages, some of which can be unhelpful. The most obvious of them is that you undermine a reputation for approachability, listening and understanding that is worth far more, in my view of leadership, than being thought of as distant, aloof and authoritarian. With military ranks and culture the accusation of being out of touch and unapproachable is an easy cliché, and like so many clichés is rooted in the truth.

Having said all that, it *was* increasingly important to me to own the plan. There were so many things that had happened that keeping responsibility for the final decision became very important to me. If I was going to be responsible then I wanted to be responsible for my plan not someone else's, at least until it did not survive contact with the enemy – at which point you trust that people know your intent and act accordingly, even if not precisely how you might have done it. But it was an indication of just how frayed I was getting that I truly lost my temper for the first time in the tour.

Of course things then change on the ground. The enemy gets a say in the execution of a plan and especially where he has the best knowledge of the ground and the population. You try to limit his ability to exploit those strengths. A good example of one of his strengths in our area was during an early patrol from PB Bariolai. Mike and his team came within a compound's length of catching an insurgent. When they realised he had evaded them they stopped at a compound nearby and asked a young teenager who the insurgent was, not thinking they would get any reply.

To their amazement the boy gave him the insurgent's call-sign, or nickname, which he used on the radio. Not only that, but he reeled off another twenty-seven names of those who were operating in our area at the time. I have likened it to my brother being able to name the entire Manchester United squad at roughly the same age. These guys were their heroes for a lack of other heroes. You could have had a game of insurgent top trumps. I sometimes wondered about meeting one of them. If I had a personal favourite, he went by the name of Mujaheed. He had delivered a furious and hilarious outburst against his fighters who had missed an ambush against us, only giving away the fact that he wasn't with them at the time. I doubt we were so very different, him and me. Same time, same place, either side of the same COIN – 'scuse the pun. That's a joke for the military doctrinaires, a small audience.

We did actually catch a local insurgent. Or at least Corporal John 'JD' Dolton and his section caught one. He was a short fat man who had driven on a motorbike into a snap VCP carried out Northern Ireland-stylee. Good tactics, a little luck and some stupidity on his part had got him arrested. He showed us where he had laid a false IED in a culvert to facilitate an ambush. He was escorted on foot down the road in broad daylight and delivered to the NDS in Sangin. We weren't ambushed on that occasion. Seeing the enemy at close quarters had taken some of the myth and mystery out of the fighting prowess of the Taliban. Too often they had been cast as shadows; by getting into the patrol bases and checkpoints they were forced out of the shadows to fight, on to ground that we knew as well as they did.

We began to have some success against the enemy. A number of IED layers blew themselves up, which might have suggested some novices. In order to try to get IEDs in on the road a variety of rather obvious tactics were being used. Tractors broke down, animals were herded across random stretches of the road and tyres were changed, all of which the sentries were alive to and now, being close enough, were able to deal with without recourse to lethal force. And with Afghan troops stationed with most of the platoons they were able to move them on very quickly. By the time I left for R and R we had not been hit with an IED for a couple of weeks. I hoped we were beginning to win that battle.

There was a change in the locals too. The arrival of the ANA in Patrol Base Shuga started a series of joint security shuras. The one in the first week of February had twenty-two heads of household attending. They volunteered to come. I began to feel the plan was working, even if it had come at considerable cost. Tom was less enthusiastic. OK they had come, but they had done nothing but complain for two hours. I wish I had remembered at the time the old adage that one needs to worry about soldiers when they stop complaining rather than when they are complaining. At least if they are complaining to you they must think you might be able or willing to do something about the problem. This is true at all levels in the chain of command: start worrying when you're doing all the talking. The same was true of our new friends around Shuga. Tom had a point. If the population left because of the fighting it would demonstrate that we were not able to bring the rule of law to this part of Sangin. If you have not got a population who are using government 'services', even if that means only the most limited security and freedom of movement, then you have lost. So whilst I remained extremely positive about all the new interaction with the locals, the deal was by no means sealed. More accurately, given the context of the number of security incidents, the whole plan was balanced on a knife edge.

I remained convinced that the only way to defeat the insurgency was to suck the life out of it. That is to say, the money that you spend on operations needs to be spent to the benefit of the population. The amount of money I had to spend was 3,000 US dollars a month. At the start of the tour I could barely spend that. I took a very simple view. Somehow we needed, and I say we on behalf of the district governor, because it was him we wanted to boost, to employ people in the same way as the Taliban did. OK there were twenty-seven Taliban 'commander' call-signs in the area, but they relied on a team of three or four local fighters each to do their fetching, carrying, scouting, and shooting. These guys were paid for their trouble to the tune of about ten dollars a day. What we needed was a project that would pay them fifteen. CO 3 Rifles had a pithy little phrase about 'using the laws of economics rather than the laws of physics.' By the end of January we were exploring the idea of putting tarmac on the 611, or 'black topping', with benefits for security, freedom of movement and the economy.

It was not all that far-fetched. The Saudis were already starting the process at the bottom end of the 611, so some interim help from the British government might mean the middle bit could be done as well. In support of this I scoped a location for a contractor camp bordering Inkerman and worked out how it might function and be protected. The idea gained some momentum in the Battlegroup and Brigade Headquarters. So it was arranged that we should have a visit from the Brigade Commander and Lindy Cameron, the head of the Provincial Reconstruction Team (PRT). I was left in no doubt by the CO that this was a huge opportunity. He could not be there, but I needed to make the case. Given this was two days before the start of Operation Moshtarak and the Brigadier was coming to us, I got a sense that this was indeed being taken seriously.

On a personal note I was on the point of leaving for R and R. Most of the helicopter flights had stopped to save the flying hours for the coming operation. The rest of the guys who were going on the same flight back to the UK had gone a few days before. In order to get out for R and R I would hitch a lift with the Brigadier at the end of the visit; I just hoped there would be room. Brigadier James and Lindy arrived with hardly any entourage – always a blessing, but particularly so given my desire to travel with them. We took them to the briefing area where the usual rather stilted military brief was given. One of my mannerisms clearly annoyed the Brigadier. He liked a direct and unequivocal view rather than a series of pros and cons. I am not that good at painting fifty shades of grey as either black or white. Lindy Cameron was rather more receptive. They were looking at 4.5 million dollars and tendering in the next month. Ye bloody ha!

We had a tour of camp lined up, but first a bit of a meet and greet with a few troops in from patrol to Inkerman from 7 Platoon. The Brigadier gathered them round for some inspiration.

'Afghanistan is the most violent country in the world,' he began. 'And Helmand is the most violent province in Afghanistan, Sangin is the most violent district in the province and the Inkerman area of operations is the most violent in the district. That you continue to make progress in the most violent place in the world is a great compliment to your fortitude and skill as soldiers.' He went on for a while longer, explaining about Moshtarak and the Brigade plan. 'Keep up the good work.'

We set off for the far end of camp to observe down the road. Just as we finished in the tower the Taliban illustrated the Brigadier's point most aptly. A burst of fire and some fairly accurate single shots zipped overhead. Lindy Cameron dived for cover. The Brigadier looked mighty pleased to be under fire before realising that we did all need to take cover. A small fire-fight ensued with our northern sangar and then it all went quiet. Tim Lush came to find us. He told us very calmly, for a man who had just come within a whisker, that there was an unexploded rocket-propelled grenade just outside his stores. The guard were marking up an internal cordon and there was a search on for any more in the camp. Thirty minutes later we were all packed up and ready to go down by the HLS. Ben was now in charge for two weeks and three days. I wished him luck and went down to wait.

As we waited for the helicopter I had, I think, one of the most extraordinary conversations that I have had with a senior officer. By way of context one must know that the Army was in a right old state at this time about the physical appearance of soldiers on operations. The image was becoming one of Vietnam. Unshaven men, with weapons and bandoliers carried in the manner of an African mercenary, did not look a disciplined force. This had been given four-star attention by an open letter from General Sir David Richards, the commander-in-chief at the time, on the subject of sideburns. The tiller had been jerked so violently on the subject of standards of dress that suddenly it became all-consuming. Shaving seemed to be at the top of the 'to do' list in Task Force Helmand, from Camp Bastion to Sangin.

Most disturbingly it became the standard by which officers judged the enforcement of discipline by their senior non-commissioned officers. I had taken a fairly tolerant line. The patrol bases had been down to three days' supply of drinking water when they were supposed to keep a month's worth. That is not to say we had beards; we did not. Nor did we grow beards as some kind of *faux* culturalism. It was dealt with as sensibly as we could. Image and self-regard are important – it is part of self-discipline – but I felt we had begun to confuse standards of dress with the values and standards of the Army.

The Brigadier turned to me as we waited at the side of the helicopter landing site and mentioned to me that my sideburns could do with a trim. I must have looked like a guppy fish, mouth hanging slack as Bertie Wooster's. Luckily I was rescued by Lindy Cameron, who rode to my aid with 'What did you say James? His sideburns? One they aren't untidy and secondly he's getting shot at every day. I think from the evidence of today he's got his work cut out.'

I smiled nervously. 'Thank God,' I thought. 'At least someone's got it; shame she's not in the Army.'

In Bastion the base rat serjeant majors were enforcing garrison standards of dress. Some of my men coming in for R and R were asked to change out of a shirt that had their blood group and Zap number marked on, as it was too scruffy. Troops had twelve hours to get a haircut once in Camp Bastion. To those coming from patrol bases, hoping for two weeks where they could really let their hair down, getting a haircut from the local Afghan barber, who used a pair of shears much like an Australian on a sheep, before going on R and R was about as enticing as cup of sick. The letters of outrage, still available online, to *Soldier* magazine continued until May, the vast majority of which defended the right of the soldier to a smart but not prescribed haircut, and more latitude in their appearance than the chain of command appeared willing to give. On the issue of sideburns the army manifestly picked the wrong fight. It felt like a smokescreen to the true cause of our trouble. My experience is that the soldier responds to context; they are chameleons in that respect. If he feels he is doing the right thing, if he knows he has the right support and feels personally valued, then he acts and dresses in a manner consistent with the values and appearance one expects of a soldier. Take any one of those away and he may well respond in a way that is consistent with a breach of trust further up the chain. As far as most soldiers were concerned it was a case of sanction not support, symptom not cause, and for those with a religious education, motes and beams.

I went on R and R ready as anyone for rest and recuperation.

\* \* \* \* \*

The necessity for the two weeks of holiday that soldiers get in the middle of a tour is a divisive subject, for several reasons. It has a disastrous effect on the manpower available for operations: we had up to 20 per cent of our manpower away at times. The fact that R and R is taken in the UK means that the air transport fleet is put under considerable pressure, and it is fragile enough as it is. If a plane is not working the delay causes a concertina effect and the people who suffer are those who are covering in a patrol base. On the other side of the coin I have no doubt that the intensity of the operation in Sangin demanded a break, probably more than one. Back in the day, soldiers would be rotated into the front line. Now there were guys who had been on the first or second R and R slots, which take place after six weeks, who would spend the best part of five months continuously in a patrol base.

Five months of broken sleep, eating rations not fresh food, daily patrols and fire-fights; five months on the front line. A few thrived, most survived but were changed forever, others crawled over the line at the end, and of course some never made it back at all.

My R and R group included Tom, who had left a replacement 2nd Lieutenant in charge of 3 Platoon. In truth he was an extra pair of hands, but Tom's platoon second-in-command, Serjeant Jimmy Houston, felt a little aggrieved that he was not now the platoon commander. He needed some persuading that, in light of experiences with 1 Platoon, if I had the backup I was going to use it. Mark, the replacement platoon commander, was straight out of the cerebral school of officers, driven to serve by the desire to see the real world. I am sure he found the world of the 611 equally as surreal as the world of the Oxford classicist. He was a good man and played the role of 3 Platoon commander for two weeks with efficient understatement that made him quite popular, even with Jimmy, by the end.

The others on the flight included Riflemen Mnguni, Apolis and Lance Corporal T. All were soldiers from the Commonwealth: South Africa and Fiji. Mnguni had been driving a Mastiff for Pat Hyde for three months. He had been blown up in Mastiffs half a dozen times already. Despite a relatively short stature he was indomitable. He found humour everywhere in the ridiculousness of it all. Carlo Apolis was a Black South African, the 'old man' of 2 Platoon. He had joined the Company just before I arrived and was a 'senior' Rifleman in every sense. He was the man with blood all over his trousers at the end of our fitness test. Lance Corporal T was a sniper. He had been a Rifleman in my company in Northern Ireland and was as rock solid as they came, in the best tradition of our Fijian association.

As we boarded the plane all those of the rank of major and above were invited into the first-class cabin of the chartered Flybe jet. The majority of us sported the well-nourished look of the senior staff officer. There were three spare seats. I asked the cabin crew if I could fetch three from the back. A few minutes later Carlo, Mnguni, T and I were horizontal for most of 13 hours, much to the amazement of our first-class travelling companions.

I was met on a cold Valentine's February morning by Rachel in the grey surroundings of the Brize Norton car park. The first week the kids would be at school or nursery, then we would go away for a few days. Not far. The four-day sojourn in Centre Parcs is a favourite of those on R and R. The thing about R and R is that it is just so normal and yet so weird. I climbed out of my uniform and into my jeans, played games with my children, had supper with my wife and meantime back on the 611 Rifleman Mark Marshall became 7 Platoon's first fatality.

Ben did not call me. We had not discussed the specifics other than that he should call if he needed to, but I needed time away and I couldn't and shouldn't try to control the situation from 5,000 miles away. Then Sapper Guy Mellors died the following day from an injury sustained when he stepped on an IED as the follow-up tried to exploit the scene and I was halfway down a bottle of red for the first time in five months. Rachel and I talked a lot about Henry and autism. The school, Avondale in Bulford, had been brilliant and they now had a series of strategies in place that seemed to be working. I set out on the long road to try to understand how an autistic child works. Rachel was already streets ahead of me. She had devoted a good deal of time when she wasn't going to the funerals of our fallen to finding out all she could.

It seemed that a gluten and dairy free diet might help. I was undeniably sceptical of the nutritionists and alternative remedy. No longer. The day Henry came off dairy and gluten was a good day. He made almost immediate progress. While we were talking a lot about family and just trying to enjoy the limited time together there were one or two things I wanted and needed to do.

I went into the welfare office. Steve Harris, the welfare officer, had gathered together those from A Company who were in work, including Mike. It was good to see Mike again, and he was full of determination to return. I understood his desire, but tried to temper his expectation. A muscle in his wrist had been damaged and no one knew how long it would be before his grip recovered. He updated me with various goings-on. Tom showed up. Tom and Mike's relationship was recovering after the blue on blue incident. I had made a strong effort with everyone involved to focus on their responsibility rather than anyone else's. The desire to lay blame and avoid censure, if left unchecked, would split us apart. Better to know what you might have done differently rather than anyone else because, then as now, try as I might, when I think of that time I cannot shake a 'How the hell did that happen?' thought from my head.

Mike was worried about the level of care being shown by the Battalion to the A Company platoon in Support Company. 'Well, you can do something about that in the next few weeks.' I was not expecting much change from the Battalion, the weekly sitreps back and forth from 4 Rifles had become a source of horror and then amusement as the list of demands grew longer and relatively more trivial by the day. For me it had culminated in a series of emails in early February where I was accused by CO 4 Rifles of putting the Radio 4 blogs ahead of my responsibilities to write reports on the corporals. In what had always been a less than comfortable relationship it was a small straw that broke the camel's back; I hadn't written a blog in eight weeks and the reports weren't due in Glasgow until April. I spoke to him as little as possible from then on, notwithstanding the minimum professional requirements. I clambered into the car with Steve and went to Birmingham to see Ricky Furgusson. Ricky had taken days to become medically stable in Afghanistan before he could fly. But flown he had, in an induced coma, from which he had been woken sometime in late January. Still sedated, he was now able to take visitors.

I hate hospitals. I don't know why, it is entirely irrational, but they just give me the jeebies. I know part of the reason: I have a very bad reaction to scarring and stitches. It is the thought of the stitched flaps of skin. It just gets me behind the knees and twice in my life the physiological reaction has been so strong I have fainted. Given what I had seen without fainting in training and Afghanistan I was pretty sure that this would be alright. Steve was warming me up for what Ricky looked like. 'Some people just can't take it. He's in a pretty bad way.' I became quietly nervous.

We got to Birmingham after one o'clock; no time for lunch just straight in. Bad idea. On the ward was Pricy, a recently retired lance corporal, another celebrated Battalion boxer, who had also been in my company in Northern Ireland. We exchanged the usual grunted greetings and I glanced over at Ricky lying on the bed.

'Holy shit,' I thought, as I turned away to take off my jacket and compose myself.

'Alright, Corporal F?' I said.

'Al'iit iir'. Ricky was speaking through a tracheotomy halfway up his neck. The hole where his mouth might have been was on his right cheek. And the doctors had planted a large graft on his left cheek for use in later cosmetic surgery. His right eye, glazed, and looking frankly pretty manic, stared out following the conversation. The other empty socket was covered in gauze. The bed lay flat where his legs should have been. He appeared semi-foetal, as one of his hands had been stitched to his thigh to try and get as much blood as possible back into the limb to heal it. He proffered his available semi-digitised hand to shake, which I carefully held.

Strange as it may seem, he was in good spirits. He yabbered away in his usual quick-fire brummie drone. Brummie through a tracheotomy was not all that intelligible. There seemed to be quite a lot about his missing legs and did I bring them back from Helmand. The previous night's booze and no lunch rapidly seemed more than just a bad idea. Hypersensitivity kicked in. The hospital smell, the ravages of an IED now stitched roughly into place and underneath an incredible human spirit trying with all his might to throw off the new found physical constraints. The doctors had slowly realised that what they had thought was euphoria was just Ricky. Steve looked at me and realised I was in trouble.

I made it down stairs into the fresh air.

'Bugger me.' I thought it might be different. I had a cigarette. Another bad idea. I began to walk back inside. Next stop Rifleman Pollock. Light-headed from one of Steve's mighty Lamberts, I went down in a dead faint. I was soon back in the land of the feeling rather embarrassed. Still, better to have come than not. I may have been embarrassed, but that is better than not being able to forgive oneself. Rumours in the Army persist of senior MoD officer(s) not going to Birmingham to visit the wounded. If it is true it would be truly shameful.

I never made it to see Rifleman Pollock. I saw and chatted to his mother; he had been taken back into a high level of care for an infection. Steve reckoned that after my experience with Furgie it probably wasn't wise to see him hooked up. We went to get something to eat and found Furgie's mother and her sister in the café. Whilst they had got over the immediate shock, the road ahead for all the families of the wounded looked a very hard one. I am glad to say that whilst hospitals still give me the jeebies, I have become familiar enough with Ricky's injuries that it no longer gives me such an outstanding reaction, but I can't pretend that it still doesn't turn me over when I think of that day in February.

Eleven months later Ricky climbed aboard his full prosthetic legs for the first time to have his Military Cross pinned to his chest by the Queen. It was, and still is, a quite remarkable story of survival and recovery. A surgeon commander from the Royal Navy, who was also at Buckingham Palace that day, turned to Ricky and said 'Corporal Furgusson?'

'Yeah... Who's asking?'

'Last time I saw you, you didn't have a face.'

She had been in the MIRT that night. From his grievous wounding in the explosion via treatment by Lance Corporal Murphy and the surgeon Lt Commander in the helicopter, to Medical Centre in Camp Bastion, to Selly Oak and Headley Court, Ricky not only survived in the face of medically insurmountable odds but also recovered to play his part unaided in the Olympic torch relay. Swift and bold.

A slightly chastened company commander returned to Bulford. The next day I had to get up early. I had agreed at some point that I would do an interview for Radio 4 during R and R. I have to say that this was pure self-indulgence on my part. Having listened to the *Today* programme on Radio 4 for many years, nay, being forced to listen to it during my first six weeks of training at the Royal Military Academy Sandhurst, here was a chance to be on the other side. I would get up at four am, be in the studio at seven forty-five, have breakfast with my brother and be back to Bulford by eleven. No great hardship there, except that I was eating into the most precious commodity of all: family time.

An MoD press officer came along to be there. As I sat down in the studio, with the Bishop of London loitering outside with a Thought for the Day in his hand, Evan Davis looked over. 'You're much younger than I expected,' he said. I noted he did not say better looking, so I assumed it was just a compliment. Anyway. Jim Naughtie bumbled into the studio. He walks like he talks, with milliseconds to spare. He asked me two or three innocuous questions about what I'd been up to. My reply included a line that I had been handed a lesson in humility seeing those who were recovering from injury. It was all over in a couple of minutes. Watching the *Today* team at work looked very much like an ops room: quiet efficiency and the occasional bustle as breaking news barged longer-term items off the agenda.

Next stop, Center Parcs. Center Parcs was a second trip through the exquisite agony of savouring the seconds and wishing it all over. One moment sliding down a water slide, or on bike rides in February sleet, then thoughts, inevitably, of the return. From jeans to uniform in one easy step. During our last twenty-four hours in Center Parcs I got a phone call, well actually I got two, both from the Commanding Officer of 4 Rifles. The first was to tell me that I had *not* been selected for the jobs I had gone in for at the end of the tour, but I had been selected for a procurement post in London. His recommendation was I should take it. I had four hours to decide with no way of finding out anything about it. It was a job in the procurement of soldiers' kit: radios, body armour, weapons and load carriage were to be my remit. I took it. At least it meant London, which was my first choice for purely geographical reasons. Three years on I am thoroughly intimate with the inadequacies of the procurement system; back then I was just naïve, as my blogs testify. The second phone call came early in the morning; it could only mean one thing. Another man down. Rifleman Martin Kinggett had been killed by a bullet on patrol.

I had to get the eulogy to the Adjutant by four that afternoon. There are some eulogies that you need to research to get exact dates, or to confirm with someone whether a particular memory you have is consistent with him as a person. I will not pretend that each Rifleman in A Company was as familiar to me as the next. But first Pete Aldridge and now Martin Kinggett were two Riflemen who needed no research, no questions – just an attempt to find the right words to do them and their contribution justice. It was a deeply unpleasant way to spend my last afternoon on R and R. Then there were goodbyes. Goodnight kisses. An early start. Uniform on. The battalion transport back to Brize. And for the first time, a near seamless transition back to Inkerman. They always seem to get you there much faster than they get you back.

I did get a chance to stop by at the Bastion hospital to see Rifleman 'Borth' Borthwick, who had been shot in the chest during the same incident that killed Rifleman Martin Kinggett. He had been rescued by Corporal Penk, operated on in the MIRT, and was now sitting up and chatting in the hospital.

This was the very same Corporal Penk whom I had ceased to fully trust in July. Below is part of the description of his actions that I wrote in Inkerman in March 2010 following the after-action review. The resulting citations, as I mentioned previously, are both necessary and iniquitous. The medals they are supposed to lead to are not based on the quality of the act, but on a quota system. This inevitably leads to questions of fairness, as they are always subject to the context in which they are awarded. Corporal Penk was ultimately awarded a Joint Commanders' Commendation for his actions as described below. I believe that at any other time and place, on pretty much any other tour, he would have got a cross of some description pinned to his chest.

Corporal Penk is a Mortar Fire Controller based with 3 Platoon A Company 4 Rifles in Forward Operating Base INKERMAN. On 25 February he was waiting to be picked up from a Check Point by a patrol coming from a nearby Patrol Base, SHUGA. As the patrol moved along the road two hundred metres from the waiting group they were engaged from two firing points. The initial fire caused one casualty to the rear of the patrol. Rfn Borthwick was shot through the torso. The section commander started to move back to collect the casualty. As he did this shortly afterwards Rifleman Kinggett was shot and killed near the front of the patrol as he tried to give covering fire. This left the section horribly exposed. Two casualties with the six remaining men under fire attempting to win the fire fight. The casualties were separated by sixty metres. The waiting group including Penk were in cover from the fire onto the section in the open. Without a thought for his own safety Corporal Penk dashed across the open ground leading the two others in the group, Strype and Bennett. The section commander was controlling his fire team to win the firefight and evacuate Kinggett.

Borthwick had been acting as his section second in command. Penk arrived at the casualty and took command of the remainder of the fire team. He organised the covering fire from Strype, and set about treating Borthwick. He gave lifesaving first aid. During this time the enemy continued to fire at the patrol with accurate single shots and bursts of fire. With the casualty prepared they had to move back across the open ground. With Bennett and two others he stretchered Borthwick two hundred metres over the open ground to the waiting casevac vehicles. He simultaneously treated the casualty and organised the covering fire to complete the evacuation with the utmost efficiency.

Borthwick was put on the Medical Emergency Response Team helicopter in a perilous condition. He was cut open and the bleeding controlled on the helicopter. The doctors in the hospital said that the only reason for his survival was down to his treatment at the scene of his injury and the speed of his evacuation.

Amongst a number of commendable actions on that day Penk stands out. For his courage to make the dash into the face of withering and lethal enemy fire; for his selfless commitment to his comrades; for his leadership of Strype and Bennett; for his initial treatment of Borthwick; for his command and control of the evacuation that ultimately led to the saving of Borthwick's life, Penk is highly deserving of official recognition.

He was clearly a top man, but he had not been in July the previous year, when I had come undeniably close to sacking Corporal Penk after that incident on the final test exercise in July 2009. In hindsight I'm very glad I didn't sack him then, because Rifleman, now Lance Corporal, Borthwick would probably not be alive today and Corporal Penk would not have had the chance to prove me utterly wrong. The cloud against Corporal Penk dispersed on 25 February 2010. He was doubly unfortunate that the CO of 4 Rifles had forced my hand with his annual report three weeks previously. He more than re-earned any loss of trust that day. He might argue and I would agree that the selfless commitment that drove him into the line of fire that day was always part of his make-up. In the end, only by their fruits shall ye really know them.

## Chapter 13

# Return to Hell

I arrived back in Helmand on the day of my thirty-seventh birthday. I even had a birthday card from Brigadier Ty Urch, my Brigade Commander in the UK, on a 'loose minute', the army's 'informal' communiqué. Entitled 'BIRTHDAY GREETINGS', inscribed it had 'Rich'. I have never been called Rich. I am Dickie to most of my army friends, Richard to my mother, and my wife on a bad day, Rick or Bigus or Dozey to my family, but never Rich.

'Have a riot', the card read, along with a Far Side cartoon of a man being hit by an old age truck. 'Hope you had a good R and R', it said, and the signature had a smiley face emoticon 'Ty ☺'. My first thought as I read it was 'You haven't got a bloody clue.'

I am only slightly more charitable now. I still have the card as a reminder of how the best of intention depends on who you are intending the benefit, yourself or the recipient.

If Evan Davis thought I looked young at thirty-six, then at thirty-seven I felt pretty old. Ben ran me through what had happened while I was away; essentially a great deal more of the same. The small arms threat was worse than at any stage, but we seemed to be doing OK defeating and avoiding the IEDs on the road. The death of Sapper Guy Mellors had been difficult. We had already experienced a couple of close calls with exploitations and this had ended in the worst possible way. The final decision had not been his. I was surprisingly calm about it. I had thought I might not be, as two in two days had been very difficult in November and here it was again. I can say categorically that these are very difficult judgements to make, nigh on impossible in fact. If the exploitation works it can be very valuable evidence to defeat the network behind the device and therefore an example of best practice, but if it doesn't it suddenly becomes very difficult to justify. Another paradox, another tragedy that got no better for dwelling on it.

And there was no time to dwell on it, because the imminent problem was in the plan for the last major operation that the Battlegroup would undertake. Whilst it was going to take place in our area, only the first part of the operation relied on A Company troops. That is to say in the second phase we had the Recce Platoon and a platoon from A Company 3 Rifles under command to assist with the escort of the engineers while we guarded the road. But the first phase had been conceived by Colonel Wadood in the newly-formed Combined Force Sangin HQ, who wanted to provide protection in depth to the road going over the western culvert. This meant occupying another checkpoint. We would return the compound we had occupied near the road and try to occupy a larger one some 300 metres south of the culvert. It meant traversing the area south of the culvert and Charlie was not a happy man for good reason.

The whole area was extremely dangerous even by the perilous standards we had already set. The target compound was at the top of a hill in an excellent position to give security. But getting there meant being surrounded on three sides by compounds that had all been used as firing points; moreover, given our experience of clearing IEDs in that area, there was more than a distinct possibility that there were a plethora of devices placed on any potential path. It was to all intents and purposes a killing zone the size of three football fields. So as we all knew very well by now, going early meant you couldn't see the ground sign and going later meant exposure to the small arms fire. Frying pan or fire? It wasn't as though things were easy as they were. The day before the operation was supposed to start Corporal 'Woodie' Haywood was shot in the neck. An inch further over and he would not have lived a minute longer, let alone be alive and well today. As it was he was quickly evacuated by a well-practiced team, the fourth rifle section commander to be evacuated of nine in the company, but not the last.

I sat with Charlie and we talked through the options for how and when to get to the compound. Eventually we settled on going early along the 611 and then through a compound we knew was occupied. There was some risk because we had used it before and the son of the occupant had been identified as a member of the Taliban. But an occupied compound was considerably safer than an unoccupied one, and if we got there before dawn we could use the ANA to talk to him and then walk where the occupant walked. Good old 'Farmer' Barma. We would then be 200 metres from the target compound and could use the time from dawn to cross the most vulnerable area, search the compound and, if all that went according to plan, we would have time to build a hasty defence of the compound by the time the enemy reaction came. One thing we were certain of was that the move to the compound, the search and the subsequent build of defences needed cover from the air.

By this stage in the tour I was utterly convinced that moving without some kind of observation from the air was asking for trouble. The enemy knew the ground too well to be outflanked by ground manoeuvre alone. So with eight hours until H-hour it was with some dismay, leading rapidly to a full array of expletives, that I heard that the air assets had been allocated elsewhere for the following day. I was at PB Blenheim with Charlie when this happened. I got in a vehicle and went straight to the Battlegroup HQ in the middle of Sangin. It was after eleven pm when I strode in; most of the Battlegroup staff had left the ops room, but luckily the CO was still about. The CO had a small cupboard of an office hidden from view, but not soundproof, in the corner of the ops room.

The conversation was a relatively short one. I made the point that he and I were asking 2 Platoon to lead a Battlegroup operation with no air cover. It was a simple point and one that he took without reply, other than to reach for the phone. He made an immediate call to the Brigade Chief of Staff. Again the brevity of the call was the most notable thing about it. Apaches on 15 minutes' notice? Next to no good because Bastion was half an hour away and too much can happen in five minutes, let alone forty-five. The Chief of Staff allocated us a drone for four hours from 0600. Charlie felt a bit happier on my return at 0100. It would not have the suppressive effect, but at least we could see what was happening. He was leaving at 0530.

The first three hours of the operation went swimmingly. Down the road at best speed, with the ANA waking a pleasingly surprised occupant, a quick walk through and then a painstaking move across 200 metres of no-man's land. 2 Platoon got to the compound, unscathed. The IED team moved in and set about searching the target compound, which appeared to be unoccupied. We knew insurgents used it. They had poured out of it to rescue the man killed in our first hellfire strike. They found nothing and by nine o'clock the place was cleared safe. No more than a couple of minutes later, just as the first members of 2 Platoon moved from the roof to more protected surroundings, the worst barrage of fire I ever witnessed, albeit from the relative safety of the Blenheim ops room 500 metres away, erupted from the buildings around the compound at close range, and not for the first time in the tour all hell broke loose. The platoon was at least in all-round defence on the compound roof, but still horribly exposed. Amazingly the Taliban had, for the first time, kept absolute radio silence. There had been no trigger on the ICOM; radio net discipline was something they had been very bad at up to this point. Commanders had previously always wanted to check on the whereabouts of subordinates or confirm how many of the 'big things' they were bringing. Even from these snippets one gets a good idea of the timing, location and probable intensity of the prospective engagement. There had been no observation of fighters moving in, nor of the local population leaving. The eye in the sky had a perfect view and had seen none of the usual signs.

The two Riflemen to move first were Carlo Apolis and Dan Owens: both were shot and wounded simultaneously. As well as lethally accurate small arms fire RPGs rained in, as did the grenades thrown over the walls from close quarters. How the hell did they get that close without being seen? The following forty-five minutes were very frustrating. Events conspired to make it the slowest evacuation we did and least successful to boot. It was well within the time that the Army wants to get casualties away. We hit the platinum ten and the golden hour but it was slow by our own standards. A radio went down in the Chinook;

there was a simultaneous evacuation from a base on the other side of Sangin. It all just happened at once. We couldn't save Carlo Apolis: he had no vital signs before the helicopter arrived and whilst the team continued to give CPR we all knew what the outcome would be. Carlo, whom I had shared a first-class cabin with sixteen days previously on the way to R and R, and chatted to on our way back about his plans for life after the tour, now breathed his last breath in a dusty compound. Pure anguish. Daniel Owens thought at first he had been shot in the leg because he couldn't walk. He had, in fact, been shot in the back. We put him on the same helicopter as Carlo and his determination has meant he has made a recovery to full fitness and is still serving.

Whilst we had taken two casualties 2 Platoon held firm. The arrival of the Apaches with the Chinook for the evacuation meant the enemy went to ground. 2 Platoon secured the compound. We had decided that the best route from the road to what would become Ullah's Post, although 2 Platoon continued to call it Carlo's until the end of tour, was through what appeared to be an abandoned compound. We wanted it removed and Colonel Wadood was happy to sanction its destruction. We had received plenty of intelligence that it was occupied by the enemy. Hours of observation from the air had revealed nothing, repeated visits had never elicited a response and yet the rumours persisted. Now that the western culvert was genuinely isolated and protected the bomb-disposal teams could go to work. When we forced entry they found five IEDs in the compound and a tunnel. It was a eureka moment: how they appeared and disappeared was now blindingly obvious. I for one had been fooled by how much the insurgents used the normal routes. The use of irrigation tunnels and deep wells to hide in had been part of our original briefs. At the start of the tour we had looked for tunnels in the fields unsuccessfully. But we had not anticipated them in the built-up district of northern Sangin. Now it was fairly obvious what was going on. And, like all the best plans, it was hidden in plain view. They had ten years of fighting the Russians and four years of fighting us, so time enough to construct an extensive network. We decided to block it. Tunnels are hellish to fight in; most of the options involve large numbers of troops and equipment. From Vietnam to Grozny the accounts of battles for the underground are some of the most horrific.

One of the more amusing moments, and there are a few in amongst all the other trouble and strife of the operation, was escorting Colonel Wadood to see his Afghan Warriors in Ullah's post. The ANA had moved in with 2 Platoon at the end of the first day with only the essential protection in place, another mark of their new-found willingness to operate as near as damn it alongside us. When Wat-a-dood and I paid a flying visit on the second day the route up through the newly destroyed compound could still only be walked. Pat Hyde had been shot at the previous day while making the same journey. He advised a low sprint across the open ground. Wat-a-dood was not a sprinter. He claimed his bad back prevented him wearing body armour and like all Afghans he rarely, if ever, wore a helmet. A beret of Frank Spencer proportions was ample protection. The CSM went first and fastest. I set off in pursuit until I realised that the good colonel would be doing no more than an amble. So I waited and ambled too. In the cover of an eighteen-foot wall fifty metres away Pat Hyde shook his head, in the manner of my colour sergeant at Sandhurst, while the colonel and I perambulated gently towards him. When in Rome… Or in the words of the 'dood, 'Insh'Allah.'

With the compound secure the focus of the operation shifted; we moved up the 611 clearing and securing each culvert. Rifleman James Mackie from 3 Rifles' Recce Platoon won his Conspicuous Gallantry Cross during this operation, throwing back a grenade that landed amongst him and his colleagues. We were at it for a week. I had barely four hours sleep each night. By the time we had finished each day and the reports had been written I found myself going back into Sangin to plead for more resources or to sort out any of the tangle of issues that arose. Any recuperation that had been achieved by the end of February had been lost by the middle of March.

Colonel Wadood was pleased with the result. He was even more pleased when we took him a week or so later to the new expanded Bariolai, where 1 Platoon had done a land grab. By this stage it was obvious that the insurgent was really quite pissed off and was making an effort in our area. Moshtarak was nearly complete; where there had been two fatalities in central Helmand, the 3 Rifles Battlegroup had lost nine in the month since it started, of which five would be in the Inkerman area. At the end of the fourth week 1 Platoon came under attack and Lance Corporal Tom Keogh was shot and killed as he manned an emergency post. Tom had been with us a month as a battle casualty replacement. He was another one of the 4th battalion's big personalities. Bulford was as grief-stricken as we were. But although the insurgents had killed Tom, 1 Platoon were absolutely lethal that day and clinically so, bringing back memories of Lydd ranges nine months previously. Seven funerals took place in the graveyard the following day. Normally the body count is the worst metric by which one can judge success, but this was different. The insurgent attacked from compounds generally from small, almost invisible, holes in walls, known in Afghanistan as 'murder holes'. Only the RPG men had to expose themselves and then usually from ranges beyond 400 metres. In attacking the base in such numbers they were going back to the tactics of the early days in Sangin. Forward Operating Base Jackson had been known as the Alamo. It was a desperate act. I was also heartened, because despite all the munitions flying around there were no claims for compensation. This was a sure but not absolutely certain sign that all of those killed had been insurgents. Locals confirmed that we had hit the right men. In their grief for Tom 1 Platoon were rightly proud of what they had achieved. They felt the enemy had been swinging for all he was worth in the last round, but that they had delivered a knockout blow. These were strong words, and only time would tell.

The time since my return to Afghanistan had been swift, bloody and bold. We mourned Martin Kinggett, Carlo Apolis and Tom Keogh, but in the midst of grief the Company continued to take the fight to the enemy. At the end of Ghartse Gahdme 5 we had new areas under our control, new levels of partnership with the ANA and most importantly new levels of appreciation and consent from the local population. It is difficult not to confuse taking casualties with a losing battle. I don't underestimate that every loss is a tragedy for family, friends and comrades; I have seen mothers wretched in grief and fathers stoic while they weep. Yet to a man these soldiers died fighting for their friends and doing the job they volunteered for. At the time I was very keen to point out that they were volunteers not victims.

At the end of the first day of the operation I had been with Carlo's section in the new patrol base. 'How are you all?' 'Oh, you know… we're fine.' 'How are the others?' A shadow in the eyes but determination and satisfaction of another hard-earned step in the right direction. In that respect we, as soldiers, are no different from other professions: if you are an actor you derive satisfaction from a fine performance in a difficult role, a lawyer revels in a winning argument. If you are a soldier there is a satisfaction in achieving a mission when the enemy has to be out-thought and out-fought. The paradox lies in that even in success someone gets hurt or killed.

In counter-insurgency that also means bringing the local population with you. To succeed in this mission the power that comes from the barrel of a gun must be exercised with clinical precision if the battle for consent is to be won. It is a complex game, but one that by now I and the rest of the company and the Battlegroup had played for five months. I estimated then that this hellishly violent period was a far greater knock for the insurgent than it was for us. It was summed up for me at the end of the operation by one Lance Corporal 'Stripper' Strype, the man who had followed Penk to rescue Borthwick, who was finishing his tour to go on a course. I knew him well, having had him under command as a Rifleman in Germany and Kosovo with the anti-tank platoon. He was one of a number I could rely on for unflinching honesty. Back in the day he had made repeated attempts to drink Germany dry of lager. The shared experience of that and three tours to the Balkans meant that when I asked a question I got the answer he wanted to give, not the one I wanted to hear. His parting shot was 'Yeah, the casualties have been bad but most of us have actually enjoyed it'. That was our reality in March 2010.

And what of the locals? While we were still slugging it out with the enemy it was difficult not to think that their tolerance might be wearing thin. *Au contraire* – at 3 Platoon in PB Shuga seventeen heads of households turned up wanting to have a chat. Tom welcomed them with his counterpart Lt Anwar rather nervously. He had been just about to set off on patrol to try and talk to owners of local compounds, as unusually they had not popped in for their usual evening chats for a couple of days. He had seen them packing their belongings up and was frankly very nervous that as soon as they left the platoon would be wide open to being overrun from close quarters. Shuga was surrounded by occupied compounds on three sides. They were the only thing that prevented the Taliban from lobbing in grenades. There had been quite enough of that from the only open flank they had on the southeast. Tom quickly discovered that all the moving about had been families packing up to move into one room in the compound so that relatives and friends could move in to be under the protection of the base. Not only that, but in a long shura they had all agreed, after some five hours, that what was required was a local school, and that the site of a local petrol station would suffice. The elders thought they would be able to resist the Taliban, but they needed our help with equipment and books. Happy, and not a little relieved, Tom passed it up on his situation report that evening. It seemed that the locals had made their choice and now we needed to back them. With any luck we would make it worth their while and the Ministry of Education would shortly get a new project.

Sangin now had a new District Governor and we were hopeful that the local state functions would begin to flourish under his stewardship. All this work was overseen by the Political Officer and the Stabilisation Advisor, British civil servants, based in the Battlegroup HQ. There was already a new health centre and local police recruiting had begun to improve, although it could not have got any worse, and there was still plenty of space in the ANP. Furthermore, the local investigator changed to try and give people more confidence in the justice system, and the mayor presided over considerable developments in the bazaar.

The advent of a new District Governor in Sangin was the most significant political advance of our time there. The previous version had been illiterate and thuggish. The new one had been a science teacher. He came from a less partisan tribe and welcomed the other tribal elders to come and talk to him. The web of loyalties in our area was difficult to fathom, but in those areas outside the fighting the traditional groupings held firm. Every time I thought I had a grip on who was doing what to whom and why in this patchwork it changed. Mainly this was because you got vastly different versions of the same event depending on who you spoke to. The new District Governor would not take long to start having an influence. Meanwhile, after a week on the road I got back to Inkerman.

Our job was to keep on top of the insurgents to let the Governor do his job and persuade others to join those around Shuga in resisting the Taliban, so the second half of March promised to be an interesting time. In military terms things were not getting any easier. We were now convinced that we faced the most difficult threat to counter, the sniper. We knew they had the weapon system, but until mid-February they didn't seem to have anyone trained to use them. We knew they had it because Rifleman 'Pan' Panchabya has still got the bullet that the medics dug out of his shoulder in December. But the accuracy of the shooting that killed Martin, Tom and Carlo and had wounded Woodie was of a different order. On the positive side by now we were getting pretty handy with the precision fire from the Reaper drones ourselves. It came at the right time. But one area still frustrated us. Despite the large shura Tom was getting ever more exasperated that we could not control the area to his southeast. It had been used countless times by insurgents, yet for a two-week period we seemed unable to get the assets in place to deliver the knockout blow. I became equally frustrated when a golden opportunity was denied by Battlegroup Headquarters simply because they had not been attentive enough in the build-up. So it was with some relief that three Hellfire strikes came in quick succession, ending the sniper threat. On the day the sniper was killed B Company in Sangin also had a success, so it remains a matter of contention as to who got the man. It didn't really matter: the murderous small arms fire to which we had been subjected went away. In its place came the latest version of an old tactic.

The insurgents had failed to get an IED in on the road for two weeks. So now they tried to fire Chinese rockets down the alleyways at Pat Hyde and his group of vehicles. Every road leading off the 611 became cause for concern. There was one particular spot close to Inkerman which had a particularly audacious IED team working nearby – by audacious I mean utterly brazen. One of their number must have been high to attempt what he tried. Call-sign 'Fazli' had been identified trying to place a battery pack on an IED in plain view. Unfortunately the gunner who was on duty in the sangar missed. It was a difficult shot at the limit of range and he had done an excellent job up to that point identifying what was going on. He might have been forgiven for thinking there was no way it was happening because nobody could be that stupid. So Fazli and his mates were giving us a bit of a headache. The insurgents had shifted their activity towards Inkerman. The area between Inkerman and 7 Platoon in Patrol Base Ezeray was the only area that did not have a checkpoint halfway between, so the central point between the bases was at the limit of accurate fire for an individual with a rifle.

It was in this area on 22 March that we identified some suspicious activity up an alley. With the Mastiffs coming up the road with a vehicle convoy the insurgents went to ground. We knew something must be up, but try as we might from the ground and the air we could not see anything in the alleyway that looked remotely suspicious. The Mastiff group stopped as we put all the assets we had onto the problem. Nothing on the insurgent radios, normal pattern of life elsewhere in the village, nothing: the Mastiffs rolled forward. Out of the seemingly flat road a Chinese 107mm rocket jetted towards the lead vehicle. Pat Hyde reckoned afterwards that his eyebrows had actually hit his hairline before he ducked into his cupola. The rocket slammed into the bar armour just behind the driver's door and exploded. Those inside said they hardly felt or heard a thing. Those of us watching on screens in Inkerman held our breath. The Mastiff, on its run-flat tyres, trundled on: a magnificent war horse. The insurgents had fired five rockets and missed with each one up to that point. They never bothered again.

It should be no surprise that the travails of the last four and a half months were beginning to take their toll. If most had 'enjoyed' it up to that point, it was fast become a test of endurance for everyone. Lance Corporal Strype was leaving after four and a half months, others had already done five and were facing another two, for a few, even if they too had enjoyed the highs, they had already expended all they had when it came to dealing with the daily grind. For all the trauma management interviews and the reassuring conversations everyone was affected. I am not a superstitious man, and before this tour there were no little foibles about the order in which I did things. I had a few bad habits, maybe, but no rituals. As the tour progressed I noticed an increasingly superstitious element creeping in. I listened to the same piece of music every night for the last three months save for the time I was on R and R. I have no idea why that began, but now it will live with me forever.

Riflemen are not usually a religious bunch but I could guarantee more prayers had been offered in the last six months than ever before. Early in the tour I heard a section praying before they went out. 'Low though I walk through the valley of the shadow of death…' it was moving and frightening at the same time. Pete Aldridge had a prayer found in his helmet. No one carried or wore a crucifix in the UK, but now they were common. You didn't find too many atheists on this battlefield. When I got back, a fellow Rifles officer told me that, in his experience, most soldiers were atheists. And others have reported the same thing from time with other nations. On the other side of the globe prayers were said every day for our safe return, just as prayers I'm sure were offered for our swift demise more locally. In hindsight it is a situation so ridiculous as to be laughable, but unfortunately it was and still is deadly serious. On the northern 611 by March 2010 there were very few atheists, though our superstitions ranged from the religious to the ridiculous. Tom put his boots on in the same order every day, inexplicable beyond the fact that it became his ritual. There were a hundred more, the small rituals of those who need everything to be on their side.

The level of threat was beyond rationalisation. Nearly one in five of the company had been injured, one in four Vallon men, one in four platoon commanders, five of nine section commanders were evacuated and all of us survived by luck rather than judgement on more than one occasion. With those kinds of odds the mental strength to continue going out of the gate begets a sense of putting yourself at the mercy of another. It is downright dangerous to believe, as the some of the Afghans did, in fate: fatalism becomes fatal fast. For most the 'others' in whom they trusted were God and each other. For some of us it was music or boots or any particular ritual that you happened to have carried out on a particular day and then got back safely, but collectively the most important faith was always in each other. It is a sense of attached detachment; you exist in the bubble of operations doing what you need to, but at the same time there is the comfort of false consciousness, an opium of the military classes. But the real danger is that you get too detached from the reality and begin to stop trying to prevent what is going to happen anyway.

For all the symptoms of wear and tear came in some form of post-traumatic stress. For some it is just an aversion to loud bangs, but that is the tip of a large iceberg. Post-Traumatic Stress Disorder at its most pernicious involves invasive memories crowding in and preventing sleep, and for some this happens while they are awake. Flashbacks occur. The body has a response to this. It injects adrenaline into you, inducing the fight or flight response: hypersensitivity to your surroundings that is good if you're in a fire-fight but not so good if you are trying to sleep, and especially not good when you have a gun and a Vallon in your hand. Three men came back to Inkerman. One just needed a break and went back to his patrol base, the other two stayed with us to the end. At platoon level there was quite a lot of angst about this situation, because the inability to patrol due to stress often initially materialises as reticence, and that means that their share of the burden is carried by the others. Yet if a man is a danger to himself and others he is the greater burden. I was reassured by a visit to 1 Platoon and a chat with Bobby, who had been equally cagey about letting a man go until he saw with his own eyes a man whose bravery was unquestioned shaking before him. I was determined to show them humanity; those young men had overspent the coin of courage. We all took an overdraft out that winter, and for some it had turned into a loan they could not repay. They would come home with us to get the welcome they deserved, not travel alone to Brize Norton with the duty driver arriving thirty minutes late.

What I never had cause to doubt was the continued collective will of A Company to fight right to the bitter end. The last operation we undertook was the clearance of a block to the south of the Gul Agha Wadi. 1 Platoon, who had endured a great deal, and who had been in the thick of the fighting for four months by that point, moved yet again into the Gul Agha Wadi, an area that might qualify, with the western culvert now secure, as the most dangerous place in the world. I remember watching them move out, thinking 'You are five days from the start of the changeover and two weeks from the end of the tour and you have volunteered to go and do this'. The clearance was one of a number of tasks we could have done to keep the insurgent on the back foot and create the space for handover. I had given Mike, who was back, having recovered just enough grip in his hand, the choice about which one they would do. He had talked it through with his team and they went for the Gul Aga Wadi. I don't think I have ever been as proud of a platoon under my command. The collective will, the esprit de corps, the determination was astonishing given what they had been through. And in what was a faultless operation they slayed a few demons and finished the tour on a high. Those fine words about the blow that 1 Platoon had dealt in mid-March turned out to be true. The enemy did not attack that day: there was no way we could have known, it was only by doing this operation that they proved it. Only afterwards did Mike admit to me that he had been a bag of nerves all the way through – me too. Both of us were going at it like ducks, trying to be all serene on top but paddling like hell underneath.

The incidents continued, but at a rate of one a day rather than one an hour. Looking back at my log it seems a good deal fuller and busier than it felt. I remember one morning in late March going into the operations room and waiting for it all to start and it just didn't. I suddenly had time on my hands. And now, having not written an audio blog for twelve weeks, I was able to backfill from all the experiences from R and R and the various operations we had undertaken. Luckily for me Radio 4 had repeated all the early ones and had filled the gap. What is written below is with hindsight the one I am most ashamed of. It is the truth, but at such an oblique angle as to be thoroughly misleading. I had been asked by the MoD to write about the equipment we had on ops, so I picked the bit I could be most positive about.

But have you got the right kit? One of the questions that came up repeatedly during my stay in the UK concerned kit. That, and where did I sleep? Well; I sleep in a sleeping bag on a camp cot. Not in great quantities but pretty comfortably. The hot water bottle became a vital companion during January. Now it is 35 degrees during the day we are into lightweight bags. Spring has turned into summer in a month. But back to the kit. The question even turned into a statement, 'Well of course you're not properly equipped!' I have an excellent rifle with a brand new sight; a new helmet, winter and summer kit that does the job and more. We travel in a range of vehicles and I generally get the choice of whether I send people out with the balance in favour of protection or mobility. And it is a balance. The laws of physics are difficult to bend. The relentless march of technology means that kit needs constantly updating but as an infantryman I have never been better equipped whilst I have been in the Army. Of course we could do more with more but we will not fail here for lack of personal equipment. General McCrystal put it bluntly last summer, we are only in danger of defeating ourselves. It is the human touch, the politics not the technology that will make the difference.

Napoleon is alleged to have said that 'Moral is to the physical as three is to one.' So the will to fight, the cause and the doctrine by which you fight is three times more important than what you fight with. I look no further than 1 Platoon in the Gul Agha Wadi to know that the spirit was willing all the way to the end, so despite my shame I still stand by the last point in the blog. But here's the bugger. The MoD decided to equip us with kit procured through a process known as Urgent Operational Requirements, and I have already recounted the worst effects of that process for 'A' Company. The MoD procured the kit in such a way that we only got to use it in theatre rather than in training. The Army has 9,000 well-equipped troops at any one time and 90,000, soon to be 70,000, poorly-equipped troops. And most importantly that includes those on the point of deployment. Furthermore, in order to get a UOR through the procurement process you have to demonstrate the urgency of the need. That is an unpleasant euphemism for a soldier having died because they could not do something they would have been able to with a certain piece of kit. What is more, they could have had that kit because it is already commercially available.

The UOR system is like taking the child with holes in his teeth to the sweet shop so that he feels better about the holes. What is more, at the time of writing, in an effort to 'balance' the budget, the MoD has cut every line of planned spending on soldier's, marine's and airmen's individual equipment. No body armour, no new rifles, no radios or rucksacks, just keep the nine thousand you got for Afghanistan. One and half billion pounds of planned spending in the next ten years, gone. That is, to continue the sweets analogy to a tortuous conclusion, like telling the once proud boy now with holes in his teeth that he will be fed on penny sweets when his teeth hurt for years to come. Of course he and our security and the interests he is there to defend will be better for it, durch.

The new radios that the most senior procurement committee in the MoD said we had a requirement for in 2009 will not be bought until 2019. You try keeping your mobile until 2019! Especially when it's the one you bought in 1999. In this one area, where our allies and enemies are making rapid strides, because it is all commercially available, Tommy is going to have to die before someone buys him the right kit. There are civil servants, politicians, generals, admirals and air marshalls and ministers who need, as the saying goes, to take a good hard look in the mirror. The military covenant in all senses of that much misused and maligned term is still broken. That is the covenant between Country and Army and in its original and correct use between the leaders and the led, the covenant in which the senior military leadership honour their position of trust as leaders of those in the Armed Services.

How many examples do we need: generals using their positions of trust in service charities to lobby government on behalf of defence firms, anyone? The newshound in the MoD put it well on getting a copy of Mike Jackson's book: 'One hundred thousand reasons why I didn't resign.'

Many a true word is said in jest. The reality is they needed to stand up for the right thing when they had the chance, not bleat in splendidly rewarded retirement. We have time to do something about this problem. I only hope those in positions of authority can right the grievous wrong that is our servicemen's individual equipment programme before it is too late for them, the future grief of their families, and the security of the country. Enough said. *J'accuse.*

# Chapter 14

# Honourable Warriors

At the end of March 2010 I began to get bullish about what was happening in our area of operations. The lines of development, political, economic, social and security, were beginning to move in the same direction, if not quite at the same pace.

All the equipment that we had been given over the tour was now beginning to pay dividends and the tactics we employed meant that we were able to strike the enemy as cleanly as possible before he struck us. There was no better example of this than when the gunner in charge of operating the Revivor balloon camera saw something suspicious: a furtive local with a walkie-talkie. We had a patrol coming in to Inkerman from 7 Platoon, about 800 metres away in the green zone. Adam flicked through the channels and caught an insurgent talking about preparing to take on a patrol in the green zone. The electronic warfare team we had welcomed to Inkerman at the beginning of March was able to use its direction-finding equipment to confirm that the channel being used was coming from the direction of the locals, so we could now positively identify them as insurgents who had hostile intent. The channel they were using was not a repeater channel, so by confirming there were no other patrols out in our area we could be assured we had our men. So far so good. They were out of range to anything but a sniper and they were all in the patrol bases. We could try heavy machine-gun, but the risk of collateral damage was too great. Luckily with a drone overhead we could bring the right degree of precision. Dinger had to bring him onto the target. Miraculously he was already nearly in the right orbit and Al, the FSG commander, by now well-practised and in the middle of his handover, organised the area to be 'cleared hot'.

Just then a second man appeared by the side of the guy who had been positively identified. The Revivor operator and I watched instructions being given until I was convinced that this man too had hostile intent against Rob and his men in the green zone. A final check on the collateral damage possibilities and then 'My commander Romeo Golf Sierra authorises engagement.' A few seconds and one large explosion later: 'Targets identified, targets down'. Given the proximity to Inkerman I launched the QRF, in the form of Pat Hyde in a Mastiff and members of the guard. They arrived on the scene as the second body was about to be taken away. They arrested the lot and brought them and the corpse back to Inkerman.

As I launched the QRF I stepped outside the ops room for a cigarette. It had taken just twenty minutes to effect that operation and something that in normal life would be the most unusual thing to do in a lifetime was just a small part of the day. This was routine business: none of the whooping or swearing that had accompanied early strikes, just turning the screw on the insurgent. I no longer thought anything of it. I wrote the report of what happened and sent it up. It was only when it came back from the Divisional Headquarters with bells and whistles as an 'exemplary operation' that it even began to occur to me how far I'd come, how far the whole team had come, or gone… depending on your view.

One of the party detained by the QRF was a senior man in our local village of Sareagar. He was someone who was well known to us and had often protested that he didn't work for the Taliban. So why was he picking up their dead? It turned out that the first insurgent we had identified had been the local commander, but not originally from our area. The second was a local man who had been forced to fight. It was his body that we had removed and it was he the locals had tried to rescue. A deal was done. We would release the body and the rescue party early the next day to allow the necessary rituals to take place before we gave offence. We would fund two projects of his choice to give him further credibility in future negotiations with the village, but we needed a regular shura with him and the heads of household from Sareagar.

He left happy. That afternoon there were two funerals in the local graveyard. Because of the Islamic requirement to bury the dead within twenty-four hours, most Afghan graveyards have a 'stranger' corner. That day one man was buried in the corner and the other in the main graveyard. Many of our 'friends' from the first Mian Ruud shura turned up that day. We took photographs from a distance but did not interrupt. A patrol went past afterwards and got a hostile reception, verbal not physical. In a bizarre turn of events the interpreter that day, a new one in our area, was accused of offering to help the Taliban. The news came in from an unusual intelligence source in southern Sangin. He was shipped back to Bastion for some awkward questions to be answered. It was the only time we encountered possible treachery from the Afghans who worked with us. We had started life with a lamentable number of interpreters in Inkerman – with Adam on sick leave we were left with two for the entire company, and they had become the limiting factor on the number of patrols we could send out. By this point we had eighteen in the area as well as a few Afghan soldiers who had a little broken English. Most of our interpreters had Pashtun as a second language, all except Adam, and it showed. The cultural indifference and on occasions hostility showed up in their translations. Some of the Riflemen, particularly Rifleman 'H' Hernandez, became extremely useful in checking the translation. In conversations with the ANA and the locals the interpreters were often doing a three-way translation from Dari to Pashtun to English. Our language skills became good. Our training had amounted to less than two or three hours, the Riflemen selected a year previously to go on the long language course never showed up amongst the battle casualty replacements for a variety of inexcusable reasons. You only realise what you are missing when someone who really knows what they are doing shows up. A stabilisation officer turned up to write a report on the Inkerman AO, and he was all but fluent; a young Tom in the Paras with good Pashtu showed up as a mentor to one of the Tiger Teams, and suddenly we were awash with information. I was lucky to have Adam. The new interpreters did not much like his privileged position, especially the ones from the listening teams who were being constantly corrected about the exact meaning of the local Taliban commanders' codes. Mention also ought to go to Colin, clearly not his real name but nicknamed so by the Company. He was a first time 'terp', thrust into the hurly-burly of our early days in Inkerman. Effete and intellectual he had a Kabul snobbery the equivalent of anything that Kensington or Chelsea could throw at the Gorbals. He was the most unlikely man to have next to you in a fire-fight and none of us thought he would last the course, yet by the end he was a revelation. I remember taking him back to 3 Platoon in Shuga where he was greeted quite literally with open arms and then a more manly clasp and bump of chests. He endured the cold nights, the tough fights and the fear, and every night he was to be found facing west towards Mecca in his religious observance. A very good man.

In amongst the successes there were a few notable failures. In resisting an attack on one of the bases we authorised fire with a grenade machine-gun. The gunner fired a burst at an identified firing point, but lost control of the third round, which ended up killing a young girl in a different compound. The family went to what they thought was their local base to demand compensation. We paid immediately, but after having been in a near-continuous fire-fight for so long, with only relatively minor injuries inflicted by us on the local population, it was disappointing to have such an incident so near the end. Our bank of goodwill was still in credit despite this incident, although we did inflict a further serious civilian casualty, not killed but a serious injury nonetheless, before the tour was through.

Despite what on other operations – Northern Ireland for example – might have become a national incident, these were so minor by comparison to what had gone before in the Inkerman AO that they barely registered with the remainder of the local national population, even if the grief of that girl's loved ones was as deep as that of any bereaved parent. I do not buy the idea that Afghans are callous when they come for money: it is part of their culture, you pay to restore honour, and it is only by treating it with disdain that one risks revenge. Thus the insurgents were not able to make anything of it, and the fact that the family came to one of our bases to talk to us was as good a sign as any that they trusted us to do the right thing, even if it made for uncomfortable listening. Our discomfort was nothing in comparison to theirs. By keeping them with us the enemy remained under the cosh.

Not only that, but we now knew that the Taliban groups in our area were divided amongst themselves. Three of the five had succumbed to the blandishments of the new District Governor and stopped fighting. It was alleged that part of the reason why we had had such a hard time at the beginning of March was because the last two groups wanted to make a point. Indeed the nature of the attacks, which were brave in the extreme, suggested something of this kind of zeal. 7 Platoon had five grenades thrown over the wall of their newly established checkpoint, Marshall's post, luckily with no one hurt, but yet again a very close run thing: call-sign 'Fazli' up to his old tricks. Serjeant Billy Bain had a 'Shootout at the OK Corral' moment when he walked round the corner at the same time as two insurgents came into the alley from the other end. Such was the surprise at both ends of the road that no shots were fired and both parties moved into cover pretty sharpish.

1 Platoon had a lucky escape where they were ambushed at close quarters. Three were injured: Corporal 'JD' Dolton had bullet holes in his kit, his shirt, but miraculously only one in him, in his wrist. In addition to his injury, an interpreter and Rifleman Dicky Sheldon from the signals detachment were both wounded. JD became the fifth and, thankfully, the last section commander to be lifted out in a MIRT helicopter.

Each platoon now had a patrol base and a checkpoint to man. The operation to resupply them that had taken eight days in early January now took less than eight hours. Even the long-term resupply into Inkerman that had taken three days on arrival came and left in less than four hours. The military tactics of holding fixed points could only really work if supported by other types of operation to disrupt the Taliban in depth. Now that Operation Moshtarak was over to our south the Brigade Recce Force and the 'Armoured' Squadron manned by the Royal Tank Regiment had three very successful operations in depth in our area. I say 'Armoured' because they came in Viking vehicles, which had a host of black humoured names. They were not very IED resistant, to say the least, so I used them in the desert checking out compounds on the edge of Sangin, interdicting the resupply of arms and ammunition into our area, much as I had wished to use the Fire Support Group in the early days. The chat on ICOM confirmed their success. They found a couple of IEDs in a cave which took two light anti-structure munitions to destroy, either a bad shot, incredibly resistant containers, or the photographs of the first one were not quite good enough. The Brigade Recce Force (BRF) went into the northern side of Jusalay aiming to have a look in the mosques that we had not quite reached in November. They were given the run around all day by small groups of insurgents, but never managed to engage them decisively.

These operations were truly over or behind the IED minefield, inserted from the desert or by helicopter, run from Inkerman using our local knowledge. And it kept the fight away from the population we were trying to protect, at least for the day, and gave the insurgent something else to think about. The Afghan National Army platoons were getting more confident by the day. They planned and conducted a cordon and search operation which 2 Platoon supported. Tom and 3 Platoon were getting on famously with Lieutenant Anwar and the ANA platoon in Shuga. Anwar was persuaded to do a reactive operation to search a property that we thought an IED team was using just off the 611. One might think that this should be par for the course, but for the ANA if a patrol had not been scheduled they would rarely go out and only after long discussion: union rules. But a quick call into Sangin to the Combined Force Sangin operations room meant that Colonel Wadood could order them to do it far more easily, the order coming back into the joint operations room in Patrol Base Shuga. Joint operations room sounds grand, but in fact the ANA manned a radio in a tent just outside Tom's operations room. Even so it made the passage of information infinitely faster than it had been.

The ANA came and led the search, Afghans giving other Afghans a sense of security. The Tiger Team started a new security shura with 1 Platoon in Patrol Base Bariolai and thirteen heads of household turned up. 1 Platoon also had an NDS – Afghan security intelligence – officer with them who made a couple of arrests of local Taliban he recognised, only serving to demonstrate the impunity with which they had moved amongst us. And for me it demonstrated that you cannot really control an area unless you are there all the time. The ANA even spent a day in Pete's Post on the Gul Agha Wadi. They were very nervous, but the day went well. In mid-March the ANA company commander who had left just before the start of the tour to go on leave and then to the UK for training came back. With the return of the good Captain Araf as their company commander the ANA got a new lease of life.

Having Araf in Patrol Base Blenheim put me in something of a quandary. Partnership should have meant that I moved my Company HQ to Blenheim. The infrastructure move was too horrendous to contemplate, but it did mean I spent a lot more time in Blenheim with 2 Platoon at the end of the tour. Lucky them! I harboured the ambition that Araf should move to Inkerman and set about plans to make it so for my successor. The locals were now attending weekly shuras in all of the bases apart from 7 Platoon. But Rob used to go to the mosque on a regular basis. The mountain – durch – to Mohammed…. In all of them the locals complained of the level of intimidation they were suffering. It was our first insight into the low-level operation of control that the Taliban had over them. I was confused. They kept talking about intimidation and yet they continued to come to the shuras; my sense was that while the Taliban were still on their backs, the free run to market that they were now getting into Sangin was worth the hassle. I attended one such meeting with Captain Araf in Blenheim. We sat in the spring sunshine and drank tea. Captain Araf was waxing lyrical about the new security in the area and at one point reduced his audience to total fits of laughter. Then all of a sudden the translation stopped. I was using a 2 Platoon interpreter and not Adam, for once. I asked him what was so funny. He protested he couldn't… it was too rude… an Afghan joke. I pressed him to tell me.

After a little persuading he said that if there is one thing an Afghan is more frightened of than any other it is the sea. In a landlocked country the fear of this unknown and mysterious beast is culturally unfathomable to someone from an island. Yet when it comes to anal sex with another man the Afghan is surprisingly tolerant. You might think that is a total non sequitur but bear with me. Many if not all of the Afghan soldiers we worked with had wives, but 2 Platoon can testify to the admiring looks their youngest, lithest, blondest Rifleman got from their Afghan partners. Yes, that's you Rifleman Gedeye. That, and the unearthly noise of 'Man Love Thursday'. I am not suggesting for a moment that these men thought of themselves as gay or homosexual. They certainly did not, for now as then being gay is illegal in Afghanistan. But it didn't stop them having sex with other men. So Captain Araf had said 'If my dick is by your arsehole and your head is in the sea, which are you going to choose?'. The assembled Afghans appreciated the vulgarity, the simplicity and the inevitability of the choice. We were finally making good on another part of the bargain and I hoped we were making them a better offer than buggery.

The tender had gone out from the stabilisation team for a 4.5 million dollar contract to black-top the road. By mid-April a preferred bidder would be selected and by the time the harvest was finished we should be paying 200 local men to work on the road. The CO had ideas about creating a local militia, as a Sangin police force, and handing over the checkpoints. All things seemed possible. The lure of the dollar was a strong incentive. This was the clincher for me. The status of the patrol bases had hung on a thread. Much had been written and said attacking the concept of tying ourselves down to guard fixed points, denying ourselves the freedom to patrol. It was all too easy to forget that to patrol out of Inkerman was to walk into a minefield. You just can't do blitzkreig because you wish it so. In further talks with locals Phil Wetherill, the stabilisation adviser, determined that after a patrol had gone to a village the Taliban used to follow up immediately. The only way to prevent them was permanent over-watch. The cost of guarding a base is a price worth paying for living amongst the people. People, and most especially Pashtuns, take time to be persuaded, time and evidence; landing outside his village, rummaging through his house and having a fire-fight with other people he doesn't much like and then moseying off to your big base surrounded by wire, leaving him to fend off the Taliban inquisition into what you talked about, is evidence for the prosecution not the defence. To persuade him you have to live it with him and, most importantly, put yourself between him and the enemy and not create a Pashtun sandwich in the manner of Mortimer Durand.

With the fighting season coming there was only one way to really secure the 611 and that was to get local men to build it and secure it, not blow it up. I was often told by Afghans that Afghans believe in what they can see. They liked the patrol bases because they could see them, but patrol bases come and go. No one would be taking a road anywhere.

Someone once told me, against my nature, to live in the expectation of success not the fear of failure. In the first week of April I fully expected success. With three weeks to go I thought we had built and secured bases that could be handed over eventually to Afghan security forces and ISAF could then secure the rest of northern Sangin. I thought we had won over the local population and that they supported us, not just because we had fought against the Taliban, but also because we were beginning to show that we could bring economic prosperity, the freedom to access government services, and a measure of freedom from the fear of reprisal. And the reason I fully expected success was because, astonishingly for all of us in an incredibly tight circle, it wasn't me saying this, it was the Taliban.

* * * * *

*Pashtunwali* is the way of the Pashtun. It is a set of unwritten ethical principles by which the Pashtun population live in Afghanistan. Most importantly it is how they judged both us and the Taliban. The intricacies of *Pashtunwali* are lost on me, but the main principles are outlined below courtesy of experience, a little cultural training and a well-known search engine. Our first aim was to protect the population. To protect them one has to win them over. In insurgency, this time courtesy of Mao, the insurgent swims like fish in the water. The rest of the population are the water. If you want to deal with the fish one can simply remove the water. And in the case of the insurgency in Malaya that is what we did, putting everyone in guarded villages, but we were not in that game in Afghanistan. Instead we needed the population to give up the insurgents of their own free will and that meant winning them over, learning to swim like the fish. In order to win the population over one has to demonstrate an understanding of and a sympathy to their culture and in the Pashtun lands of southern Afghanistan that meant *Pashtunwali*. To offend any of these codes was to dishonour the Pashtun and if you have no honour in Pashtun-dominated southern Afghanistan you might as well leave.

The Pashtun must show *melmastia* (hospitality) and profound respect to all visitors. Interestingly this is regardless of distinctions of race, religion, national affiliation or economic status, and he must do so without any hope of remuneration or favour. Pashtuns will go to great lengths to show their hospitality. This is why forced entry into compounds is such a problem: it is a slap in the face to their requirement to invite you in. Now think of all those videos of troops bursting through compound doors and walls.

*Nanawatai* (asylum), derived from the verb meaning 'to go in', is used for the protection given to a person who requests protection against his or her enemies. These people are protected at all costs: in many cases even people running from the law must be given refuge until the situation is clarified. It can also be used when the vanquished party is prepared to go in to the house of the victors and ask for their forgiveness. It is a peculiar form of 'chivalrous' surrender, in which an enemy seeks 'sanctuary' at his enemy's house. A more famous example of this code, and one that got a lot of airtime in our training, is of Navy Petty Officer First Class (PO1) Marcus Luttrell, the sole surviving member of a US Navy SEAL team that was ambushed by Taliban fighters. Luttrell evaded the enemy for days before stumbling upon members of the Sabray tribe who realized the wounded SEAL needed assistance. He was taken to the village and protected by the tribal chief, who even sent word to nearby US forces of his location.

*Badal* (justice) means to seek justice or take revenge against the wrongdoer. This applies to injustices committed yesterday, 133 years ago or 1,000 years previously if the wrongdoer still exists. Justice in Pashtun law needs elaborating: even a mere taunt (or '*paighor*') is regarded as an insult, which can only usually be redressed by shedding of the taunter's blood and, if he isn't available, then his next closest male relation. This in turn leads to a blood feud that can last generations and involve whole tribes with the loss of hundreds of lives. There were many who saw our presence in Helmand as a desire to seek justice for previous losses, particularly at the battle of Maiwand.

*Tureh* (bravery) is the idea that a Pashtun must defend his land, property, family and women from incursions, wherever he or she might reside. A Pashtun should always stand brave against tyranny and he should always be able to defend his property, family, women and the honour of his name.

*Sabat* (loyalty) must be paid to one's family, friends, and tribe members. Loyalty is a must and a Pashtun can never become disloyal as this would be utterly shameful for them and their families.

*Imandari* (righteousness) describes how a Pashtun must always strive to think good thoughts, speak good words and do other good deeds. Pashtuns must behave respectfully towards all creation, people, animals and the environment around them. Pollution of the environment or its destruction is against the *Pashtunwali*.

*Isteqamat* (trust in God) refers to the god known as 'Allah' in Arabic and 'Khudai' in Pashto. The notion of trusting in the one Creator generally mirrors the Islamic idea of belief in only one God (*tawheed*).

*Ghayrat* (self-honour, or dignity) decrees that Pashtuns must maintain their dignity. Honour has great importance in Pashtun society and most other codes of life are aimed towards the preservation of honour or pride. They must respect themselves and others in order to be able to do so, especially those they do not know. Respect begins at home, among family members and relatives.

*Namus* (honour of women) requires that a Pashtun must defend the honour of Pashtun women at all costs and must protect them from verbal and physical harm.

We had been given a brief that as a result of the infighting amongst the various groups that there might be some attempt to reach out to us. I passed this on in very general terms, telling the platoon commanders if it happened in our area that we should on no account arrest those concerned, but try to make arrangements for them to come to Inkerman or go to the District Governor, who would be happy to speak to them. On 18 March a section from 7 Platoon led by Corporal Fox were conducting a VCP outside Patrol Base Ezeray. It was something they did very regularly. If the VCP stayed in place for more than thirty minutes the locals seemed to get to know about it and diverted their route. The passage information was remarkably good and testament to the control the Taliban still exercised in our area. But in the first ten minutes we could usually find out about what was going on in the bazaar and pick up local gossip on a one-to-one basis with people who hopefully would not be identified for recrimination.

As they were readying to leave two men walked over to talk to them. The conversation that they had was barely credible. The two men claimed to be representatives of the 'Military Committee of the Upper Sangin Valley'. They gave their names and a short speech that was reported to me as 'The committee recognise you as honourable warriors and we wish to talk'. This was outreach in reverse. Corporal Fox was highly suspicious, as was Rob for various reasons, but at least they did not arrest them. That would have been to immediately dishonour them. He took their names and the name of the group they claimed to represent and invited them to come to the patrol base to meet Rob or to go to the District Governor. Rob was unconvinced: he had begun to doubt Corporal Fox for a variety of reasons that ultimately meant he was returned to Kajaki days later, and also because that was the last he saw of them and it was the last conversation that I had with any of my team about what was happening. But they did go to the governor and the names checked out as being from the group that Combined Force Sangin and the stabilisation team most wanted to talk to. In March 2010 the heads of the Taliban Civil and Military Commissions contacted the District Stabilisation Team to confirm that they had stopped those fighters under their control from laying IEDs, but made it clear that out-of-area Taliban could not be stopped. On 29 May 2010, a formal offer of peace with the Upper Sangin Valley was made by eight of the most influential leaders and was swiftly followed by overtures from tribal groups in the south of the district. It opened a dialogue that resulted in a peace offer being on the table in September 2010 before the 3/5 US Marines smashed their way into the china shop.

The reasons why they wanted to talk were multiple. My personal belief is that our part in all this was simply to have demonstrated that we were on the side of the population, we would protect them with our lives, offer stern resistance to the enemy, but we were willing to talk. This had been achieved by months of fighting, yet in hindsight the door to dialogue had only really been opened by the relationship developed over two months with the elders of Mian Ruud at the start of the tour. In the early conversations we had constantly stressed the desire to open up a dialogue with the Taliban, which had aroused some anger in the early shuras, but had not fallen on deaf ears. Our words then had been backed by action. We had not arranged for the release of the brothers, but we had managed to allow the family to see their boys in prison. The bases were in and the road to market was free. That road was due for a considerable upgrade. In short our offer was beginning to look far better than the Taliban's. By early 2010 all of the out-of-area fighters had congregated in Mian Ruud. You might ask why they weren't offering stiffer resistance in central Helmand at that time, but maybe they thought they could come and attack what they perceived as the outpost when there was overwhelming force being applied elsewhere. This congregation of fighters in Mian Ruud we had not formally identified at the time, but it explains why February and early March were such hectic times and why they might have been persuaded to talk. It certainly wasn't solely down to our conversations with this group, there were factors outside our control that had also helped bring them to the table.

Further north up the valley a local drug baron had got into a fight with the Taliban and been shot. This did not go down well with the locals who produced most of their poppy for this man. It was strange, as the narco barons were often cast as the villains of the piece, but in this instance he was preferred to the Taliban. We seemed to have had an ally in a most unlikely place. Taken altogether the Taliban were losing the population.

As the enemy picture became clearer I was very hopeful that from the ashes of the bombing of Sangin in 2006 something approaching peace could eventually be delivered. If it could happen then not only would we have fought honourably, but perhaps we would also have helped achieve the mission. It certainly was not over. There were still shooting incidents in the middle of April, whereas the year before there had been none while the harvest was conducted, but I felt that we were nearly there. My penultimate and final reports to my CO can be summarised thus:

The story of the northern 611 looks increasingly positive. The prospect of local employment at the end of the Harvest, an increased ANA presence, troops permitting, as well as an improvement in route security for ISAF will be a good note to handover on.

The handover to B Company 40 Commando went well. Ten days is a long time for a handover and by the last two I felt very much like a spare part. Mark, my successor, was clearly itching, as I had been six months earlier, to make the changes he thought necessary and enact some of the things we had left behind. Naturally he wanted to do them his way. To their credit there was not a murmur of criticism from them. Something I was thankful for. The lull in activity during the harvest would hopefully give them time to find their feet, and for the plans we had made to come to fruition. On 19 April I handed over to Mark with a grip and grin photo under the very same flagpoles where Iain and I had handed over. The only difference was that now the Afghan flag was ascendant over the Union flag. I sent my last, five-word sitrep to HQ and allowed Mark to write up what had really happened that week. It read 'The end of the road – durch.'

On 21 April 2010 I was the last member of A Company to step onto the Chinook out of Inkerman. Pat Hyde was just ahead of me and it would be normal for the company sergeant major to count everyone through and step on last himself. No communication was necessary, or possible, given the noise of the rotors as he watched me loiter at the tail. I was having my Mel Gibson moment from the film *When We Were Soldiers*: first into the field, and the last off it. He did me the honour of indulgence, not for the first or last time.

## Chapter 15

# Coming Home

As we flew into Camp Bastion there was no overwhelming sense of relief or elation or any other hyper-emotion. I was just exhausted. I did not feel tired and I did not feel empty. I did not feel anything. I have described it since as being 'emotionally cauterised'. Nothing is perceived as it once was and yet everything looks the same. The months of adrenaline, caffeine and nicotine, waking up with jaw aching from clenched tension in the night, the grief, the fear, the elation – in comparison the nature of life even in Camp Bastion, especially in Camp Bastion, so near and yet so far, is suddenly, epically, awfully mundanefully dull.

We gathered and held our last memorial service, reading some of the eulogies to our fallen. I was encouraging everyone to 'talk about it' all as much as possible. While we had waited two drawn out days after handover in Inkerman before flying out I had talked to Mike, Charlie, Tom and Rob about their views of the tour. I asked them if there was anything they wanted to get off their chest about things I had ordered them to do or not to do. As we chewed over the hows, whys, and whens I tried to impress upon them the scale of what they had been through. They had joined up with the Army in Iraq and Afghanistan. They had signed on with operations of this type in mind. It was all they had ever known.

Their steel had been forged in the hottest fire. I laughed to myself as I thought of trundling round in Landrovers in Bosnia when I had been at their age and stage. Op Palatine had been a different kind of operation; the whole Battalion had returned in one piece, not a single shot had been fired in anger, and the greatest danger was being in a road traffic accident. If it were true for the officers, the same was true for this generation of Riflemen, most of whom had been in the Army for less than eighteen months. As we left Inkerman I thought that we were part of a new reality for the Army. I thought those who would follow might be luckier than us, and hopefully had been given a better chance of success by our effort. We would all find out that even by the bloody standard of Afghanistan, the winter of 2009–10 more than matched any other as the most sustained period of violence ever tolerated by the Army in the twenty-first century and probably since Korea. The period turned out to be unusual even in the context of the last decade.

After weeks and weeks of living on the edge of existence, three fresh meals a day and packing up seemed disastrously ordinary. The light at the end of the tunnel, the tune in the tedium, was the prospect of reunion with our families, now delayed by the Icelandic dust cloud. At the beginning I dearly wanted all of us who went to Afghanistan in October to return home together in one group – a vain hope – and now I wanted those that were still there to be together for the journey home, but that too seemed too much to ask. 'Efficiency' dictated we be split into two packets. We were supposed to meet up at the transfer onto the charter but my group never made it in time. Cohesion is an important aspect of morale and yet here again, at the very last, we were split up. Half of us spent twenty-four hours in an airport terminal in the middle of the desert, the agony of waiting before the ecstasy of reunion; regular fare from the boys in light blue, but maybe this time, much as it was easy to, they could not be blamed for the vagaries of subterranean volcanic explosions in Iceland.

There was another stop to be made. The Army has learned that sending people from fire-fight to fireplace in a matter of hours enhances the sense of dislocation that can bring trouble and at worst be a step on the road to post-traumatic stress. So despite our enforced stop in the desert there was another period of enforced fun to be had. I had done my best to get out of it. We had been out of the Forward Operating Base for a week and most of the Company had been off the front line for ten days or more. I met the same stock answer from those in charge of the move. You have to spend a day in Cyprus – orders is orders. After three such conversations I gave up. The rest of the group couldn't help but hear the bulk of one of the calls: not the best way to deliver bad news, but they were satisfied that little more could have been done. We were on the beach at ten o'clock the following morning, having got in at three am, and were required to do a swim test before we were allowed in the sea. Really? In the face of the Mexican standoff I took the plunge and the rest followed, albeit grudgingly.

The next twenty-four hours in Cyprus were indeed a great way to relax and by mid-afternoon just about everybody had 'bought in'. There was another infantry company on the same flight, commanded by a guy I knew from a course. We were able to share a beer while our respective companies tried to out-sing each other that evening. As night ended the Senior NCOs, Pat, Jona and Jimmy, intervened before anyone regretted taking the competition to what appeared would be its natural conclusion. The Riflemen went to bed. I had a 'moment' with a corporal who had joined us for the last eight weeks of the tour from B Company 4 Rifles. He had replaced Corporal Furgusson and was a good man. He decided that that the 'no beer in bed' rule for the Riflemen did not apply to him and was considerably disappointed when I made him pour his secreted stash down the sink. He had the humility to apologise the next day. I couldn't blame him for trying; I was pretty keen to have a few more myself, but turning up to Bulford glassy-eyed was not the way we should come home. It would have shown a distinct lack of respect for those who had travelled before us, nursing wounds, on life support or carried off draped in a flag.

So on Sunday 25 April, many having spent nearly 300 days of the previous 364 apart, we were reunited with our loved ones. For all the talk of 'only' doing a six-month tour, the reality is more like a year, so needless to say we were given a very warm welcome. I remember stepping off the bus and seeing not only large crowds of families, but also TV cameras and microphones galore. It was all very public. Emily wanted a big hug and got one, as did Rachel. Henry was confused by cameras and crowds and clung to his mother. It was great to be home, but I knew there would be others watching. Who probably could not bear to watch those happy scenes that they would have given everything to share. Nor were the wounded there. CO 4 Rifles had decided that it would not be appropriate for them and us. I now regret not making my case for their participation more strongly: they deserved the accolades more than we did.

I was partly to blame for this press exposure. When I had phoned Rachel from Cyprus she said they had played my last blog. I had formed the idea for it in the middle of March and it was the only one that took more than half an hour to write. It was all the names and nicknames of the company, just A Company, in a list and then an exhortation to remember the fallen. Rachel told me it had made people stop and cry: even John Humphrys had been moved. I had, rather randomly, limited it to the names of the guys who had set out from Bulford six months previously, more than anything to keep it to a reasonable length. There were at least 200 more who should have been named and all of them feature in some way, named or unnamed, in this narrative. For it was above all a team effort, yet I neglected to record the true scope of that team and their sacrifice which was great as ours.

I Salute you
Ricky, Ginge, Sonny
Legs, Owens, V, Ed, Smudge,
Rolfy, Archy, Cam, Hitch, Eddie, Lips,
Monty, Bobby, Sam, and Thorpy,
Kristian, Ronnie, Craig, and Dave
Bethan, Jodie, Colette, Hayley
Fish, Morgs, and Murph.
Two Toms, two Tells, and a couple of Macs
Ash, Cat, Gaz, Bremner, Danso, Fletch, and Hoyley
JD, Louie, Michael, Nash,
Sakiusa, Ollie, Pan, and Ratty,
Tapps, Vinny, Will, Woody, and another V

Topsy, Robbo, Preecy, Pete,
Guy, Furgie, Ruby, Cunny, and Coxy,
Browny, Axel, Bab, Cadell, and Nathan
Mike, Niall, Knighty, Johno
Waka, Patch, Gumbo, Compass, Cookie
Cameron, Anthony, Jovilifi, Nash,
Ken, Ray Ray, Tommy T,
Grevo, Grandad, Gorm, Goody, Gonzo, Ginge
Vinny, Trev, Tony, Toby, Bertie
Reading, Payney, Paul, Martin, Mark
Needs, Ned, James twice, Pablos and Picker
Chico, Chip, Chase, Charlie, Coxy, Coyne
5 Dans, Dave squared Dudley, Dole, Dicky, Devo, Decks, Dean, and Daz,
Stuart, Stripper, Steven, Stephen, Stan, Spencer, Spence
Smithers, Slumdog, Sin, Si, Scouse, Sarg, Bridgey, Borth, Bertrand, Bags
Ben, Pat, Fred, Charles, Michael, Tom, Ed, and Jessie, Jonna, Jimmy, H.
These are the men and women whom I have had the privilege to lead
Mothers, brothers, husbands, sons and daughters I salute you.

Carlo, Martin, Tom, Sam, and Pete for our tomorrow you gave your today.
Age will not weary you nor the years condemn,
At the going down of the sun and in the morning we will remember.

This list was the one broadcast on Radio 4 which, in the context of everything I have written, does a considerable disservice to a number of people. In the fifth paragraph on the first line sits Robbo. Rifleman Ross 'Robbo' Robinson had been flown home from Afghanistan with a broken back after he had been injured in the IED blast that had killed Sam Bassett. It hadn't stopped him getting to his feet and Valloning the path for his friends' evacuation immediately after the explosion. Rifleman Ross Robinson had been at Headley Court getting treatment on his back when we returned. He had seen a number of 1 Platoon as they returned through injury or on R and R and had had long chats with Mike, his platoon commander. He returned to Bulford on 28 April and, now on his feet again, he went out with the platoon. It was an emotional evening. In the early hours of 29 April he was hit by a van on the A303, walking back to Bulford from a local service station, and killed. It was a cruel blow. Rifleman Robinson had been an early example of fortitude and bravery in the face of serious injury and his efforts were to be publicly recognised. His Queen's Gallantry Medal was awarded posthumously to his family.

Rifleman Robinson's QGM represented, as did all the other awards the Company got, not only recognition of his actions, but also the actions of all those on the tour who happened not to be seen or not selected from the profusion of incidents and acts of selfless bravery I saw every day. It is with an unfortunate regularity that soldiers get killed on return from operations. The army tries to warn them about a reduced ability to calibrate risk. If your yardstick is lead and buried homemade explosive, other risks seem insignificant. Whilst the manner of his death was an accident, it was Afghanistan that killed him almost as surely as if he had been shot.

Also not included in that list of 22 April 2010 are the men of 7 Platoon, C Company, 3 Rifles, one of whom, Rifleman Mark Marshall, gave his life to the cause. Rifleman Philip Allen, who was attached to A Company from 2 Rifles and was killed by an IED on 7 November 2009, is also missing from the list, as is Lance Corporal Michael Pritchard, who was attached to A Company from the Royal Military Police and was killed by 'friendly' fire on 20 December. Nor did I include the Explosive Ordinance Disposal, EOD or bomb-disposal teams, two of whom, Sapper David Watson and Sapper Guy Mellors, gave their lives trying to clear the area of IEDS for us. They all more than deserved to be mentioned, for they too laid down their lives in support of our efforts.

Despite these unknown omissions the list had caused the press to suddenly take an interest in coming to see us. We were going to get our fifteen minutes of fame. When Rachel and I spoke from Cyprus I said that I would try to limit the time I spent with the formalities of arrival. No such luck. There turned out to be more than an hour of chatting to families, press and friends. In the Army, 'good with media' is not a compliment, but Riflemen are far better spokesmen than the spokesmen because people believe them. I wanted to select a few of my best talkers to front up: I had no desire on this occasion to be Company spokesman when there were better alternatives. It seemed that no one had organised anything to take advantage of this opportunity. No photo op, no lines to take, men just randomly plucked from family greetings. By luck more than judgement those interviewed did themselves proud that day as well, combining the pleasure of coming home with due respect for those who had not come home alive. I find it a subject of horrible fascination that the Army information operation is so poor. If you are going to persuade people to fight for you or with you the information operation is crucial. It feels like organising a credible message through the right medium to the key audience is some way beyond our current capability. You need people who are going to talk about the things they are doing or have done in a way that is accessible and credible to all the people who matter, in this case friends and family, and in Afghanistan that includes the local population and the enemy.

With the crowd dispersing and media beginning to head off to file I went with Rachel and the family to collect my bags. We got home in time for tea, then children's bath and bed. I got out of my uniform, into my jeans and we cracked open a bottle. It was great to be home.

One of the other lessons the Army has learned is that a period of leave immediately after a long and trying operation is also a recipe for disaster. Even following a fairly uneventful six months in Kosovo over the millennium the Battalion gave us six weeks off at Easter as soon as we stepped off the plane and there were twenty divorces in a population of 200 odd families that year. Of course there is no precise cause and effect, but it is far better in the long term psychologically to step down to leave through a period of 'normal' work. There are a host of leadership maxims about the maintenance of discipline in barracks after the rigours of the front line. And like all good maxims taken to their zenith they become ridiculous. I don't contest that it is important, but it is just as important not to pretend that things are 'normal' when they are different. We came back to work three days later. There was a medals parade to see to which, now nestled back in the bosom of 4 Rifles, was a chance for the Battalion to recognise eleven months of commitment to Afghanistan, as well as A Company's return. We were going through rapid reintegration and as a result I certainly felt the creative tension between the recognising the difference and reintegrating the Company. More than anything I was determined to enjoy leading a 'double' off the parade square.

On a personal level I know I was ecstatic to be back. I did not feel an overwhelming sense of joy at the time, however – I didn't feel anything much, only when I was really provoked. I know because there is a recording that I did in early May, an interview at home as a wrap-up for *Today*, which I have listened to, where the happiness just in my tone of voice is there for all to hear. It sounds to me now like sheer unbridled relief at safety, joy of union, and the still bullish satisfaction that we had done a hard job the right way.

On 4 May, the day before our medals parade, we had supper for the families of the fallen. It was an evening of raw emotion for them and a small glimpse for me into what had been the almost daily experience for the welfare office and for Rachel. We have all experienced grief: new grief is a harsh and unforgiving place, and that had been the front line for those who we had left behind. It was just as transformative for them as any of us in Afghanistan. So when the Duchess of Cornwall came to visit us on 5 May for the medals parade with her leg broken from a walking accident in Scotland the celebration was considerably muted. Her Royal Highness had been a friend to us in the Upper Sangin Valley: we were never far from her thoughts. Several large Duchy of Cornwall packages had made their way to us in Afghanistan to be shared among the patrol bases. Shortcake and ginger snaps with your corned beef hash – surreal, but very gratefully received and a welcome show of support for us. I forget which comedy genius suggested that Tim Lush had forgotten the Earl Grey and the cakes to go with them. The Cohiba cigars that came with the biscuits were waiting for a time when we got together the Inkerman stalwarts at a more suitable moment. During the tour my daughter had been presented to

Camilla when she came to visit the families. Emily was alleged to have said she was a 'bit old for a duchess' before dropping a much-practised curtsey. Luckily, she now had a chance to make amends.

The final practice for the medal presentation, Royal Salutes and double off the square was done to the sound of the band and bugles of the Rifles. Furgie, Pollock, Dan Owens, Ben Nash and others who could not march through injury, were seated in a tent having participated in as much of the rehearsal as they were able. As I barked the orders in my best parade-ground voice the band struck up the Regimental Quick March – 'Ta da-der -e -da'. I was transported back to my camp cot and those crazy fatigued winter nights. It was my ritual come back to haunt me. I had put some Regimental tunes on my iPod in case they were appropriate for an occasion in Inkerman; the Regimental birthday perhaps, or as part of a quiz or.... Then the Regimental Quick March and the Regimental Double, *The Road to the Isles*, appeared late one night in January on iPod shuffle and it became my ritual. Random. But to hear it now transported me straight back. In 1998, at Sandhurst, I had marched off the square as a newly commissioned officer to a version of this tune; I had listened to it every night for nearly four months, now 'doubling', knees high at a military canter, at the head of the company, looking over my right shoulder at the men, my men, our men wounded in battle, saluting, to this tune... My heart was thumping, a lump well and truly jammed in my throat, tears pricked and welled, but never fell. Blinking rapidly and breathing deeply we came to a rambling halt off the parade ground. I turned to look at the platoon commanders. Charlie was as affected as I was.

'I'm glad we did that before this afternoon.'

'Me too.'

If there was sadness it was thinned by joy and the celebration diluted by respect. Families came from all over the UK to see their heroes and heroines. We had military visitors who had worked with us, but had left Helmand up to a month before, including a section from the troop of Engineers who had supported us so well. Jodie, our medic, whose family came down from the valleys of South Wales, just came up and hugged me. Her parents said 'We listen'd on the raadior, she wordn't tell us nuthin'. But we knor thanks to yo'.' And with that I felt reassured that in the best way it had been a worthwhile thing to have spent a few hours explaining what we were doing and a little bit of why. They were not the only ones who said as much. By the end of the day I felt that although I would have written almost exactly the same thing in a weekly or monthly newsletter, somehow being broadcast on the BBC had given it more credibility for the people whom I had always known were the most important of any who might listen. If they understood marginally more about what we had been through it might help them understand without having to ask awkward questions. There were a few other personal highlights from that day: my mother's confused look as her daughter-in-law appeared to be on first name terms with HRH; a beer with Ricky Furgusson without falling over; and, to the accompaniment of *The Road to the Isles*, whoops cheers, and the applause of those assembled, doubling off the square with A Company of Honourable Warriors.

\* \* \* \* \*

Meanwhile, back in Helmand, our best-laid plans were beginning to fall apart, not on the ground, but in the next phase of operations that were being planned for Sangin. We had left twenty-two ISAF bases in Sangin District in April 2010, nine of which were in the Inkerman area. According to local elders, reporting to the stabilisation adviser, there were assessed to be 250 Taliban left in Sangin District. The plan that would have seen a contractor base in Inkerman in May 2010 did not come to fruition. In its place was a smaller black-topping project for the road that started from the middle of Sangin. It did not employ 200 workers, it only employed twenty workers and achieved only 1,500 metres in six months. In other words it only just reached the area of operations it was supposed to help at the end of the summer fighting season and then only barely passed PB Blenheim.

At some point in the early spring the decision had been made to hand over Sangin to the US. From June 2010 3rd Battalion 7th United States Marines (3/7 USMC) started to deploy to Sangin. Over the summer the UK Royal Marines from 40 Commando 'demilitarised' the northern 611: in other words, they took all the bases out. This was done from July 2010 onwards. I am not certain where the order to demilitarise came from. It would seem likely that it was the US Marines who asked and UK Brigade that gave the order, but it doesn't really matter. What matters is whether those now in charge could protect the local population who had nailed their colours so firmly to our mast in March, or would the Taliban be back to exact revenge? On 20 September 2010 40 Commando Royal Marines handed over to 3 Battalion 5th US Marines who had taken over from the 3/7th. The 3/5th Marines were nicknamed the 'Butchers of Fallujah' for the way they had fought there. I think that's all you need to know. If you want to know more then journalist Ben Anderson's book, *No Worse Enemy* is a good place to start. The number of patrol bases in Sangin, on the day the UK officially handed over to the US Marines, was reduced to six.

In September 2010 the honours and awards were announced for Op Herrick 11. I had by that point handed A Company over to my successor and was safely ensconced, suited and brogued, in Whitehall. Corporal Furgusson was awarded a Military Cross. Rifleman Reece Terry and Rifleman Ross Robinson (posthumously) were awarded the Queen's Gallantry Medal. Charlie, 2 Platoon

Commander, Corporal Chico Bryant and Pat Hyde were mentioned in dispatches. Corporal Penk was awarded a Joint Commander's Commendation. Ed, Tom, Lance Corporal Hall, the 2 Platoon medic and Rifleman Needham were awarded NATO Meritorious Service Medals. I was honoured to receive an MBE. There has been recent discussion about removing 'For God and the Empire' from this award, and I have to say that it seemed a bit out of date given what it was earned for. If OBE generally stands for 'Other Bugger's Efforts' then this MBE definitely stands for 'My Boys' Efforts'. It is the property of the men of A Company Group, which I have the honour to wear. That is not humility, it is just a fact. This account could easily be construed as their citation for that award. Overall I was pleased that every rank bar two had received recognition and on the announcement of the list I was kindly invited back to 4 Rifles and my successor as OC allowed me to say a few words to the whole Company. All I had to say was that those who had received recognition did so on behalf of the entire Company; they had the honour of wearing them, but they had been earned by everyone, including those who had paid the ultimate price. It is the truth and the only thing one can say when a minority of those who were written up got an award.

The iniquity of the honours and award system is that it is based on quotas with a kind of points system for an operation, with each award using a number of points. So some of the usual markers for the higher level awards were ignored for A Company. Saving life under fire is usually a marker for a military cross – but not for corporals Bryant or Penk. Repeated acts of courage, in the face of the enemy or not, usually lead to a similar level of award, but not for Pat Hyde. I feel particularly aggrieved on his behalf because if you had to choose one person from the whole of A Company and probably from the 3 Rifles Battlegroup, and therefore, given our situation, from the whole of Helmand, who deserved greater recognition, it was Pat Hyde. He had been blown up seven times with direct strikes on his vehicle and been within fifty metres of a further seven, at one point being no more than three metres from a device that went off in the Gul Agha Wadi. I knew he had become talismanic, because I heard it every day from Riflemen from all over the Battlegroup how much inspiration they drew from his example. Somehow we did not find the right words to get him the recognition he surely deserved, which is one of my few lasting regrets. But it is the iniquity of a system that sets a quota on bravery that is in the greatest need of reform. Just because we have always done it that way does not make it the best way we could do it. There were others further up the chain of command who were using up the Herrick 11 quota of points that might have been better bestowed on the brave.

DSO during Op Herrick as a whole might stand for 'Dodgy Strategy Ordered' with the notable exceptions of Charlie, Ian and Giles, amongst a few others. I hope those in receipt of such a prestigious award for distinguished service on active operations did deserve it in and of itself. I am not in a position to judge them as individuals or know what earned them the tribute. What I do know is that the majority of recipients conceived operations that won them the award at ever-greater risk to others. It was all with the best of intent, but seemingly without regard to the actual resources to achieve the job and, most damagingly of all, with little or no regard to strategic continuity from one commander to another. An operation may indeed have been well led, but what we now know is that from 2006 through Panchai Palang (Panther's Claw) to Moshtarak and beyond there was little or no strategic continuity. Here is one such example among many.

Having taken on six patrol bases on 20 September in the last two weeks of October the 3/5 lost nine Marines. In their seven-month tour in Sangin twenty-five US Marines were killed and 200 wounded. In summer 2009, 2 Rifles had thirty killed, in winter 2009–10 3 Rifles had thirty-two killed. The bases went in and 40 Commando had sixteen killed that summer, half the number of the previous fighting season. But the US had taken them out and the casualties rose again.

In December 2010 the peace offer from the Taliban was still on the table, but by January 2011 there were assessed to be 1,500 Taliban in Sangin district. The promise that the local leaders had made that they could control their own men but not the out-of-area fighters was proving deadly. So why had all these fighters arrived in Sangin? In February 2011 the BBC television programme *Panorama*, courtesy of Ben Anderson, showed US Marines blasting a path through occupied compounds back to Wishtan Patrol Base, which had housed B Company 1 Scots during our time in Sangin. They blasted any residual goodwill away with it, providing the Taliban the perfect opportunity to turn the population.

In March 2011 the US claimed, reported in the *Guardian* and other places, a strategic breakthrough in Sangin, having 'pacified' the local area, something that had 'eluded the British'. By March 2011 3/5 US Marines had reconstructed a further sixteen patrol bases, bringing the total back to twenty-two, exactly the same number that had been in Sangin twelve months previously, when the peace offer first went on the table. Also in March 2011 my successor Mark, in Inkerman (now renamed Shamsher), was awarded an MBE for Service in Afghanistan. Both his commanding officer and mine got DSOs, as did his Divisional Commander and my Brigade Commander. His Brigade Commander was awarded the CBE. All for very distinguished service, all high points in the quota, well done. The irony can be lost on no one that his company bravely took out the bases we had bravely put in and the Americans had now bravely put back again. All very brave, but ultimately flawed without continuity. DSOs all round.

The British General, now in receipt of his long-sought DSO, who handed Sangin over to the US, told me that it was 'a morally courageous decision'.

Which book on moral courage does this come from? Tough calls need to be made on operations and when victory was within sight in Sangin defeat was snatched from its jaws. It was the moral courage of a tragic hero. Anthony had it in a nutshell when Brutus was called an honourable man. The handover of Sangin, the morally courageous decision of an 'honourable' warrior. It gets to a point where it doesn't matter who is right or wrong about the tactics of patrolling or over-watch, the combined effect of changing the tactic every six months is to lose the trust of the population, as no one trusts people who can't make up their minds. To lose the population is to lose the war.

So, one might ask, who has taken responsibility for this fiasco? A fiasco that caused the death of over 100 British and American soldiers in a twenty-four month period and injured six times that many. Whilst some of the stimuli for these decisions were undoubtedly political, it is a succession of Brigadiers and Generals who might sleep a little less easily in their beds, their 'strategy' never examined from above, but bravely carried out by those below. In my view, to describe the last of these vacillations as 'moral courage' when the peace process had started is beyond belief. Sangin had become iconic for the Army, the toughest place to go. Even if I am critical of the tactics and strategy of some of the Battlegroups that had occupied Sangin, they had all sacrificed themselves to the cause. To hand over this area to the US and allow them to declare a strategic breakthrough, unanswered, is to dishonour those men. The US Marines cooked up the British leftovers and presented it as a gourmet dish. I will confess that not all of the new US patrol bases are in the same locations as the ones we had built. We had placed ours due to resource constraints and for the purpose of tactical restraint. I left my successor with a map of northern Sangin showing where I would have put patrol bases, given a free hand, and it did not include having one in Inkerman. I don't know, but I would hazard a very strong guess knowing the physical and human geography, that the US laydown looks rather like the dots on that map of April 2010.

The US strategic breakthrough is equally unbelievable given the facts. Declaring victory or strategic breakthrough is a necessary prelude to withdrawal, but the facts are more than just inconvenient. The military ordinance involved in the building of those bases again, the bombs and the bullets to achieve that, if the other fifteen bases are anything like Wishtan or in any way similar to our experience, will have been considerable. The Taliban may have been bombed into submission, but the population will be ripe once again for the plucking when the US has gone. In two years the Taliban will have control of Sangin again. I confidently make that assertion, but I would be happy to be proved wrong. I could not wish a life under that kind of regime on anyone. In June 2011 Barack Obama announced the return of 33,000 US troops sent for the surge, including those based in Sangin. In the summer of 2012 1/7 US Marines based in Sangin had six killed and thirty-nine wounded. There are now just two patrols a week in Sangin by the US Marines based there. In another *Panorama* of February 2013 Ben Anderson showed US powerlessness in the face of the corruption of the local police. And of the twelve most recently elected officials in Sangin four have already been killed by the Taliban. Some victory.

The problem is a question of honour and of trust. In this respect it is a human issue rather than an 'Afghan problem'. If I were an Afghan in the Upper Sangin Valley I would no more trust ISAF than stick my head in the sea. It would be for the following reasons. In 2006, 3 Para came to Sangin, fought the Taliban to a standstill and reduced the bazaar to rubble in the process. Will Pike was the company commander. He has been quoted as reflecting at the time:

> We seem to be stretching ourselves dangerously and things seem to be run in a rather haphazard way. Clearly there is always a risk but it is the risk of unnecessary death, with little being done to minimise those risks, that makes me angry. The strategic direction of UK operations in Afghanistan seems ad hoc, poorly co-ordinated and not very well thought through. There does not seem to be a UK plan for Afghanistan or Helmand.

But 3 Para had done one thing, albeit rather destructively. They convinced the local population that we were serious, even if we picked the wrong side and most of the locals thought we had come back for revenge. Then, in 2007, the locals rose up against the Taliban in a *levée en masse* and we stayed in our bases. The Taliban put down the uprising in the most brutal way. But in the second half of 2007 we created new bases: Inkerman, Blenheim and Downes. And in 2008 we put more patrol bases on the 611, partly for the deception for the move of the turbine to Kajaki, but at least it had the effect of telling the locals we were still serious and we would be there for the locals at last. In 2009 bases were taken down, the centre of Sangin was controlled by a corrupt Afghan Police force and 45 Commando used intensive patrolling tactics to keep the place as 'secure' as they could. The security operation in the summer of 2009 had been undone by 2 Rifles' contributions to Operation Panther's Claw, Panchai Palang, and the advent of a serious IED threat. This engendered the change of tactics of 2010 when we put in fifteen patrol bases and then took them out again in a ten-month period. Six months later the US had put them back in. You simply could not make this up. And it is summed up by one word – tragedy.

Afghanistan has all the elements of a Shakespearean tragedy, except, of course, that it is all too real. I perhaps muddied the idea of the Afghanistan tragedy with the description of the general as Brutus, the 'honourable' man. The model of the Aristotelian tragedy begins with a tragic hero; in this case that role does not fall to one man but to a body of men, the British Army. The protagonist must begin as someone of importance or fortune, as indeed the Army has been in our history. He cannot be perfect, though. Well that is true enough of this Army, feted now in the streets our county towns, but with nasty little flaws that show up in Basra in the death of Baha Mousa, Camp Breadbasket, in Kenya, Malaya and in Afghanistan.

. The audience must be able to relate to the hero, so Aristotle said the hero must have tragic flaws that balance his otherwise good character. And maybe, even hopefully, this book goes some way towards showing that the Army is indeed in part a reflection of what we would like to believe about our Army. But one might also recognise that the Army has flaws. Ironically Aristotle usually made this flaw hubris, an all-consuming pride that causes the individual to ignore a moral tenet or a divine warning. What made us think we could tame Helmand with 100,000, let alone 10,000, or, laughably, 3,000? Armies have marched into Helmand many times before and most times come out with their tails between their legs. Any reading of the culture, the history or the politics should have prevented us taking on Helmand. Who advised this and who took the advice? General Richards' idea that we will be giving forty years of commitment to Afghanistan looks increasingly tenuous and now more than faintly ridiculous. Hubris was to the fore.

These flaws culminate in the humiliation, defeat, and death of the protagonist. This should invite the audience to feel a great pity for the character because he can be related to, and the audience can put themselves in his position. The people of Dorchester waved and cheered and gave us a fantastic reception on our return, they felt our pain. Pity the heroes. As an Army we are close to withdrawal from combat operations in Afghanistan. It may be dressed as victory, but it will be the white paint on the grave. Even with our combat role still intact, the area we now control is a tiny percentage of the territory. Yet we are told of continuing progress and it is true in this postage stamp, but not in Afghanistan as a whole. Again it is such an oblique view of the truth as to be instantly discreditable. Helmand is roughly the size of Wales and the area we control roughly sits between Swansea and Cardiff: the Taliban have the run of the rest. When we leave those in the area we control will pay dearly for siding with the security forces, even though they had little choice, as they will in Sangin. The 'step down in 2013' will end all notions that we can commit to the security of the Afghan government, let alone the Afghan people. It will only be a case of whether the Afghan forces can keep the Taliban from chasing us out; whether we reach some kind of accommodation directly with the Taliban or whether it will be a fighting withdrawal.

On the home front the political humiliation of the Army is complete. The Army will lose twenty per cent of its manpower in the next five years and fifty per cent of its equipment funding. It has been reduced to being the nation's doorman for the Olympics, albeit a very polite cheerful one. There is one act left, for the tragedy must end in a catharsis. The catharsis is where the audience lose their feelings of anxiety and fear and finally reach a sense of completion. I fear the Army's is some way off.

There are several things that need to happen before catharsis for the Army. We must end the folly of the TA as the formed units' first reserve. The budget does not and will not stretch that far. We need our defence equipment plan in balance and sharpish. By balance I do not mean with a bunch of zeros at the bottom of the balance sheet. The current equipment plan in the MoD is so badly out of balance precisely because it has been achieved by accountancy rather than the balance of military effect. Any system of choosing the equipment priorities that plumps for a 230th jet over any new body armour is rather obviously flawed. If we want a meaningful Army in the modern world we need to give them the requisite individual and collective protection and mobility, as well as twenty-first century communications. The Army will tell you it is the best we have ever had, which is true, but what they won't tell you is that it is nowhere near the right, type, standard, quantity or quality to keep pace with our allies or defeat our enemies. Two more years of the current madness and the only thing between us and our enemies will be the will of the Army to fight. I have little doubt in the Army's will, it will be what saves us. It saved us at Calais, but the Army deserves far, far better from its military and political leadership. And that is what the Army needs most of all, because from Napoleon to Slim to now there are no such things as good soldiers and bad soldiers, good units and bad units: there are only good and bad officers. The crisis of leadership that has affected our banks, our press and our politics is as prevalent in our forces. We need senior officers who think in terms of their soldiers' needs rather than their own, who have the moral courage to stand up for the right thing, not sell their rank and access to the highest bidder. As an aside, on the tenth anniversary of the start of the Iraq war, given what we now know about the lead-up, it seems even more astonishing that no senior military officer resigned. Were they all convinced by the shreds of evidence? We need an army where we talk of proportionality, not sideburns. In the last six years Afghanistan has been the highest profile posting for any commander, but I'm not sure we want much more dodgy strategy ordered, especially by those who have been rewarded for that failure. There is simply no military benefit to staying any longer, the Army knows that. The morally courageous decision, the honourable act, is to bring our Army home now.

These words will be of no comfort to those who mourn the dead from Afghanistan. We all wanted to fight for a cause worth fighting for, knowing that death might come. I could never say that they died for nothing because I know they did not. Their lives were laid down for their friends in the service of their country and greater love hath no man than that. Their sacrifice will serve as inspiration, and a reminder to current and future generations. It may yet also serve as a warning: that sacrifice on its own, however honourable, is not enough.

Those in the chain of command who tap in to the inspirational reserves of will of the next generation need to make sure that they are doing so in the best interests of the country.

If their sacrifice achieves that, it will have been worth it.

*N.B.*

Exhortation of the Adjutant of the Royal Military Academy Sandhurst and its Old College Sergeant Major, circa August 1997:

'To those who did well, well done. To those who did not do so well, you know who you are, do it better next time.'

And, delivered from a 6ft 7in Scots Guards Regimental Sergeant Major to a quivering Officer Cadet:

Mr Streatfeild, *that* was the worst example of Rifle drill I have ever had the misfortune to witness. If you do not start seizing, striking and grasping the Rifle, your world will shortly become one of pain and suffering. Now get a *fucking* grip.

*Appendix 1*

# Orders

**HOLD and BUILD**

(1)  HOLD and BUILD in Sangin District Centre.
(2)  Write, implement and refine the Sangin Local Security Plan.
(3)  Write, implement and refine the Upper Sangin Valley Local Security Plan.
(4)  Write, implement and refine the Sangin Kajaki Local Security Plan.
(5)  Partner ANSF.
(6)  Conduct systematic baseline census operations in the AO.
(7)  Identify opportunities for reintegration within boundaries.

In order to SECURE Sangin, PROTECT Kajaki dam, DISRUPT insurgents in Upper Sangin Valley.

Out of all that CO Rifles had given me this likely mission. For CO 3 Rifles had come to the conclusion that things had to be done differently. He therefore decided to bide his time before deciding on the approach. I know some in 2 Rifles were aggrieved at how stiff an ignoring he gave them during the handover, but only time would tell who was right. In any case, for the time being he told me to:

**HOLD, INTERDICT, IDENTIFY**

(1)  HOLD Forward Operating Base Inkerman.
(2)  DEFEND the Ground Defence Area (the immediate vicinity around Inkerman).
(3)  INTERDICT Enemy Force capability and influence.
(4)  Advise on, implement and refine the Upper Sangin Valley Local Security Plan.
(5)  Conduct Influence Ops in line with BG Plan.
(6)  IDENTIFY Consent Winning Activity and Reconciliation opportunities.
(7)  be prepared to reinforce Nolay for Company Group Ops.
(8)  be prepared to support BG Ops (Company-)

In order to PROTECT the deepening security effect in the vicinity of Sangin District Centre.

I then got to the crunch point. On 19 October I was on my feet in front of my command group, some of whom I had only met a week before, and they needed to be persuaded that this was the plan. A Company would protect the deepening security effect in Sangin in the following way:

The decisive moment in the counter insurgency battle is when, in the mind of the Afghan, he decides to support government forces rather than the insurgent. Getting to this moment is a process, taking people from simple awareness of our presence, through mutual understanding to mutual trust and then support for what we do. Autumn, winter and spring give us an advantage: patrolling is physically less degrading providing appropriate warm kit and food are taken. Arcs are greater giving the opportunity to use our superior marksmanship at range. Foreign fighters often return home for the winter giving the opportunity to influence tier three insurgents amongst the local Afghans.

We will continue to familiarise everyone here with the Inkerman AO. All platoons are to conduct green zone, desert and village patrols. All platoons are to conduct at least one patrol with Afghan National Army TIGER team in this familiarisation phase. During this phase all commanders are to use an interpreter to gain information from Afghans. All platoons must gain an understanding of how tactics, techniques and procedures are to be adapted to our AO. All members of the Company must be comfortable using an interpreter for the purpose of gaining answers to standard information requirements. This information will form the basis of future operations. This familiarisation phase will finish when the maize harvest is complete and the Upper Sangin Valley security plan is confirmed.

The principal population in the Inkerman AO is in SAREAGAR. A Company will PROTECT this population. A COMPANY will attack the IED network and seek to NEUTRALISE insurgent influence in SAREAGAR by influence operations, information operations and consent winning activity. At the end of the harvest A Company will patrol to Jusalay and Jokhoran to conduct HTM (Human Terrain Mapping) and collect basic information. The Company will also then patrol at full strength into MAZAK, MIAN RUD, to conduct HTM and collect basic information. Subsidiary tasks will be to FIND insurgents logistic support and DISRUPT insurgents influence. This too is a process. It will involve a number of patrols to the same areas to build background information, identify insurgents' weakness, DISRUPT insurgents' logistic support. And most importantly, build and exploit relationships with the local population.

In addition A Company will support Battlegroup operations. A Company will plan to conduct operations with B Company 3 RIFLES on our inter Company boundary in order to interdict enemy routes into SANGIN from the Upper Sangin Valley. A Company will investigate and plan to emplace a patrol base in the Green Zone and in SAREAGAR to extend the security provided by ISAF. A Company will conduct ALL operations as far as possible in partnership with ANSF. The arrival of the Tiger Team is of considerable benefit. A Company will aim to partner an ANA Platoon in Forward Operating Base Inkerman by January 2010. Interspersed with routine patrolling will be intelligence led patrols to interdict insurgent influence and capability.

Our operational capability must be sustained for six months and beyond. Base routine, force protection and logistics are the foundation from which we launch. Routine is founded on our standard operating procedures these are covered in coordinating instructions. Force protection is critical to sustaining operations. Commanders must check on personal hygiene, cleanliness and serviceability of personal equipment. A high standard of cleanliness in living accommodation is required. This check is to be done weekly. Commanders must check that individual protective equipment is worn at all times on duty in the Forward Operating Base and on patrol. The resupply operations, Op LOAM and Op GRANITE, are critical operations for sustaining the base. All platoons are to be familiar with these operations. Platoon Sergeants must identify logistic requirements to the CQMS in good time. There can be significant delay to routine resupply. Therefore the CQMS is to hold stocks forward and create robust accounting measures within the base. Logistic issues are to be identified early and the Chain of Command informed. Trauma Management interviews must be conducted seventy-two hours after an incident and when necessary thereafter. Close liaison between commanders and the doctor is required to sustain the Company Group. On-going training is vital to sustain operational capability. Vallon training, Barma skills, med training, rules of engagement training, weapon handling tests and a rifle target practice are to take place every month.

The main effort is to PROTECT the deepening security effect in SANGIN.

I then dished out the following tasks common to each of the platoons and groups under my command;

- DEFEND Forward Operating Base Inkerman from one of the guard posts (They each got a different one.)
- DEFEND the immediate area around Inkerman (Again a different area for each.)

- INTERDICT EF capability & influence in the vicinity of Forward Operating Base Inkerman. (And again.)
- Conduct human terrain mapping
- Increase ISAF influence with Afghans by identifying consent winning activities, cash for work projects and reconciliation dialogue opportunities
- Conduct ground familiarisation and improve situational awareness
- Conduct Op MINIMISE on orders
- Provide force protection through good health & hygiene
- be prepared to REINFORCE Forward Operating Base Nolay
- be prepared to act as Quick Reaction Force on orders
- be prepared to partner an ANA platoon
- be prepared to occupy a Platoon Base on orders
- be prepared to support Battlegroup operations in depth
- be prepared to CLEAR & SECURE to facilitate Op GRANITE, Op LOAM & Air Drops

In order to interdict enemy capability and influence in the vicinity of Sangin.

*Appendix 2*

# Embedded Partnering at Platoon Level

## *Lt Charlie Winstanley*

2 Platoon, A Coy 4RIFLES moved from Inkerman to Patrol Base Blenheim in late November 2009 as part of BG(N)'s new partnered force laydown to 'achieve greater coordination with (and development of) ANSF through embedded partnering'. Prior to our arrival the 7-man Operation Mentoring and Liaison Team (OMLT) team from 2YORKS had been working with the ANA platoon at Blenheim for two months. They had made significant headway in developing the ANA's patrol tempo – from three patrols a week during HERRICK 10 up to five or six patrols a week. On these patrols the OMLT would carry the electronic counter-measures equipment and Vallon for the ANA as they patrolled with them. The OMLT would have to not only plan the patrol and provide the tactical direction and intimate security, but also mentor the ANA on their low-level drills.

The benefits of embedded partnership are clear. It improves the local national perception of security within their villages, and bolsters their confidence in both the ANSF and ISAF through joint patrolling. It allows an 'Afghan Face' to be put on more operations, and helps develop the ANA indirectly by setting an example and by freeing up the OMLT to focus purely on mentoring rather than on force protection.

Numbers for partnered patrols have been fluid. The arrangement agreed was that every ISAF section would have ANA soldiers attached which would be mentored by a member of the OMLT team. Initially five ANA were attached to the back of each section, but this tended to result in the ANA taking a passive role in the patrol, especially for the commanders. Subsequently the two ISAF Vallon men leading the section would be followed immediately by an ANA Vallon man. The ANA section commander follows the ISAF commander with a dedicated OMLT mentor and interpreter. The remaining ANA are split amongst the section. This fully integrated approach forces the ANA section commanders to take an active role in directing their men, and partners ISAF-ANA equivalents to give more scope for development of ANA low-level drills. It provides the freedom for the OMLT to focus entirely on mentoring – such as checking the commanders' map reading and the Warriors' fire positions, Valloning and patrol formations – and maintains a discreet ANA command structure.

Using this configuration we have conducted six partnered patrols per week of increasing ambition. One of the greatest restrictions of Partnering is the limitations that it places on patrol taskings. Whilst it has improved, the ANA's lack of confidence means that they are often unwilling to patrol out of their comfort zone, which is limited to the permissive urban areas towards Sangin DC. Partnering allows us to conduct in-depth human terrain mapping and Local National interaction in these areas, but can prevent us from pushing regularly into new places with the ANA. This situation has been mitigated by supplementing Partnered patrols with ISAF-only patrols which allow us to patrol into higher risk areas and also maintain a higher tempo patrol matrix. Levels of training and equipment also cause issues. Their BARMA drills are continually improving, but remain at a level where I would not be happy to allow ISAF troops to follow without their own Vallon man. They are lent Vallons and night sights by the OMLT. The ANA are not allowed to carry our electronic counter measures equipment, and so this burden remains with ISAF troops. Fire control measures are a constant battle, and continue to be a primary factor in deciding how the ANA fit into a patrol.

Patrol planning is conducted weekly but remains only superficially partnered: myself and the OMLT commander will decide what we want to achieve in the week, and then discuss timings and taskings with the ANA commander. The ANA commander is increasingly forthcoming with his own patrol ideas, including arrest operations and night lurks. The ANA patrol matrix is not very flexible: they are unwilling to patrol at certain times of the day – specifically mid-morning when they have men committed to the bazaar patrols and over lunch – and are very keen to stick to the agreed weekly patrols without deviations. The result is that when a reactive patrol is required this is inevitably ISAF-only.

With more troops and assets, the ANA are gaining in confidence and tactical ambition. Throughout Op Herrick 11 they have conducted partnered patrols into areas unthinkable only 2 months earlier. If partnering continues to evolve to meet the developing capabilities of the ANA it will go on to push them towards a level where they can take control of the security situation themselves.

*Appendix 3*

# OC A4R COY – CO's Weekly Assessment Report as at 28 January 2010

**Intro**

The fight for the 611 is well and truly on. The resupply effort which had been going on for three days at the time of the last assessment report lasted a further four days. The total cost: one killed, six wounded and two MASTIFFS. Balanced with that were the successful visits of the ANA to PB SHUGA and Pritch's Post which has precipitated ANA orders to move fifteen warriors to PB SHUGA.

**Enemy Forces**

The enemy made life particularly difficult this week. The anti-tank mines on the 611 were a first for the INKERMAN Area of Operations. There has been an increase in devices aimed at dismounted patrols. These have been offset into dead ground from the sangers and detonated to little effect against MASTIFFS and dismounted patrols. The Anti-Tank device was surface laid with a bag of earth for a quick cover. Insurgents can lay these devices extremely quickly. There was significant ground sign which was noticed too late. It appears that insurgents were prepared to lay Vehicle Operated Pressure Pad IEDs that threatened both Local Nationals and International Stabilisation Force freedom of movement. The insurgent successfully engaged a dismounted patrol to push them onto a device in the Gul Agha Wadi (GAW). The difficulty of securing the same piece of ground without a permanent presence is increasingly challenging. The inevitable pattern setting is easy for the insurgent to target. The insurgent was also able to identify the Observation Posts and was able to conduct grenade attacks eventually resulting in two walking wounded casualties. The insurgent suffered some attrition with one being neutralised in the GAW and potentially another by the AH in support of the CASEVAC of one of our casualties. The insurgent is having a little Local National difficulty. There has been some talk of locals calling the insurgents to a meeting regarding IEDs on the 611.

## Friendly Forces – now and to come

The attrition has meant that the Fire Support Group has been entirely rebalanced along the 611 providing specialist capability and temporary Battle Casualty Replacements to give the Patrol Bases maximum patrolling capability. It leaves the risk with INKERMAN but the Artillery and Mortars are picking up the slack. Routine patrols at the end of the week involved a number of shuras and mini shuras. The most pressing need is the upgrade to the PBs to be able to welcome the ANA. This will involve another resupply starting on 30 January. We are planning for forty-eight hours and we will attempt more simultaneity in order to give the best chance of achieving the three runs. If all goes to plan engineers will open the arcs onto the area of dead ground to the West of 7 Platoon. Improvised Explosive Device Disposal Team will search a new part of PB SHUGA and the engineers will be able to make SHUGA more liveable for the Afghan National Army. In addition the REVIVOR Balloon will move to Patrol Base BLENHEIM and we shall get Helicopter Landing Site matting to BLENHEIM to try and open the HLS there for normal use. Finally a Jackal vehicle will move to BLENHEIM to assist with moves to Forward Operating Base Jackson in Sangin.

My fervent aspiration is a deliberate operation to fix the culverts. I am aware of various plans for the Vulnerable Points and I have submitted various suggestions. But the way to reduce the current casualties is to remove the requirement to clear and hold the VPs on every move down the 611. This cannot come too soon.

## Wider Picture – people, governance, influence etc.

The mosque project in the vicinity of PB BARIOLAI and the electricity transformer project have both reached the District Development Authority and we await progress. Two other Mosque projects will be taken forward to the MSST. We await the information on local schools and details of the new health clinic.

We have found a potential recruit for the ANP. The caveat to his willingness to join was that he wished to have his family relocated.

A small but important point is that no one seems to have an English to Pashtu dictionary in HELMAND. This should be standard issue to interpreters. It might improve their reporting.

We have not been able to confirm the LN meeting with insurgents in regard to the 611. However every walk in and every shura continues to respond positively to our presence.

Most significantly this week the ANA participated in a security shura with 17 LN heads of households at SHUGA. All parties were very pleased to be there, all the right messages were passed and the mutual backslapping went on for most of the morning.

**Admin and command issues**

Eight new radios were very gratefully received this week.

A three month warning is on the cards for a Rifleman from 7 Pl. The Adjutant has the details.

The supply of water in the PBs is the greatest admin problem. Our best laid plans calling them Check Points rather than Patrol Bases for Permanent Joint Head Quarters in London means that the 'small groups' water pumps are not officially required. We are investigating whether ANA funding would be able to provide a pump for the wells. The water would have to be boiled for washing. This would ease the requirement but not remove it. We are also in the process of ordering more water carriage packs.

**Summary**

A difficult week in terms of casualties with 42 and 41 bearing the brunt. But the prospect of the ANA in SHUGA and BARIOLAI is extremely heartening. The fact that locals around SHUGA actively encouraged the move is more heartening still.

*Appendix 4*

# Rules of Engagement: an analysis of current application and effect in Afghanistan

I tried to look at both the theory and practice of rules of engagement examining the effect of our rules of engagement from three perspectives: the local national or Afghan perspective, an insurgent perspective, and the effect on friendly (ISAF) forces. For the purpose of the analysis the principles of the Law of Armed Conflict (LOAC) were encapsulated thus:

Principles of LOAC:
- Military Necessity 'engagement will reduce EF mil capability & FF will benefit militarily'
- Distinction 'everything feasible to verify objectives not civilian'
- Discrimination 'attacks will be directed and not indiscriminate'
- Proportionality 'acceptable balance between military advantage and collateral damage'
- Humanity 'it is prohibited to cause unnecessary suffering and injury'

The law of armed conflict was framed at a time when the opposing force would be relatively easily identifiable. The architects sought to protect the civilian population in this context. It is far more difficult to achieve that distinction in Counter Insurgency Operations (COIN). In COIN one might argue that there are instances where the protection of the population is achieved by targeting insurgents using civilian objects for a military purpose. In this case the remainder of the local population are not only prepared to tolerate fire against the insurgents under these circumstances, but on most occasions actively support it.

The alternative view and one that has engendered the current direction on rules of engagement is our current understanding and practice of the implementation of Card A. Self-defence has become the fall-back position of much of what might be considered as at best unnecessary but at worst offensive and disproportionate. Below is the mantra that is given at every ROE lecture. Its effect has been the destruction of many communities in Afghanistan.

'If you honestly believe there is an imminent threat to life and there is no other way to stop the threat, you may use force up to lethal force to prevent the threat. Any force you use must be necessary and proportionate and you must stop using lethal force once the imminent threat has passed, At all times you must take all precautions to minimise the risk to innocent civilians.'

The village of Jokhoran is, as I have already described, one and a half km NE of Forward Operating Base Inkerman. This village is now inhabited by one family and a Mullah, the compounds large and deserted. The locals tell of a once prosperous village. Its destruction through 'self-defence' had rendered it uninhabitable. It was assessed to be used by fighters as a bed-down location. It had become a training ground for insurgents.

The commander of the International Stabilisation Force, Stanley McChrystal at the time, gave the following direction in regard to escalation of force. 'The dynamic between not wishing to deny the right to self-defence but the encouragement to resist using all the available means to crack the nut is all too evident. Constraint in practice but not in principle.' The then Task Force Helmand guidance on escalation of force is summarised by the following quote. 'The use of non-kinetic and non-lethal kinetic warning equipment must be maximised in order to reduce the necessity of lethal options. This will help maintain the support and confidence of the local population.' This is underpinned by a three-step process. The three-step process can be summarised as follows: the Standard Operating Instructions provide commanders with training and operating frameworks for reducing the likelihood of unnecessary force escalation incidents. Without removing flexibility from commanders, it mandates minimum baseline standards for VCP, cordon and convoy procedures and equipment. Ultimately, it is for commanders and soldiers on the ground to act responsibly and within the law. Troops at all times retain the inherent right to exercise lethal force in self-defence. 'All personnel may move immediately to the application of lethal force under an inalienable right to self-defence if their perception of the threat so demands.'

The aim of all this direction was to explain to soldiers under what circumstances they could engage and to try and assist them in their judgement about when they should engage. The result was a mechanistic view of the rules. Judgement and flexibility were reduced in practice. This led to 'honest belief' issues where the fall back position is to Card Alpha engagements rather than using judgement as to the effect on the LN population or the insurgents. Another issue with the linear view as outlined in the TFH guidance is that every engagement where a soldier escalates is treated as a one-off event, leaving less latitude for judgement to be informed by experience. It can be captured in graphical format, as in Fig 1.

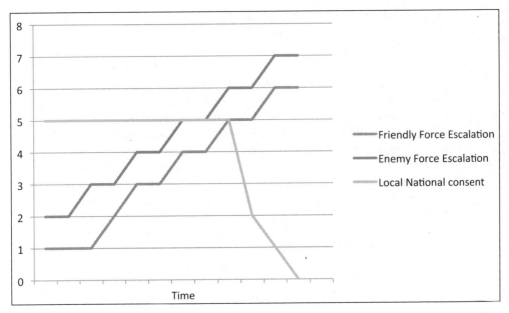

**Figure 1**

This has multiple effects. The start point is that the insurgent knows when to act and when to move. He can judge his activity through time to overmatch or avoid our escalation. There is no better manifestation of this than scouting. He will scout brazenly until warning shots are offered and then take more care. He will engage with small arms from a firing point for fifteen minutes before he moves because he knows that we will not engage with indirect fire or heavy weapons until other effects are exhausted. At every stage he is able to change his activity to out-manoeuvre the escalation. But COIN is not principally about the enemy. It is about local national perception of security.

In this case the local national appreciates our restraint but is frustrated by a lack of effect. If the contact persists then the escalation will reach the point where crops are destroyed or at the very least his family are rightly frightened of the firepower we are bringing to bear. The effect on friendly force troops is to better understand what 'should' be used in which order, but ultimately reduces our ability to out-manoeuvre the insurgent and therefore leads to a sense of frustration.

A slightly broader view of the implementation of ROE came to the fore during 2009, encapsulated in the phrase 'courageous restraint'. There had been much encouragement from the chain of command to demonstrate courageous restraint. A graphical representation is given at Fig 2 on p.216.

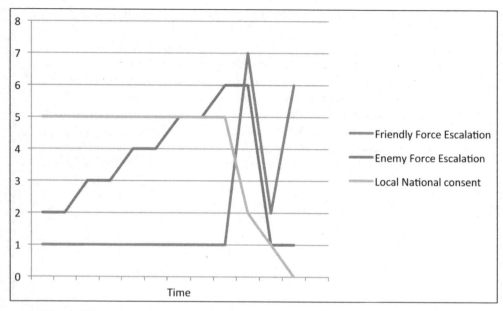

**Figure 2**

In this case ISAF troops are encouraged not to escalate in the face of insurgent provocation. The rationale is to protect the mission. From the local national perspective this is designed to enhance their consent for ISAF operations by demonstrating that we take utmost care to avoid civilian casualties. From the insurgent's perspective it has yet to have any discernible effect. It may frustrate them because they are not getting the gratification of ISAF reaction or overreaction. Alternatively it may embolden them in the face of perceived ISAF passivity. The graphic at Fig 2 above indicates that at some point ISAF troops will have to escalate to defeat an intolerable threat to life. This could potentially mean that ISAF would have to use greater force than they would have had to if they had neutralised the threat initially. The logic of this line of argument culminated in my view that there was a high likelihood for courageous restraint to diminish the overall perception of security in the mind of the local national.

For troops on the ground courageous restraint had some physical and moral effect. It is very difficult for soldiers to understand that they are going to be put at a greater risk than they need to be by their commanders. The tactical impulse and operational imperatives run in opposite directions, creating either disagreements over tactics or moral tension and very often both. The tactical collision would be injury of troops caused by inaction or restraint. Tension is caused by the perception that the collision is unnecessary. Commanders are in post to manage both of these aspects, but I argue that if only a broader view of

ROE were taken it would limit the difficulties of the concept of courageous restraint.

Fig 3 below attempts to show that enemy action will end at a certain point during escalation. Commanders have to manage the escalation to a point where the insurgent action halts. There is a danger that over-escalation will undermine locals' perception of security and even turn the locals against security forces. Having escalated to this point there is a danger that this level of escalation will become the norm. This becomes the usual level of violence which is open to political exploitation by the insurgent. And whilst it has prevented insurgent activity, it has built such a lasting resentment as to be ultimately self-defeating.

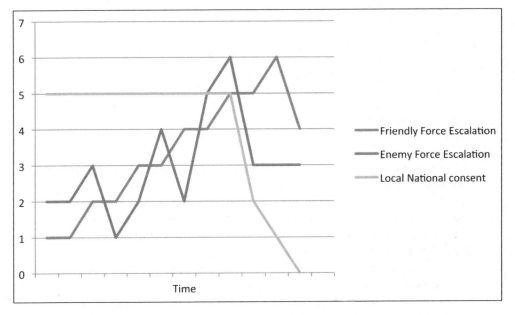

**Figure 3**

The solution to this problem is to find a method of training and implementation that attracts the political benefit of restraint and gains the consent of the Afghan, but has the desired effect of neutralising the insurgents. The third aspect to take into account is the perception of ISAF troops that they remained unconstrained to 'do their job'. The solution is characterised graphically in Fig 4 on p.218.

Escalation should not be viewed as a single event. The graphic indicates a reduced amount of Afghan consent in the face of escalation. However, there were times when Afghans in the Inkerman AO actively encouraged harder measures against the insurgents on their behalf. For better application of ROE one should not only look at the mechanics of escalation and training. Application is informed by training, but patrol experience and judgement of the situation on

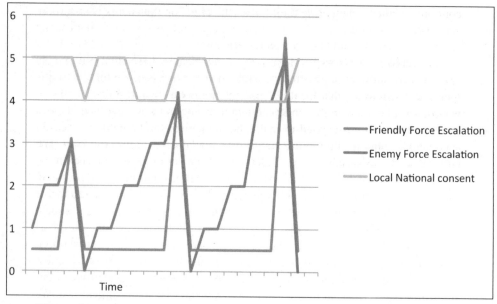

**Figure 4**

the ground is more critical to local consent and neutralisation of the insurgents. Rather than step up through the escalation measures one should spike them or spot them to have the desired effect. Retrospective analysis of some of the engagements in the Inkerman AO indicates that an early use of proportionate lethal force would have had a better effect than textbook Operational Training and Advisory Group lessons on escalation.

The logic of this argument is that after a period a soldier will know what level of escalation is appropriate to a situation. This means a far higher level of responsibility for an individual soldier. There is no room for prophylactic fire. Or the stats game that is still played by members of the fires community. In a COIN environment it is about being clinical in the contact, or 'clear-eyed' as COMISAF put it.

What one needs to be clear-eyed about is the effect of our implementation of ROE on the local national population. A final vignette by way of example. Forward Operating Base INKERMAN came under persistent and accurate Mortar Fire. The locating radar worked out the firing point. ROE clearly state that counter mortar fire can be fired by mortars or guns on location by radar.

Counter mortar fire was fired at the second and fourth insurgent volley. The following day two more separate volleys were fired. They were inaccurate but landed in close proximity to local national compounds. No counter was fired. In the after-action reviews it has been argued that we showed courageous restraint on day two. From a local national perspective we allowed the fire to continue, further endangering their lives. The effect on the enemy is uncertain. The effect on friendly troops was to engender a feeling that lives, both theirs and local nationals, had been risked needlessly.

To overcome these issues there is a strong argument for a more complete approach to the implementation of ROE. A more dynamic understanding is required; I still argue that local perception should be its start point. For ISAF troops, moral responsibility and accountability needs to be devolved. Troops can therefore feel unshackled to make the judgement but be held more easily accountable. This would require a cultural shift in current army thinking. The cultural shift should have several elements. Application of ROE needs to be made truly accountable. The Card Alpha honest belief syndrome must be cured. Cultural understanding of what is expected by local nationals should be a theme in both training and application. Mission focus rather than task focus will help to set the working parameters for all cap badges. Courageous restraint represents a step forward, but has the innate potential to undermine the 'popular support' that will be 'decisive to either side in this struggle.' If we are not to defeat ourselves then we need to place local national consent at the forefront of our application of ROE. That means being able to neutralise the insurgent fast. We must retain the flexibility in principle and practice. Mechanistic or overly restrictive application facilitates insurgent manoeuvre, undermines LN consent and ISAF confidence.

These problems persist to this day. The cry goes up that soldiers are too afraid to fire in the face of potential prosecution. I think there is strong evidence to suggest that they are not afraid enough. We are not at war. We fight in Afghanistan at the invitation of the government of Afghanistan. If we are to enforce the rule of law we must abide by the rule of law. The lack of investigations and prosecutions with regard to the adherence to the law of armed conflict, especially in regard to proportionality and discrimination, is evidence not necessarily of a conflict well fought, but might well hint at a lack of judgement and of moral courage on the part of soldiers and commanders alike.